P9-AOY-658

A Practical Guide to Industrial Development

PRAEGER SPECIAL STUDIES IN
INTERNATIONAL ECONOMICS AND DEVELOPMENT

A Practical Guide to Industrial Development

Richard S. Kaynor
Konrad F. Schultz

FREDERICK A. PRAEGER, Publishers
New York · Washington · London

The purpose of the Praeger Special Studies is to make specialized research monographs in U.S. and international economics and politics available to the academic, business, and government communities. For further information, write to the Special Projects Division, Frederick A. Praeger, Publishers, 111 Fourth Avenue, New York, N.Y. 10003.

FREDERICK A. PRAEGER, PUBLISHERS
111 Fourth Avenue, New York, N.Y. 10003, U.S.A.
77-79 Charlotte Street, London W.1, England

Published in the United States of America in 1967
by Frederick A. Praeger, Inc., Publishers

Library of Congress Catalog Card Number: 66-26565

Printed in the United States of America

Dedicated to our wives,

Betty and Gwynne

ACKNOWLEDGMENTS

The authors are grateful to the many people who have helped in the preparation of this book. Several merit special recognition.

Professor Frank Shallenberger of Stanford University was most generous with his ideas and time.

Dr. José Manuel Illán, former Under-Secretary of the Treasury in Cuba, was very helpful, particularly with those sections of our book dealing with finance and banking.

Emerson Ross kindly read the entire manuscript and made a number of very helpful suggestions.

We are most appreciative of the work of our indefatigable secretaries, Margarita Pelleyá and Esperanza Silvestre, without whose persistent efforts these pages would have never been completed.

Finally, and importantly, we wish to thank Pamela Johnson who took time out from her own writing to read this work and make many useful suggestions.

CONTENTS

PART II. THE IDENTIFICATION OF INDUSTRIAL INVESTMENT OPPORTUNITIES

LIST OF FIGURES

LIST OF TABLES

ABBREVIATIONS

AID	United States Agency for International Development
ADELA	Atlantic Development Community Group
ADL	Arthur D. Little, Inc.
CACM	Central American Common Market
CIAP	Interamerican Committee of the Alliance for Progress
CED	Committee for Economic Development
CIPM	Council for International Progress in Management, Inc.
DLF	Development Loan Fund
ESAN	Escuela Superior de Administración de Negocios
EXIM BANK	Export-Import Bank
IBEC	International Basic Economy Corporation
IBRD	International Bank for Reconstruction and Development
ICA	International Cooperation Administration
IDA	International Development Association
IDB	Inter-American Development Bank
IFC	International Finance Corporation

INP	National Planning Institute
INPI	National Industrial Promotion Institute
IMF	International Monetary Fund
LAFTA	Latin American Free Trade Area
OAS	Organization of American States
OECD	Organization for Economic Cooperation and Development
RTAC	Regional Technical Aids Center
SID	Society for International Development
SPTF	Social Progress Trust Fund
SRI	Stanford Research Institute
UNESCO	United Nations Educational, Scientific and Cultural Organization

A Practical Guide to Industrial Development

INTRODUCTION

Recently, the developing countries of the world have experienced a rising wave of expectations, created in part by the press, television, movies, and the transistor radio. Desires for material possessions have been awakened, and competition between the free world and the Communist Bloc to assuage these needs is rapidly increasing.

Industrial development, as an integral part of over-all economic development, must aid in increasing developing countries' economic advancement by helping them make better use of their internal natural resources. In the developing countries most available agricultural land is now under cultivation, and too few jobs are being created each year to take care of those entering the labor market. It is industry, therefore, that must help to provide employment for the growing populations. In addition, since many developing countries rely on one or two main export items, their entire economies react to the fluctuations in world market prices. Industrial development can help in this area.

Another recent phenomenon is the mass migration from the countryside to the larger urban centers in many of the developing countries. This problem, with all its attendant social and economic evils, can be eased by the judicious use of the various means of industrial decentralization in outlying areas. The regional development corporation's role in this decentralization is discussed here. Industrial development normally carries with it a number of helpful side effects, including increased domestic savings, the creation of a capital market (stock market), and the creation of technological and managerial skills that are so desperately needed.

In outlining the problems and challenges of industrial development, this study places heavy emphasis on small business and the small businessman; for a viable, competitive small business sector is an essential ingredient of the free enterprise system and can create the stimulus necessary for contagious industrial expansion and development. Modern, progressive, small and medium industry represents the necessary complement to large (often foreign-owned) industries, mining or agricultural complexes, and government-sponsored basic heavy industries.

For the purposes of this book, a "small business" is defined as one whose capital investment does not exceed $50,000 and whose work force is no more than thirty. A "medium business" is one having no more than a $250,000 capitalization and no more than 100 employees. Any business with more than $250,000 capitalization and more than 100 employees is "big business" in the developing countries.

The term "entrepreneur" refers to an individual who is, to some extent, an innovator but who also functions as a manager. He is able to deal with the basic problems of organization, and he has the courage to go out into the money market and put together a business enterprise.

This book is divided into four principal sections. The first section treats the development institution, specifically the regional development corporation, from the standpoint of what a development organization can do to be effective. The second portion of the book deals with the identification of industrial investment opportunities. The third section is concerned with industrial promotion. Here a blueprint of a typical effective industrial promotion program has been constructed. The final section deals with the avenues of finance that are available to businesses of all sizes.

It is our hope that this book will serve as a ready reference for the student of industrial development, for small and large businessmen in developing and developed countries, and for those working in development organizations all over the world.

PART I

THE REGIONAL DEVELOPMENT CORPORATION CONCEPT OF INDUSTRIAL DEVELOPMENT

CHAPTER 1 INTRODUCTION TO REGIONAL DEVELOPMENT CONCEPT OF INDUSTRIAL DEVELOPMENT

Today, concepts, policies, and methods of industrial development are being analyzed in a great number of countries. Considerable progress has already been made. But in order for any policy or method to be implemented, an effective instrument is needed. As a result, industrial development or promotion institutes, productivity centers, industrial advisory institutes, and other similar institutions are functioning in many countries. But these organizations often discover that the problem of developing an entire country is a complex task that may exceed their capabilities. On the other hand, the goal of many countries' economic policy is a more balanced development of all the country's regions. The prime motivation for such policies is a more economically rational and equitable geographical distribution of investments.

An overdeveloped, overcrowded principal city, along with deserted, badly neglected provinces, is a phenomenon that many countries are trying to fight. To decentralize economic activity in accordance with economic criteria is one of the important challenges that planners, politicians, and businessmen in many countries will have to face in the near future. Diseconomies created by huge urban agglomerations and deserted provinces can be particularly serious in nations whose continuing development depends on avoiding wasted resources.

Just as governments and business firms have found it useful to decentralize their functions in order to more effectively administer the whole country, industrial development planners, too, are finding it necessary to decentralize economic and industrial development efforts. In response to this necessity, the "regional development corporation" or "regional industrial development corporation" is emerging today in a number of countries. Such institutions serve to apply modern industrial development techniques and concepts intensively on regional and local levels. They are in direct contact with regional or local development problems so that they can work out solutions specifically fitted to the local situations, and they have the means to carry out their policies directly without administrative delays. They become the instrument for translating regional or local aspirations into specific action based on local resources and skills. They thus become valuable defenses against overcentralization and against cumbersome bureaucratic processes in the capital city.

If organized properly, a regional development corporation allows special attention to the small and medium local industries that account for a large share of industrial output and employment even in highly industrialized countries but are often neglected in national industrial development schemes.

This type of organization typically covers an area with a population of at least 2 million. The exact size of the territory or population served by a regional industrial development corporation will vary greatly with circumstances. The regions may coincide with political subdivisions or may be determined by such considerations as economic complementary, geographical boundaries, or cultural affinity. If the area or population is too small, too large an effort will probably be wasted; if it is too large, the drawbacks of overcentralization will make themselves felt.

The kind of organization discussed here is one whose efforts are concentrated primarily on industrial development in the broadest sense. Such efforts may include building an economic infrastructure and developing agriculture, education, and training, because industrial development is closely connected to and dependent on the development of these other activities. However, the starting point of all considerations is industrial development, and the guidelines in this study are primarily directed to development corporations whose central and basic task is industrial development.

In both highly developed and newly developing countries today, regional development corporations that focus on industrial development have become important, effective tools of economic progress. They can be found all over the world: in the Canadian prairie provinces, in the southern United States, in southern Italy, in many Latin American countries such as Brazil and Peru, in Pakistan, the Philippines, and in many other nations.

In small countries, one national corporation is usually sufficient. In this case, the guidelines for regional corporations in larger countries apply with few modifications.

It is one of the purposes of this book to serve as a guide for the organization of regional industrial development corporations and for the practical work they have to perform. The advantages of a regionalized approach to industrial development will be discussed, followed by an explanation of the functions and organization of regional development corporations in the industrial field.

ADVANTAGES OF THE REGIONAL APPROACH TO ECONOMIC DEVELOPMENT

The regular governmental functions of a country are structured on various levels: the national level, the regional level, the provincial or departmental level, the city level, and the village level. Besides an internal political and economic structure, a country is usually connected with some type of international structure, in the form of membership in either the United Nations, Common Market or trade associations, defense treaty organizations, or international educational, social welfare, or scientific organizations. Countries have found that the multiple functions of government cannot be carried out from one central point, but rather that decision-making and executive authority have to be distributed over the country in a decentralized manner. If this were not the case, the administrative apparatus would become clumsy, slow, and monolithic: Many important matters would probably not be attended to; and individual, regional, or local participation in national activities would be smothered.

Many newly developing countries find that economic development requires an administrative apparatus separate from those through which normal government functions are performed. The normal government organizations are not staffed or equipped to handle development functions, or they are already overburdened with the performance of their normal functions. As a result, special economic development organizations have been created in many countries, such as national planning institutes, industrial promotion institutes, special development finance institutions and banks, special organizations for the development finance institutions and banks, special organizations for the development of infrastructure, and industrial advisory services. But often these special organizations are organized only on the national level, so that they concentrate only on national problems. Even though such organizations often set up regional or local offices, financial and personnel shortages often do not permit their work to be very profound or far-reaching outside of the capital cities. Even more important, regional interests are often overlooked by national agencies. Sometimes regions are functionally subdivided among the different organizations: As a result, regional interests are often disregarded and the participation of the people of the region in the developmental process and especially in the decision-making process that should preceed developmental plans is reduced to a minimum. Any developmental process, if it is to be effective, has to involve as many people as possible in order to mobilize the energies, imagination, and drive of a broad segment of the population for economic development; this is especially true in newly developing countries where trained individuals are scarce.

In order to achieve this end, it is often found convenient to regroup and institutionalize the national development functions on the regional or even local levels and to try to provide maximum opportunity for popular regional or local backing and participation. This can be achieved through the formation of regional or local development corporations which combine the development functions and coordinate them into one integrated regional program. Such institutions are designed to carry out the national industrial development functions of planning, research into development possibilities and project studies, promoting these possibilities among potential investors, financing for development, and providing for advisory services for development on a regional basis.

This structure of development activity is shown in Figure 1, which shows that each national institution in charge of a principal function of economic or industrial development delegates this function on the regional level to regional development corporations. There are links between the national organizations and the regional development corporations to assure horizontal coordination on all levels. The regional development organizations may in turn delegate some of their functions to local organizations.

The type of regional development corporation with which this study is primarily concerned could, for instance, be based on an assembly or governing body made up of elected or appointed representatives of the economic development institutions on the national level, representatives from the national government, representatives from the most active economic elements of the area (the "live forces" of the region), and representatives from the regional government. The "live forces" of the region could be represented by the chambers of commerce and industry or similar industrial organizations, agricultural

FIGURE 1

DEVELOPMENT FUNCTIONS

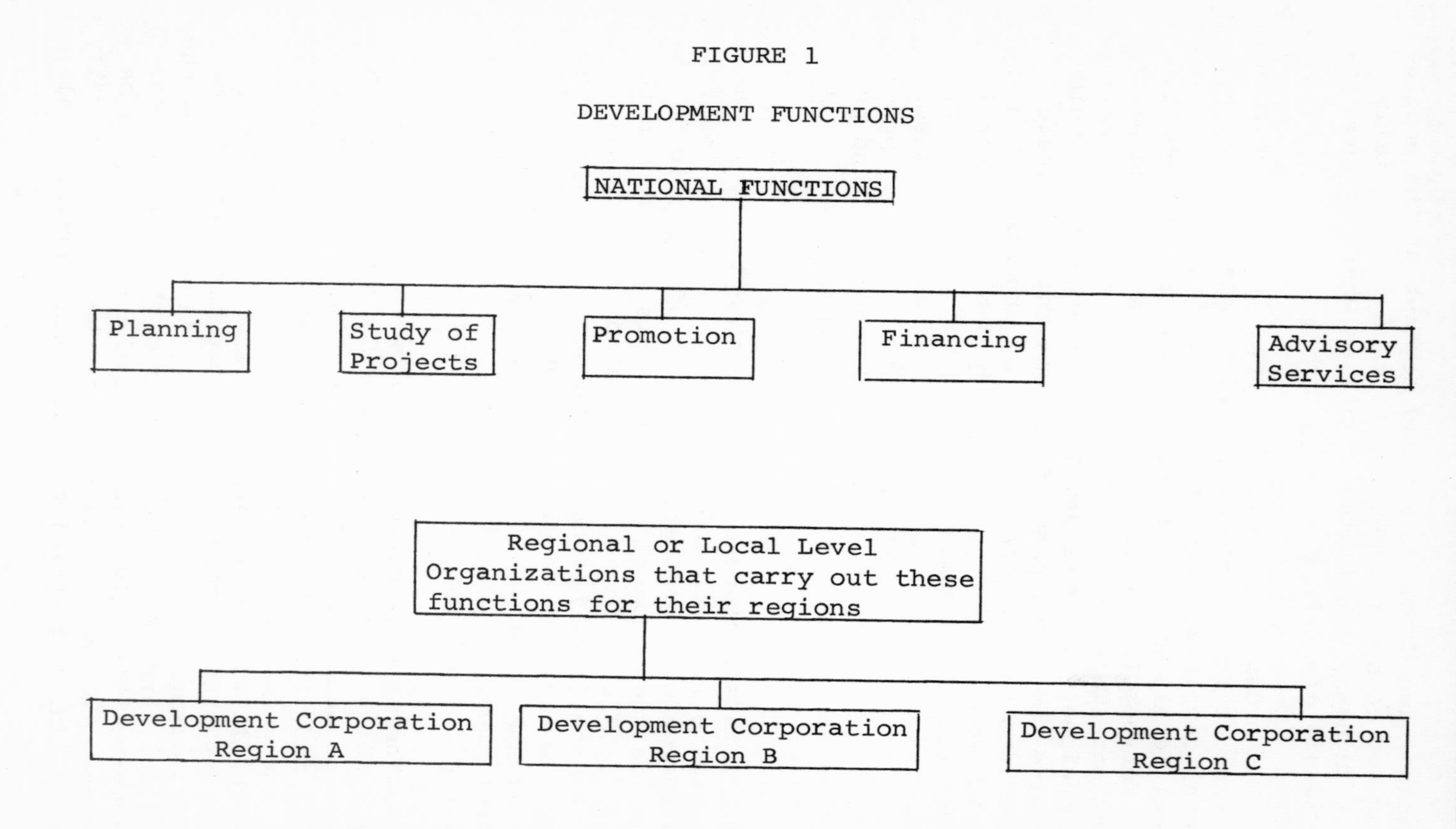

organizations, professional organizations, labor unions, universities and similar educational or research institutions, or other elements that play a vital role in the development of the regions and whose participations and support must, therefore, be secured. The governing body or assembly selects a board of directors, forms special committees, and names a general executive who appoints his staff. The development corporation thus becomes a focus and a clearing or coordinating house for all economic and industrial development efforts coming from within the region or from the national or international level to the region. Such development corporations can contribute greatly toward uniting all the region's development plans and efforts in one organization, and it can become a spokesman for all the region's economic and industrial development interests.

ORGANIZING A DEVELOPMENT CORPORATION

The first step in organizing a regional development corporation is to identify the leaders in business, the professions, government, civic affairs, the labor unions, and other organizations that can contribute to a well-functioning organization. No segment of the population, especially the active groups within the population, should be left out. The next step is to interest the leaders in a plan for a development corporation and to work out an organizational structure with them and define the functions it should fulfill. This should result in a complete proposal for a regional corporation with an organizational chart, a description of purposes and goals, and a plan of how these goals can be reached, and the necessary budget.

The organization may receive its funds from public sources or such private sources as contributions from existing businesses. Regardless of the source, membership of the governing body should include key spokesmen for both sectors. Even if all funds come from public sources, the private sector of the area should be well represented, and, if possible, should even have a majority. For example, here is the composition of the governing body of a development corporation financed entirely with public funds: (1) the president of the governing body, named by the president of the country; (2) four other persons, designated by the central government, who should be experts in management and finance as well as in industry and agriculture; (3) one member of the city council of the principal city of the area who is to represent the interests of the other municipal governments as well; (4) one representative from a special public works board in the region; (5) one member designated by a private industrial promotion committee in the region; (6) two representatives from the chambers of commerce of the region; (7) one representative of the agricultural societies of the region; (8) three persons representing the professional organizations of the region, namely lawyers, engineers, and doctors; and (9) two representatives from the labor unions.

It is evident that in each specific situation a different form of representation must be worked out since different groups vary as to interest, power, dedication, and leadership ability. Appointments should be for staggered terms so as to assure continuity from one political regime to the next. The membership may be as large as 100, but in this case an executive committee should be appointed of no more than five persons. If the governing board is too small and important organizations and groups are not represented, this may alienate them and cause them to refuse to cooperate with the corporation. The governing body may meet as often as monthly or as infrequently as yearly.[1] The function of the governing body is to outline the broad policies and goals of the corporation and to monitor its performance in reaching these goals and complying with established policies. The governing body delegates executive responsibility to a director or manager who appoints his staff.

The director or manager is then responsible for working out a program of industrial development for the area which then has to be approved by the governing body. "Industrial development" is used here in its broader sense, referring to all activities that contribute to the prosperity and progress of the region involved. Thus industrial development may include, in addition to industry in the narrow sense, such activities as agro-business, mining, fisheries, forestry, and tourism. Agriculture is usually excluded since it represents a special field which in many countries is the responsibility of special organizations. However, agro-business, such as warehousing, and marketing of agricultural products, may be included. Thus a development corporation's organizational structure is determined by whatever activities it undertakes in the following fields: industrial development (in the narrower sense) including small industry and handicraft development; development of the industrial infrastructure of power, water, sewage, ports, possibly roads and railroads, and industrial parks; commercial development including agro-business and marketing of agricultural products; and tourism development.

To this could be added community development and any other special activities that may be required by the particular region involved. In Puerto Rico, for instance, the Economic Development Administration has a special rum promotion division. A development corporation in the Andean highlands of Peru has a special division for the creation of handicraft centers since these centers provide employment and introduce organized work methods.

Some development corporations have found it necessary to develop certain basic industries under their own initiative. Once the success of these industries has been demonstrated, they try to sell them, wholly or partially, to private investors. The danger of publicly owned and managed industries is that their managements may be determined by political or social welfare considerations, rather than by purely economic considerations. Such a policy can lead to chronically deficitary enterprises which no private investors want to take over and which represent a constant drain on the financial resources of the development corporation. To avoid such situations and to assure the success of corporation-owned and-managed industries, a separate division should be formed in the corporation from the moment the project has entered the planning phase. Otherwise the regular organization of the corporation, which might be overburdened with the execution of a major project, could fail to give sufficient attention to its other responsibilities. The management of the corporation-owned industries should be completely independent of political or other influences that are extraneous to running an industry efficiently and it should be responsible to the corporation only to the extent that the management of any private company is responsible to its board of directors--that is, with respect to its performance in administrative and technical management and with respect to its profits. In many cases, corporations have found it advantageous to sign over the management of their industries under a management contract to reputable and experienced firms familiar with the type of industry concerned.

The president should be a leader of such stature and prominence that he can impart to the organization some of the status it needs to be effective. He can be an outstanding political, civic or business, or professional leader who enjoys the respect of the public and of the other members of the governing body. He must be able to unite the governing body in support of a clearly defined development program and to inspire enthusiasm and confidence throughout the whole organization.

The general manager must be a dynamic organizer, capable of attracting highly qualified personnel and building them into a strong and active organization. He must be a man of vision and ideas, who sees development opportunities, has them studied, and employs all resources and personal contacts at his disposal to turn plans and projects into realities. He must be possessed by a sense of urgency and dedication to the cause of development. He must have the confidence of the president and the members of the board of directors and of the public in general.

Many development programs or development corporations fail because their leaders are not the real leaders in the area or because their leaders do not have the competent technicians and specialists to give their plans and programs definite shape.[2] People with leadership qualities and technical knowledge in the development field or technicians with specific knowledge and experience in the methods and techniques of development are scarce almost anywhere. A development corporation will therefore have to start with people with the most promising backgrounds and performance on their former jobs and will then have to train them in the special tasks at hand. In order to attract top quality people, a development corporation should not skimp on salaries or other incentives. Development is a critical field; therefore a successful program can have tremendous impact on the region which will more than compensate the initial expenses in salaries for high quality personnel. The general manager, the president, and the members of the governing body will do well to undertake study trips to other regions or other countries to get firsthand knowledge of the working methods and programs of successful development corporations elsewhere. Such trips will also give them an opportunity to learn about training opportunities for the technical staff of the corporation. On the basis of a carefully conceived training plan, the technical staff will then participate in training courses abroad or with other development corporations in the country.

A development corporation will also do well to engage the services of an industrial development advisor from the beginning. Such experts can be of great value in guiding the corporation executives and staff in their planning and programming and in specific development methods and techniques. Such experts are available from international institutions, research and development institutions in the industrialized countries, and through the technical aid programs of the major industrial countries.

This organizational structure would have to be adapted to the situation and circumstances of each specific corporation. According to the volume of

FIGURE 2

ORGANIZATION OF A DEVELOPMENT CORPORATION

Governing Body

Executive Committee

Outside Advisors

Legal Advisor

President

General Manager

Head of Planning Section

Assistant

Administrative Assistant

Head of Special Section

Head of Tourism Section

Head of Commercial Development Section

Head of Infrastructure Section

Head of Industrial Section

SUBDIVISIONS OF THE INDUSTRIAL SECTION

Head of the Section and Head of the Sub-Section Medium and Larger Industry

Secretarial Pool

Head Sub-Section Small Industry and Artisans

Market Research and Marketing specialist

Designer

Production Techniques and Cost Specialist

Management and Cooperating Specialist

Services

Production Techniques Specialist

Management Specialist

Financial Analyst

Financial Analyst

Finance Specialist

Market Research Specialist

Chemical Industries Specialist

Mechanical Industries Specialist

Food-Processing Industries Specialist

Specialist in Other Industries Important to the Region

Promotional and Publicity Specialist

work required, more persons can be added to each section.

The Industrial Section

Small Industry and Artisans Section

The Industrial Section is divided into two sections: one for medium and larger industries and one for small industries and artisans. This division is recommended to insure sufficient attention to small industries and artisans. It is usually easier to work with a small group of medium and larger industries than with a large group of small industries or artisans, and a staff responsible for the whole spectrum of industries would tend to devote its time to work in the medium and larger industry field.

The functions or activities of the small industry and artisan section are: (1) conducting market studies within the country and abroad for small industry products in order to open up new markets; (2) conducting surveys of existing small industries in the region and their products; (3) conducting simple feasibility studies for new small industry; (4) designing and redesigning small industry products to adapt them to consumer tastes and needs; (5) conducting studies of improvements in production techniques and methods; maintaining constant contact with sources of technical information within the country and abroad, such as research institutes within the country and abroad, the technical aid agencies of various industrial countries, of the United Nations, of the OECD, and of other similar organizations; making cost studies and cost analyses; (6) providing technical training of small industrialists and artisans at various levels; (7) assisting with the purchase of raw materials, machinery, and tools; (8) providing quality control assistance and assistance in shop layout and organization of work flow; (9) providing assistance in obtaining lower freight rates and selecting the best means of transportation; (10) providing assistance in the selection of the best distribution and marketing methods within the country and abroad; organizing expositions, trade fairs, and fashion shows; (11) encouraging potential entrepreneurs who want to establish new small industries; (12) arranging for the financing of new or improved industries, both for equipment and for working capital; (13) providing assistance to the management of small industries; (14) evaluating loan requests and requests for equity capital participation from small industrialists and artisans; providing technical and administrative supervision of loans made to small industrialists and artisans; (15) providing help in obtaining loans from commercial banks or commercial firms; and (16) providing assistance in the organization of sales and production cooperatives throughout the region.

To fulfill these functions satisfactorily, the staff of this division should have special qualifications.

The person heading the division should have experience in different artisan and small industry activities. He should be experienced in the organization of small productions, in financial management and accounting, and in business management in general. He should be knowledgeable about cooperatives, about marketing and distribution, and about exporting manufactured goods. If artistically oriented small industries and artisans seem to offer the most promising possibilities in the area, he should have at least a basic knowledge of artistic design and general trends in consumer tastes within the country and abroad. He should be able to deal with small manufacturers in an effective way and should be skillful in public relations.

The market research and marketing specialist should have knowledge of marketing and sales promotion techniques and methods. He does not need an academic or professional degree; for instance, he can be a student of economics at the local university. He should be familiar with the small industry and artisan manufacturing activities and products of the region.

The production techniques and cost specialist

could be a student of industrial engineering or industrial economics; he must be familiar with production statistics, analysis, and determination of costs and comparative cost studies of small industries.

The management and cooperatives specialist could be a student of economics or a recent graduate in the field with some experience in business organization and the ability to organize working groups. He should be able to interpret statistics and should have a good knowledge of accounting. He should also be familiar with the small industries of the region.

The designer should have a good knowledge of the commercial arts and a deep understanding of local art; he should be knowledgeable in sculpture, in industrial design, and in modeling. He should be able to read mechanical drawings and to introduce new products and designs.

Medium and Larger Industry Section

This division could be in charge of the following developmental activities: (1) planning industrial development of the region in collaboration with the planning office in the corporation and with other governmental agencies working in industrial development, such as the industrial promotion institute of the country, the industrial bank of the country, the ministry of development, and others; (2) undertaking general economic studies, including studies of the natural and human resources of the region that might be important to industry; studies of market and technological trends which can serve as guidelines for the longer-range industrial development programs; and an inventory of all industrial activities of the area; (3) seeking and identifying industrial investment opportunities; (4) undertaking feasibility studies, both preliminary feasibility studies made by the staff of the section and final feasibility studies made by specialized firms or consultants contracted from outside; (5) undertaking industrial promotion activities through the preparation of specific investment prospectuses on industrial investment opportunities in the region; the preparation of general investment prospectuses on the economy of the region and the advantages it has to offer to investors; general promotional work through developing close contacts with potential investors from within the country and abroad and sponsoring speeches, seminars, conferences, displays, and trade fairs; the organization of community and industrial development groups in other smaller towns and communities in the area; and distribution of literature, guidance, and assistance to them as required; (6) offering extension services that include providing technical literature to the businessmen of the region. Such literature can often be obtained at relatively low cost through the technical aid programs of industrial countries, the United Nations, the OECD, and other similar organizations. Another such service is providing industrial advisory services in management and production technology to the existing and new industries in the region; (7) offering financial services, including receiving and evaluating loan applications and providing information on other sources of financing from within the country or from international or foreign sources; supervising the loans made by the development corporation; and preparing loan application from the development corporation to sources of outside financing, such as the World Bank, the International Finance Corporation, private banks, and the Agency for International Development of the U.S. Government, to supplement the development corporation's funds.

To be able to carry out these activities and functions, this division's personnel must have special qualifications.

The head of the industrial section should be an industrial engineer or industrial economist who is experienced in making feasibility studies and who is familiar with industrial finance. He should be able to plan, program, and organize the work of his staff. He should know English in addition to his native language.

As can be seen from Figure 2, it is usually advantageous to have as industry specialists engineers with special knowledge and experience in chemical, mechanical, and food-processing industries or other industries important to the region.

The market research specialist should be an economist with experience in market research; his work supplements that of the industry specialists.

The financial specialist should be experienced in banking and financial management, for he will be responsible for evaluating and processing loan applications and for preparing loan applications from the development corporation to sources of outside financing.

The background of the promotional and publicity specialist should be in journalism and public relations with emphasis on financial and business writing. He should be an effective speaker, well versed in all methods of communication.

The Infrastructure Section

This section will be in charge of identifying the infrastructure requirements for industrial development in such areas as water, sewage, power, industrial parks, access roads to industrial raw materials, port installations, and possibly housing facilities for workers and employees. It will also make plans and studies as to how these requirements can be met. It will cooperate closely with other governmental agencies responsible for infrastructure projects in general, that is, road and port authorities, urban planning sections, power companies, etc. It will supplement the work of these entities keeping in mind the special needs of industry rather than competing with them or duplicating their functions. One of its more important projects will be feasibility studies for industrial parks.

Ordinarily all that is needed is a small staff consisting of a civil engineer as head of the section, an assistant engineer, and a draftsman. It can draw on the services of the staff of the industrial section for such special projects as market research or on the services of specialists contracted from outside.

The Commercial Development Section

Many newly developing countries have found that one of the major obstacles to industrial growth is an archaic system of marketing and distribution. This is particularly true of agricultural and fisheries products. In many Latin American countries, for instance, products like fish, fruit, and vegetables are sold to the consumer at three or four times the prices paid to the producer. On purely industrial goods the mark-ups may not be quite as high, but distribution costs may nevertheless raise the price to the final consumer to such an extent that the product is no longer within the reach of large consumer groups. This is partially due to inefficient marketing methods, to the practice of a high margin and low volume rather than a low margin and high volume, and to cartels of distributors who keep profits artificially high. Often it is the policy of distributors to pay producers lower prices for greater quantities whereas the consumers usually get only insufficient amounts at high or exorbitant prices.

Often producers and firms in the outlying provinces of a country suffer most from such practices since they are often unable to organize their own distribution firms in the principal cities of the country where the major markets lie.

The export markets are often closed to firms in outlying provinces since they do not usually possess the special knowledge of export markets and exporting techniques and they cannot pay the high fees charged by export firms in the principal cities. Small firms are particularly hard hit in this way.

The commercial section of a development corporation could be responsible for studying means of overcoming these difficulties and for carrying out practical schemes designed to improve domestic and export marketing for the firms in the region, particularly smaller firms. Such measures can consist of helping businessmen to start distribution firms operating on the low-margin high-volume principle, helping in the establishment of special export firms serving the industries of the region, providing financing and guidance for the construction of storage facilities for agricultural and fisheries products of the region, and helping transportation companies to expand and improve their operations. The work of this section could also include market studies for the principal products of the region and an educational program for the region's businessmen in marketing and advertising techniques through special courses, seminars, demonstrations, and the distribution of literature. It may also assist in the organization of trade fairs both in the region and outside of the region to make regional products better known to buyers in other sections of the country and abroad.

Normally, it will be sufficient to staff this section with a specialist in marketing who is thoroughly familiar with the businessmen and the products of the region aided by one or several statistical or promotional assistants who can arrange displays and exhibitions. He will work very closely with local business organizations, chambers of commerce, farmers' associations, etc.

The Tourism Section

In regions where tourism can make a substantial contribution to increased employment and income, it may be useful for a development corporation to include a special tourism development section within its organization. The work of this section would include the identification and study of tourism facilities such as hotels, beaches, country clubs, and hunting lodges, stations for stocking rivers and lakes with fish, projects for restoring historical sites and buildings, and access roads to scenic areas. It could also work on training tourist guides, hunting and fishing guides, waiters, and similar service personnel. It may help to organize conventions in the area to bring in business and professional men who will bring revenue to services and who will become better acquainted with the economic and industrial potential of the region. It can promote sports festivals and celebrations involving the particular historical or cultural features of the region, such as folk dancing and native costume festivals, wine festivals, fishermen's festivals, handicrafts exhibitions, and historical plays. This section could also publish information for tourists and maintain contact with tourist agencies in other areas of the country and abroad. The section should work closely with local governments, the chambers of commerce, cultural organizations, schools, universities, and its national tourism promotion agency (if the country has one).

The head of this section can be either a teacher of history or literature with organizational talent and a special interest in the area's civic life and cultural activities or a person with a background in the travel agency business familiar with the region and its possibilities for tourism. According to the magnitude of the job and the importance of tourism to the region, he can be given one or more assistants experienced in hotel management or travel agency work.

The Special Section

If the special section is concerned with a special industry or group of industries, it will probably work on improving quality and efficiency in the industry or on making prefeasibility and feasibility studies for industrial projects. It may work on problems of export marketing and on the organization of workshops and marketing programs for small industries. This section usually requires a combination of engineers, economists, and businessmen from the fields concerned.

The Planning Section

The head of the planning section works closely with the general manager and the different section heads as well as with the president and the executive committee in planning the work of the development corporation, in identifying the most promising fields of development of the department, and in determining the activities which should be emphasized. He also ascertains that the development plans of the regional corporation are in accord with the over-all policies and plans of the national government. If the country has a national planning institute, he will be in close contact with its executives and he may become the regional representative of the planning institute. He is responsible for the over-all development in the region, and with coordinating the plans for each section in respect to the general plan. Specifically, his functions include: (1) research and analysis concerning the resources and the development needs of the region in order to formulate over-all development objectives, priorities, and long-term plans; (2) assistance to the president, the general manager, and the section heads with respect to annual programs and specific projects; (3) recommendations to the president and the general manager about specific programs and projects proposed by the section heads, in order to maintain integrated programs within the agreed objectives and priorities, and within the resources available to the development corporation; (4) maintenance and dissemination of basic economic data for use of the section heads, private businesses, and other agencies in the region; (5) coordination with national, regional, and local organizations with respect to national, regional, and local development planning; (6) assistance to the section heads with respect to methods of carrying out programs and projects; (7) evaluation of the progress and results of the development plans and programs; and (8) assistance to municipal and town authorities in local community development and planning.

The head of this section should be highly qualified, preferably an economist, with experience in planning, programming, and evaluating projects and performance. His professional experience, personality, and stature should be such that his advice and guidance will be appreciated and respected by the section heads, the general manager, and the president. He can be given an administrative and statistical assistant to facilitate his work.

Outside Advisors

Industrial Development Advisors

The development corporation should make use of outside development advisors in establishing and executing its programs. Most of these advisors will have to come from abroad, because developing countries do not usually have experienced persons in this field. Well-selected advisors can bring pertinent international experience to bear on the problems of the development corporation and can supply valuable independent viewpoints. The services of experienced industrial development consultants should be engaged for at least one year, during the initial and planning phase of the corporation. Such advisors can be recruited either directly, from research and consulting firms specializing in industrial development, or through the technical-aid agencies of industrial countries, such as the U.S. Agency for International Development.

In addition, a development corporation should make full use of all available technicians and experts available in the country and abroad. Often these technicians have already been brought into the country by other national organizations such as productivity institutes, planning institutes, national industrial promotion institutes, ministries, or technical training organizations, and it usually is possible to extend their visits so that they can stay in the region concerned. They can be of great value in giving training courses for the personnel of the corporation and businessmen in general or in advising on special problems that the corporation may have to face.

The help of members of volunteer organizations, such as the Peace Corps of various countries, can be a significant supplement to local personnel, particularly in connection with small industry and handicraft programs.*

The Development Corporation As an Institution Builder

Institutions are the instruments through which plans and projects and provisions for services can be realized. The development corporation is itself such an institution. But economic and industrial development touch on such a variety of fields that the corporation cannot possibly enter into them all. It needs other institutions with which it can work and through which some of the development objectives can be reached. If such institutions or organizations do not already exist, the development corporation must try to encourage their formation. Such organizations as industry and trade associations, cooperatives, institutes for applied research that would directly benefit the industry of the region, private consulting firms, industrial park enterprises, training centers for skilled workers and technicians, and financial institutions like private equity investment companies and industrial finance corporations can contribute to economic and industrial development. Universities can be supplied with specific research proposals in the fields of the life sciences, engineering, chemistry, civil engineering, and especially economics and business administration. Students and professors are usually grateful for any practical research projects--for which they may even be paid--and can become dedicated and valuable collaborators in the tasks to be performed by corporations. Thus, for example, a development corporation can engage the economics and business administration department of a university to carry out an industry analysis which can serve as a basis for the loan program of the corporation or other financial institu-

---

*The functions of legal advisor and administrative assistant to the general manager are the same as those required by any governmental or industrial organization, so that they do not require any special discussion.

tions, or it can engage the science or engineering department to investigate the raw materials of the area that are best suited for building block manufacture.

Industry and trade associations are of special importance in the growth of smaller and medium industry.[3] An association offers a point of contact for people outside the region who are interested in the industry of the area. The outsiders may be buyers of commercial products from the capital city or from abroad, potential investors, or government or development corporation officials studying ways in which to assist smaller and medium-sized industry. An association can also serve as a clearing house through which its members can receive information of interest to them, such as marketing information, publications on relevant legislative matters, and information on new products and production.

Through associations manufacturers can work together in cooperative marketing activities, joint showrooms, trade fairs, and bulk purchasing of raw materials, in setting up common storage facilities, and in establishing industrial parks. In this way, smaller firms can achieve some of the economies of larger scale operations.

In other cases the enforcement of quality controls and other standards can be made more effective. Working together in an organized manner, small and medium manufacturers can more effectively make themselves heard outside of their region in legislative matters, in government tenders, or in purchases. Also, associations can more effectively organize training courses for their members.

Community development is another broad field in which the development corporation can act as a catalyst and form new organizations and institutions. In some countries, the chambers of commerce or similar organizations are already active in this field; in others, special community organizations may have to be formed. Such organizations can consist of a governing body that represents all or most of the active elements of the community, a small professional staff--very often only one director, his assistant, and a secretary--and a series of special volunteer committees that cooperate with the director in such fields as tourism, external promotion, finance, community development (in the narrower sense), and research and information. Such community development organizations or citizens committees can be formed in the principal city of the region in which the development corporation is located, but they are particularly effective in the smaller towns where they may assume some of the functions of the development corporation itself, acting as its local representative. The relationship between the development corporation and community development organizations is usually a loose one without any formal chain of command through which the development corporation provides guidance and stimulus to the community development organization. Coordination is achieved through close contacts between the two organizations, effective communication, and cooperation in working toward the same goals.

The following are some typical projects which community development organizations in smaller to medium-sized towns can undertake in the over-all field of industrial development: maintain an up-to-date file of statistical data on the local economy; compile an inventory of industrial sites and vacant buildings; cooperate with other local or regional groups; make a study of water resources; sponsor a local industrial development seminar with expert outside speakers; publish a folder to advertise tourist attractions; catalog and promote places of historical interest; conduct a campaign to have business and professional conventions held in the area; sponsor a festival, perhaps one that is associated with a local product; sponsor a "Business Education Day" when teachers and students visit local industries; conduct a series of meetings to promote a better business climate; sponsor a "clean-up paint-up project" in local communities; establish a legislative study group to represent the area's interests to political officials; work to obtain government support for better highways; study means to improve trucking service; sponsor adult education courses and promote vocational training; conduct a fire prevention and education campaign; promote the establishment of a local planning commission; promote and publicize city beautification projects; promote landing strips for light aircraft; finance and build a speculative industrial building; sponsor a labor-management forum; and plan, finance, and promote a small industrial park.

Small rural communities of a certain size should also be included in the over-all drive for development. It is important that as many citizens as possible participate in development planning and action, and that the effects of development reach even the remotest hamlet. In this way the markets for industrial products are widened and the region becomes more attractive for new industries by offering them a larger local market. For this reason, community development groups can be organized even in small rural communities. They may be organized like the groups in medium or smaller cities, except that for economic reasons they will probably not hire a professional director. All the work will be done through elected and volunteer officers and committees formed for each kind of project. Typical projects for rural community development organizations would include the following: clearing roadsides of debris; planting trees and flowers; promoting electric lines and telephone service; assisting in getting right-of-way for lines; donating poles; maintaining a farm equipment pool; organizing a volunteer fire department; sponsoring a pest control program; setting up a first-aid station; testing the water supply; maintaining statistics on those citizens who want jobs; sponsoring an agricultural fair; participating in a community-improvement contest sponsored by the development corporation of the larger region; erecting markers at points of historical interest; exchanging visits with townspeople; showing farms to city people and showing industries to farm people; establishing a handicraft center; sponsoring recreational programs for young people; getting uniforms for athletic teams; installing plumbing facilities in schools; improving school grounds and play areas; repairing churches and improving grounds; promoting small business ventures; getting outside help in promoting industrial jobs;

building a community center; showing educational motion pictures; raising funds for community projects through roadside markets; stenciling names on mail boxes and entrances; providing picnic areas along highways and inviting city people to use them; cooperating with agricultural workers in a soil-testing program; arranging for guest speakers on such topics as crop rotation, fertilizer application and drainage; promoting efficient livestock management and parasite control; setting up a farm marketing organization; arranging classes in forest management, pruning, thinning, and fire and insect control; arranging a program on family financial practices, savings, insurance, and record keeping; setting up a community food canning facility; arranging for visits of portable X-ray units or for other public health programs; promoting better bus service to cities; encouraging citizens to vote in elections; and building a small air strip for emergency use.

The establishment of handicraft centers is an especially significant project. In communities with a particular handicraft tradition, the setting up of such centers may often be an effective way to preserve this tradition and thereby an effective economic activity with possible far-reaching cultural and sociological implications, as well as a means of turning the handicrafts tradition into a modern, design-oriented industry. To establish a handicraft center, first a building has to be set up in which all artisans of one or several trades can be jointly located; this building can usually be contributed by the community itself. With outside help, specifically that of the development corporation of a larger region, modern equipment and machinery can be bought with which the craftsmen's work can be made more efficient without necessarily changing the character of the articles made. New products that can be made with available skills can be introduced through the handicraft center. The center can be managed by a handicraft technician trained for this purpose, who is provided by the development corporation. If a center has started as a unit in which production is organized in a more efficient manner on a group basis, it may evolve into a marketing unit for handicraft products.

Training for Industrial Development

The quality and experience of a development corporation's staff and the degree to which its administrators are familiar with the problems of development and with the methods and techniques that can solve them are of fundamental importance for the corporation's success and effectiveness. It is also important that the business and professional men and the civic leaders with whom the corporation will have to deal be familiar not only with the specific problems involved in improving and expanding their businesses, but also with the general problems of economic and industrial development and their possible solutions in the region concerned. A development corporation with the best plans and programs and with ample financial resources will fail without a well-trained, experienced staff and a sympathetic governing body that understands the kind of problems with which the corporation staff has to deal.

In general, experienced workers are scarce in newly developing countries and regions. The curriculums of schools and universities do not usually include the problems of development, and local business, professional, and civic leaders have only very general notions of the needs and requirements for development and the actions that must be undertaken to accelerate it. Therefore, special arrangements for development training must be made by the development corporation. The possible forms of development education are training on the job, formal training in courses and seminars in the region, formal training and visits abroad, and training in the universities.

Training on the job in development institutions is much like training within industry: Students learn from their supervisors, from outsiders, from each other, from books and technical publications, and from their daily work experiences. Part of the reason for having outside advisors working in a development corporation in daily close contact with its personnel is to give the development corporation personnel the benefit of the advisors' greater experience in various aspects of development. A development corporation should assemble a library of pertinent general and technical books and should subscribe to periodicals in the field. Staff members and top executives should be encouraged to study this material.

Before a development corporation starts its work, members of the staff and the board should participate in a training seminar covering all aspects of development: planning and programming, research and development, promotion, advisory services, small industry development, and organization for development. Such a training seminar can be arranged with the help of outside advisors, prominent government officials, and business leaders from the capital city who are experienced in development and who can act as speakers and discussion leaders.

An effective seminar can meet for one to two months. It can be divided into two sessions: the first before the participants have started to work, and the second a few months after they have had a chance to get a practical, direct knowledge of the problems with which they have to deal. They can then share their experiences and discuss the problems they have encountered with the advisors and speakers.

Besides a training program for staff members, professional and civic leaders and members of the governing body and the executive committee should participate in special courses, which can meet at night or on week-ends so that they do not interfere with the participants' other commitments. This course can be directed by the outside advisors and by guest speakers from the capital city or abroad: technical experts, governmental leaders, or business and professional leaders who are concerned with economic development and who have experience in this field.

Another kind of formal training is study trips to other sections of the country or other countries where well-functioning development corporations or development programs exist. Selected staff members, the general manager, the president, and members of the executive committee and the governing body, as well as leading local businessmen, professional men, bankers, and civic and political leaders should undertake such trips. The trips can be arranged in the initial planning phase of the corporation through the contacts of industrial development consulting firms, and plans should be made for such trips to be repeated periodically after the corporation has started its operation. A firsthand look at other successful development corporations and an interchange of ideas with the personnel of these corporations, which can be continued by mail, will help the corporation to start in the right direction. Participants must, of course, realize that the experiences of other countries are only partially applicable to their own country, so that the approach to development taken by a corporation must always be adapted to the region for which it is responsible. It must be a result of the creative thinking and determined action of the responsible officials of the development corporation itself.

Institutions in several countries are giving particular attention to policies and programs concerned with industrial development by offering courses to persons working at various levels in government and development institutions. These include the following:

The Economic Development Institute, Washington, D.C.

The International Bank for Reconstruction and Development offers a general course in economic development for a limited number of senior officials--usually not more than twenty-five--from the developing countries. This course includes general aspects of economic policy and development, historical aspects of development in various countries, fiscal policy and public finance, monetary policy, international trade and finance, agriculture, industry, social factors in development, and project appraisal. The course lasts about six months. In addition, the institute offers various special courses, such as the one on preparation and appraisal of development projects.

Program in Economic and Social Development, Graduate School of Public and International Affairs, University of Pittsburgh, Pittsburgh, Pennsylvania

This course is aimed primarily at the professional training of high-level administrators. It focuses on the problems of the developing countries. Most of the participants are enrolled in the Master's program. Some may be admitted to study on a special or nondegree basis. Short-term, intensive, nondegree courses and programs are offered, including a twelve-week summer institute for senior persons in economic, social, and industrial development.

The Institute of Social Studies, The Hague, Netherlands

This institute offers a six-month diploma course in economic planning. The course content includes tools for planning, theory of planning, planning procedures, and case studies.

The International Summer Course on Industrialization, The Hague, Netherlands

This program has been organized in cooperation with various ministries and institutes in The Netherlands. It provides a general introduction to industrialization, including such subjects as manpower requirements, industrial development planning, and infrastructural development. For participants who wish to remain longer than six weeks, special arrangements may be made to undertake field trips to other European countries. These courses are usually held in July and August; closing date for applications is June 1. Courses are given in English and the participants are not required to have college degrees, although it is preferred that they do.

The International Course on Small-Scale Industries, The Research Institute for Management Science, Delft, Netherlands

For over ten years this course has been given for international participants engaged in promotive industrial development and to managers of small industries. The course, which lasts six months, is given twice a year. The program includes a general study of small industry management, small industry and economic development, the role of small and medium industry in Europe, and international activities in the field of industrial development. Each participant is assigned a special program of field work related to specific industries. The courses begin in January and in July.

The Japan Productivity Center, Tokyo, Japan

This center administers a one-year consultant training course for small industry extension personnel. In the near future, a shorter course will be offered in English to participants from other Asian countries. The program should also be of value to participants from other parts of the world.

The Scandinavian Seminar on Smaller Industries Development, Copenhagen, Denmark

This seminar was held in 1963, but it is not known whether it is being continued. Denmark has also held summer seminars on the development of cooperatives, which emphasize agricultural cooperatives, for there has been very little development of industrial cooperatives in the Scandinavian countries.

The Small Industry Extension Training Institute, Hyderabad, India

This institute functions to promote the growth of small industry through training, research, and service activities. The training is directed particularly to small industry extension officers in India, although qualified applicants from other countries will be accepted. It covers three main fields: development, management, and extension. The basic course lasts for sixteen weeks.

El Instituto Tecnológico y de Estudios Superiores de Monterrey, Mexico

This institute offers courses partially patterned after the Massachusetts Institute of Technology. Degrees are offered in agriculture, industrial engineering, science, letters, and economics.

The German Institute for Development Policy in Berlin (Deutsches Institut Für Entwicklungs Politik)

This institute was recently founded to train German technicians in developmental work. However, it is understood that applicants from other countries are accepted. Courses are related to all aspects of industrial, agricultural, and social development.

In addition to these programs, there are various other courses in institutions in the United States, Europe, and the Near East. The above list consists only of the most important courses, and it is by no means exhaustive.

Training in the universities in most newly developing countries, as in most industrialized countries, is not usually tailored to the needs of development. A development corporation can, however, try to influence the universities to include special courses on industrial and other development. It can also encourage development-oriented thinking in the universities by giving the students and professors research projects on problems involved in the work of development corporations.

Notes to Chapter 1

1. See John McKinley Conway, *Organizing for Industrial Development*, Pamphlet (Atlanta, Georgia: Conway Research Institute, 1963).

2. *Ibid*.

3. Eugene Staley, *Methods of Industrial Development* (Paris: OECD, 1962), pp. 201-34.

CHAPTER 2 REGIONAL PLANNING AND PROGRAMMING FOR INDUSTRIAL DEVELOPMENT[1]

Every country has established a general legal and institutional framework within which private or government enterprise may operate. Within this general framework there are needs whose fulfillment require planning. Among these needs are the need to establish the major goals of economic development, the need to utilize limited public financial resources for the nation's requirements, the need to maintain financial stability, the need to provide for problems of unemployment or underemployment, the need to raise the economic level of depressed areas, the need to plan for more balanced economic development of all areas, and the need to improve productivity in all economic areas. To a large extent, such planning is the responsibility of such national agencies as the national planning institute, central reserve banks and legislatures.

A national industrial development policy and plan provide the necessary framework within which regional plans and specific industrial plans can be developed. The main elements of a national plan include a national policy for industrial development, general goals, assurances and incentives for the private sector, priorities for industrial development, encouragement for the small industry sector, priorities for the use of available or anticipated public funds, utilization of international-aid programs, provision of basic utilities, development of manpower and natural resources, improvement of productivity, and tariff protection. The national industrial plan is, of course, only one element in a general economic development plan providing for rational and integrated development of all sectors of the economy.

An analysis of the problems and shortcomings of national planning is outside the scope of this study, which concerns the work of development corporations and other regional and local agencies and the planning and programming needs of regions. National planning cannot be done in the absence of regional and local planning, and, conversely, regional and local planning depends on national plans. All levels of government are involved in the planning process.

Development corporations responsible for regional or local economic development have a vital role to play in the planning field. Specific projects and programs adapted to the needs, resources, and markets of the regions must be defined. The corporations and other local organizations are responsible for implementing plans and programs and they must advise national agencies which projects are feasible for implementation.

Planning and programming are, in effect, parts of the same process. Planning might be regarded as the strategy of industrial development in that its function is to formulate the main goals, while programming could be regarded as the tactics of industrial development in that its function is to formulate the how and when of a plan. A program is more specific than a plan and it usually refers to a relatively shorter period of time. Each program has specific objectives and a time set for completion.

In the following section, the major planning needs of a typical regional development corporation are reviewed.

PLANNING AND PROGRAMMING NEEDS AT THE REGIONAL OR LOCAL LEVEL

Basic Information

Planning and programming cannot proceed effectively until a corporation has acquired information about the physical and manpower resources in the region, about actual and potential markets for industrial products, and has gathered current statistical data regarding manufacturing production, sales, and regional imports and exports. Some of this information can usually be obtained from national agencies with sufficient resources and manpower to undertake expensive studies within a framework of national research and statistics. Usually, however, investigation of mineral, forest, and marine and other physical resources has to be carried out by regional development corporations because no such information is available from national agencies.

Development of Natural Resources

Developing natural resources involves analysis of resources needs for the development of the area in order to formulate general objectives for development and for long-, medium-, and short-term priorities. The natural resources of a region are one of the main bases for industrial development. Planning must be done in coordination with other organizations directly concerned with agricultural, mineral, forestry, and marine resources.

Development of Manpower Resources

A second major element in industrial development is the availability of skilled and semiskilled labor. One of the most immediate preconditions for manpower planning in any region is an inventory of present manpower resources and an analysis of industrial manpower requirements for a period of about ten years. On the basis of such an analysis it is often quite possible to obtain financial assistance for building technical schools through the technical assistance programs of individual countries or the International Labor Office.

Development of Financial Resources

A third requirement for industrial development is the availability of finance of various type, for both equity and loan capital, short-term, medium-term, and long-term. Studies, analysis, and plans are required to determine the amount of financial resources required and the institutions needed to distribute the available financing in the most effective manner. Also, loan requests which the corporations might present to international agencies or the technical assistance agencies of various countries require a great deal of research and planning.

Development of Infrastructure

Industrial development also requires a strong utility base in the form of power facilities, roads, ports, transportation facilities, etc. Long-range planning must be undertaken in connection with other organizations for the necessary development of the infrastructure of the region.

Development of Industrial Parks

In many countries industrial parks have been found to be one of the most effective ways of stimulating industrial development. A tremendous amount of planning and research is required for these parks, research which must continue even after construction has been completed. Planning for industrial or commercial zones falls into the same category.

Development of Community Services

Industry is attracted to an area to a large extent by the community facilities available to the management and staff. The whole community should be involved in planning for the improvement of schools, hospitals, recreational facilities, and city cleanliness and beauty, but the corporations can take the lead in instigating planning and programs for these purposes.

Development of Industrial Services

Since manufacturing industries require a large number of industrial services, planning and stimulating such services is a part of planning new industries. Such services include printing, electroplating, machine repair, tool sharpening, trucking, and banking and insurance.

Development of Commercial Facilities

Perhaps the key determinant in the decision as to whether industries should be established in a region is the existence of an actual or potential market and of marketing facilities. Planning for industrial development must also take into account the need for commercial facilities such as wholesalers, retailers, importers and exporters, brokers, commission agents, and advertising firms that can market the products of industry at home and abroad and stimulate and expand markets.

Development of Tourism Facilities and Programs

For some areas tourism can become a major industry. Often the development of tourism is left to chance and circumstance; however, a conscious planning effort is needed if full use is to be made of a region's tourist potential. For artisans and small industry, tourism often represents a major market. Also, to stimulate interest of potential investors from abroad or from outside the region, the tourism approach can be effective.

Planning Incentives for Industrial Promotion

Financial incentives to industries that locate in the area require careful planning. Such incentives as tax reductions or exemptions, freedom from local taxes, and provisions for reasonably priced industrial lands and buildings require careful planning and coordination with national plans and the plans of other regions. Often such concessions are granted without any special planning and research, and the tendency has been for one area to go ahead without regard to the plans of other areas.

Planning for the Improvement of Productivity

One of the main weaknesses of industries in newly developing areas is the low level of productivity. It is necessary, therefore, to develop, in addition to national plans, regional plans and programs for the improvement of productivity in collaboration with national productivity agencies or centers.

Establishment of Priorities for Industrial Development

Industries differ greatly with respect to the contribution they can make to the growth of the region in terms of creating employment, either directly or indirectly, opening up possibilities of other industries, providing technical training opportunities, substituting imports, or contributing in some way to industrial progress. Therefore, definite priorities have to be established on which study and promotion will be concentrated.

Planning for Industrial Location

Many newly developing countries and regions as well as highly developed areas fail to plan for the location of industries in accordance with economic considerations. Often the location of new industries is left to chance, and the result is often uneconomical location or the formation of an industrial agglomeration that is too large even for an inadequately developed region. Coordination in this field with the plans of other regions within the country is needed here, too.

Planning Small Industry Development

The development of small industry is as essential for over-all industrial development as the development of large industrial plants or complexes. Even in highly industrialized countries, small and medium industries account for a large share of total industrial output and employment. However, when industrial development efforts are concentrated on large industrial establishments, small industries are frequently neglected; the result is distortions, deficiencies, and diseconomies in the industrial structure of the region or the country. The development of small industries requires definite plans, work programs, and budgets.

Planning of Work Programs and Budgets

A development corporation needs to plan rationally for its annual work programs and budgets. With limited financial and manpower resources available, a corporation must necessarily concentrate on priorities which must be reflected in work programs, budgets, and personnel and administrative procedures.

Moreover, the results of programs must be constantly evaluated in order to avoid future mistakes and make use of past successes.

RESEARCH AND DEVELOPMENT ON A REGIONAL LEVEL

It is an established principle in economic theory that natural resources, human resources (including management resources), and capital are the main factors of production, so that the wealth of a country or a region depends on how well endowed it is with these factors and how well it is able to combine them into productive units or enterprises. In our times, when accelerated economic development has become one of the most urgent tasks facing humanity, knowledge of resources and capital and their combination into productive units cannot be left to intuition, chance, or favorable circumstances. Instead, it is necessary to gain a profound, systematic knowledge of the factors of production and of the possibilities that modern technology and organizational methods offer to combine them into productive units. This is the research task for economic development. As is the case with research in any field, the procedure is to first establish facts and figures which are confirmed by tests and experiments, and then to formulate hypotheses to explain and interrelate the facts in the form of logical, meaningful concepts and systems that enable prediction. The third step is to test these hypotheses by applying them to the reality of facts and figures. The final step is to apply the knowledge thus gained in trying to plan new beneficial courses of action, new projects, or remedies for existing problems.

Practically, this means that a development corporation has to study systematically all the factors that determine industrial production--the population, their skills, their education, their numbers, their growth rates, their migrations, and their customs; natural resources--their location, their quantities and qualities, the methods for their exploitation, their commercial and industrial applications, and their conservation; the capital of the region--savings, profits, investments and hoards, the origin of capital, and the best ways of directing it to industrial development; markets and marketing methods and their improvement; the concrete industrial possibilities based on available resources and markets; and the infrastructural requirements necessary for development of the economy and especially of industry.

Finally, a corporation must study methods to stimulate people to invest in productive enterprises. All this can only be done by determining who can do this research and how. After all these steps have been taken, concrete shape can be given to the programming of development plans, the concrete measures by which plans can be translated into realities. If research and development is omitted, programming is likely to be deficient and erroneous in meeting the goals set by planning.

As a first step in organizing its research program, a development corporation must organize a basic data and information bank.

Data and Information Needed

First, general background information is needed. This includes information about the geography and climate of the region; about population, particularly its economically active segment; about economic regions and chief centers of industry; and about major sectors of the economy other than industry, including agriculture, mining, and infrastructure. The very nature of this background information indicates that most of it is nearly constant, so that only a new census would justify updating it.

Information on human and natural resources must also be acquired. This includes information about the quantity and quality of all natural resources (mineral, water, marine, and agricultural and forest resources), and detailed information on population, population trends, training and education, and migrations.

Key economic indicators must be ascertained. This includes information on regional income or gross regional product, total and by major sectors of the economy, in current and constant values; the index of total industrial and agricultural production and output in selected critical industries; the cost of living and wholesale prices; wage trends; and such international indicators as the country's balance-of-payments and balance-of-trade situation. The compilation of this set of data is a formidable task, but it is of great value, particularly if it is periodically updated.

Data about the investment climate is another kind of information to be obtained. This set of basic economic data includes information on the attitudes of government toward private business, especially its industrial and commercial policy; data on international markets and agreements which affect industries in the region; taxation; tax exemptions; labor legislation, social security legislation; finance, money and banking policies; infrastructure developments and policies; public and private institutions in the region; and the support given to economic development and industrialization and their projects. This type of information also requires frequent updating.

Specific industry information is necessary. These data concern the supply and demand for the products of specific industries of national importance or regional or local interest; their price situation; availability and cost of raw materials; power and other utilities; labor force factors; production; and technology.

Information about specific industry can be

expanded into industry outlook surveys as a further tool of orientation, planning, and decision-making. The industry outlook survey can determine which industries in the area could make the most progress in the coming years or which ones are likely to be in a critical situation. It can determine which products have elastic demand so that the introduction of improved techniques, resulting in lower cost production and lower prices, would lead to increased consumption and output, resulting in turn in greater employment opportunities. It can define the key problems in each industry, such as supply of raw materials, marketing, effect of government regulations, competition from domestic or foreign industries, need for technical assistance, need for assistance in purchasing equipment, shortage of working capital, transportation, shortage of skilled labor, credit needs, adequacy of present sources of credit, and expansion potential.

A development corporation should keep as complete and up-to-date an information bank as possible. Moreover, its personnel should keep abreast of recent events by reading domestic and foreign technical and economical publications, by attending conferences, and by undertaking study trips.

A development corporation can then proceed to make specific development studies.

HUMAN AND NATURAL RESOURCES, RESEARCH AND DEVELOPMENT

Research into the human resources of an area implies a qualitative and quantitative analysis of the total population, its growth rates, its division into rural and urban population and into sexes and age groups, the labor force, the health, nutritional, and housing conditions under which the population lives, and its social and cultural aspects such as migration, stratification, mobility between different groups and classes, the role of the family, education, and attitudes toward change and progress. On the basis of this research, a human resources development program can then be worked out.

Human resources development includes the whole sphere of education: basic education, vocational training, training of technicians and middle management personnel, higher education, and training of managers. In none of these aspects of education can a development corporation act exclusively or become involved too deeply. In most countries, other institutions have been charged with the responsibility for these fields. However, a development corporation can act as spokesman for economic and industrial development needs before the responsible institutions. It can try to coordinate, to help, to stimulate public and community action, and to assist in financing school buildings, equipment, or scholarships. Thus its main function consists in identifying needs for technical or vocational training in the region, setting priorities, and cooperating with other institutions in meeting these needs.

An important part of education for economic development is training and stimulating entrepreneurs. Although many newly developing countries have organizations responsible for high-level manager training, there is generally a lack of organized effort to train and stimulate small industry entrepreneurs and managers. On the other hand, capable small industry and entrepreneurs and managers are in critically short supply in many countries. There is often enough capital, raw materials and abundant unskilled and even skilled labor, but there are not enough entrepreneurs and managers. Surveys in a number of countries have revealed that most small business failures are due to management deficiencies. A development corporation seems to be the logical organization to fill this gap in management training. Training and stimulating smaller industry managers and entrepreneurs through identification of the most promising candidates in the area, training courses, seminars, stimulation of self-training, and courses abroad can become a promising new field of activity for a development corporation. It can represent a valuable complement and insurance to corporation-sponsored small industry loan programs.

A development corporation can contribute to a

systematic inventory and evaluation of the natural resources of its territory. Special knowledge of agriculture, mining, fisheries, and forestry requires the development corporation to employ specialists from research firms or governmental agencies. Such studies should be oriented toward producing concrete suggestions for the development of natural resources in the form of a short-term development program.

MARKET AND MARKETING STUDIES

Market and marketing studies of the area and of different cities in the area are needed as a basis for identifying industrial opportunities, and they can serve as promotional tools for attracting investors.

Market and marketing information can be published in the form of a marketing guide for the region. A study that can serve as a basis for such a guide could include information about the following factors: (1) the consumers of the area: their incomes according to regions, ages, sex groups, occupations, and sectors of economic activity; their tastes, preferences, habits, customs, and attitudes; (2) forms and costs of transportation in the area; (3) forms and costs of storage; (4) the wholesalers, retailers, and other intermediaries: their functions, their services, and the prices of their services; (5) suggestions for improving the area's marketing structure and for establishing other new types of distribution and distributors for agricultural and industrial products; (6) projections of the future of markets and marketing in the region; (7) present markets and market projection for a large variety of products; (8) investment opportunities in the marketing field; and (9) export markets for the products of the region.

It may be advisable to contract a marketing specialist to carry out such a study if the development corporation does not have any specialized personnel on its permanent staff.

Identification of Investment Opportunities, Prefeasibility and Feasibility Studies

Studies of the resources of a region are of value only for specific projects that can employ these resources by transforming them into products and services and finding and developing markets for them. Shrewd businessmen will find investment possibilities on their own, but in an area where people are still largely unfamiliar with industry this process is likely to be slow and must be accelerated through outside initiative. The identification and study of investment opportunities thus becomes an important function of a development corporation.

Development corporations, therefore, must be constantly on the lookout for investment opportunities. They can look for ways to process or semi-process the raw materials into semifinished or finished products. In many newly developing regions, processing industries are the most natural industries, for they represent the first step from an agricultural or mineral-oriented economy to an industrial economy. They often stimulate production of raw materials, create new markets, or widen existing markets. Usually, it is easier to find investors for these industries since many people who have accumulated wealth in agriculture or by exploiting natural resources, are accustomed to invest in processing industries.

Other methods of identifying investment opportunities are to see what imports could be substituted economically by domestically manufactured goods; to study industrial projects in other countries with a similar economy; and to identify existing industries or new industries being built to ascertain what products and services they will buy from other industries. These methods climax in an input-output analysis to identify investment opportunities.

Even with the most sophisticated techniques available, this work has to be highly practical and cannot be carried out wholly from behind a desk. The development corporation staff has to be in constant contact with businessmen whom they must seek out by visiting factories and by keeping themselves available to anybody with ideas and suggestions. To facilitate contact, a committee of knowledgeable businessmen and corporation personnel can be formed to identify investment opportunities. Such a committee makes the work of the corporation personnel more effective, and it also stimulates the interest and support of the public for the work of the corporations.

The next step is to view the industrial opportunities in terms of more detailed factors, such as the availability and quality of raw materials, labor and management personnel, markets, production and distribution costs, and competitiveness of the new industry with other domestic or foreign producers. Also, the desirability of the project from the point of view of an over-all development plan must be checked. If the project can withstand these tests, it can then be presented in the form of a prefeasibility study.

A prefeasibility study includes an estimate of the total investment in fixed and working capital; an estimate of the cost of raw materials, labor, depreciation, administration, distribution and other possible costs; and an analysis of the markets. All these estimates need to be only approximate, and no aspect of the study has to be dealt with in great detail. No great specialization in any field is required for such a study except a familiarity with industrial processes in general, with markets, and with industrial costing. If the economists and industrial engineers working for the development corporations do not already possess such knowledge, they can acquire it in training courses and seminars and through practical working experience.

Prefeasibility studies are useful for attracting investors, since it is usually all they require. If they are interested in the project in question, they will make complete feasibility studies of their own according to their own specific requirements.

Industrial Location Factors

Prefeasibility studies and promotional activities can be effective for attracting investments to a region but often they are not enough. A region with unfavorable location may face sizable odds in the struggle for promoting investment, and, consequently, it must investigate possible means of overcoming this handicap.

The location of an industrial firm is relevant to three of its functions: the procurement of raw materials and their transportation to the factory; the processing of these materials and their conversion into finished and semifinished products; and the transfer and distribution of products from factory to markets or to the consumer.

The first and the third of these functions essentially involve transportation and its related functions of materials handling and storage. If, as is frequently the case, transportation costs constitute a significant part of the cost of a product, the factory making that product will be located where transportation costs can be kept to a minimum. If the cost of bringing the raw materials to the factory is substantially higher than the cost of moving the product derived from these materials, then the factory will have to be located near the source of raw materials. This condition obtains when the processing operation involves an appreciable reduction in weight from raw materials to final products. Familiar examples of industries falling into this category are sugar refineries; metal refineries and cement plants; and fruit, vegetable, and fish canneries.

The opposite situation holds true of certain industries in which the costs of transportation and the distribution of finished products are higher than the transport costs of their ingredients. This is the case with perishable commodities like ice cream, bakery products, and bottled milk or bottled drinks, which take on considerable weight during processing and require speedy transportation to the consumers. It also holds true of those processing and packaging industries whose essential function is to mix and package in small lots materials they receive in bulk shipments.

A number of other important locational factors also impinge on the manufacturing cost of industry. They include the availability and cost of basic utilities such as water, power, gas, of transportation services, and of waste disposal and sanitation facilities. They cover the cost and suitability of land, of factory buildings, and of storage areas, as well as the availability of banking and credit institutions and of industrial facilities and services such as work and repair shops and foundries. They include the existence of suitable roads on which raw materials and finished products may be transported without seasonal interruptions or delays. They also include the availability of skilled and unskilled labor and the price that has to be paid for that labor, and, in many cases, they also include the availability of technicians and managers, and the investment in health, education, recreational, and cultural facilities that must be made to attract and keep qualified personnel. In addition, they include the nature and level of local taxes and the extent to which tax incentives are obtainable. The stability of the political situation and the tranquility of the labor market is a factor. Not all of these factors are significant to all industries; the relative importance of each depends on the nature of the product, the scale of operations, the level of technology, and the extent of competition. Generally, however, regions outside of the capital are at a disadvantage with respect to many of these points, in addition to often being far from the major markets.

It is necessary that a development corporation study means of overcoming locational disadvantages. A more balanced development of the whole country also serves the national interest. Gross imbalances of regional development results in high costs of agglomeration in the highly developed areas and in social and economic tensions in the less favored areas. In many countries it is the function of a national development plan to determine a desirable degree of decentralization of the economy. Development corporations can study and propose specific development incentives that could compensate the locational handicaps.

A development corporation can present an integrated, mutually complementary package of incentives for a region characterized by unfavorable locational factors that includes the following elements: industrial parks, tax incentives, transportation subsidies, and infrastructural and community development.

Industrial Parks

Experience of lesser-developed regions in many countries has shown that industrial parks can represent an effective means of overcoming locational disadvantages and attracting new industries. An industrial park study should include studies of the suitability of the city in question as a location for an industrial park; the selection of the site for the industrial park; the characteristics of existing industries and their requirements of relocation and expansion; estimated demand from existing and new industries for space and buildings in the industrial park; layout; the financial feasibility in which the total investment, the operating costs, and the receipts from the sale of land and buildings and from rents and operating fees are computed; the organization of the park, its statutes, and its regulations; means of financing the park and obtaining suitable management; and proposals for implementing the project in phases, with definite responsibilities assigned to all divisions of the corporation and other organizations concerned.

In order to determine which tax incentives would be most effective for particular types of industry and their location, a financial and economic analysis of industries in the area should be conducted. Tax incentives should be determined on a national basis in accordance with an over-all regional development plan, but a development corporation can study the incentives best suited to its region.

High transportation costs raises the overhead of industries that depend on markets in other areas or those that have to bring in raw materials from other areas. A transportation study undertaken by the development corporation can determine how this situation can be remedied through freight subsidies.

Infrastructural and Community Development

Studies should also be made to determine which infrastructural investments are most needed in the region to stimulate and attract industry. On the basis of such a study, priorities can then be determined. Such established priorities can serve to prevent the possibility that decisions of infrastructural investments are made on the basis of purely political considerations.

Industries are attracted by the facilities and conveniences a community can offer, such as educational facilities, hospitals, recreational facilities, parks, and cultural activities. Many newly developing regions, however, do little to develop their facilities from this viewpoint. The first step in this direction is to undertake a study to identify community needs, to survey the resources available, to formulate objectives in the light of needs and resources, and to formulate alternative lines of action and priorities. The corporations can take the lead in studies for infrastructural as well as community development planning by forming local action groups, contracting experts and advisors, and promoting this kind of initiative for industry.

Community support is essential for industrial development. A development corporation should undertake public relations programs designed to keep community and business leaders fully informed of industrial development plans and the reasons for them.

Because of the sheer volume of necessary studies and the degree of specialization involved, a development corporation cannot undertake them alone. It can function as general coordinator and stimulator, but it will have to farm out the bulk of the work. In so doing, the development corporation can promote the establishment of private or university-sponsored research groups.

So far, the universities in many newly developing countries have been functioning as traditional kinds of institutions of higher learning, uninvolved in the specific research requirements of their environments. Those that have engaged in studies for economic development have been limited by inadequate funds, by inadequate research contracts from business and industry, or by their inability to compete with the prestige of foreign research groups. Many developed and newly developing countries have met their need for research in their area's specific development problems by creating university-sponsored research institutes. These institutes can engage in such research tasks as, for example, the extraction of tanning extracts from the region's tropical woods, the elaboration of local grains into more palatable and more easily marketable products, or the possibilities for commercial utilization of the different species of edible off-shore ocean fish that have so far been unused. In addition to conducting new research, these institutes could also keep informed about the latest discoveries and developments abroad in order to utilize them for their own local industry and business. Special efforts should be made to apply science and technology to the particular industrial conditions in the region involved, rather than to duplicate research already done elsewhere.

At first, research institutes will need the financial and promotional support of the development corporations on whom they will also depend for contracts. But experience in a number of countries has shown that once they are established, they themselves will promote their services among private industry, and they will convince businessmen of the benefits of applying scientific procedures to their problems.

In addition, a development corporation can assist already existing private research firms by giving them orders, or they can encourage private industrial firms in their research efforts. For instance, private firms can be encouraged to undertake research into their specific problems, and the development corporation could finance such research through loans if it appears that the firms will be able to repay the loans through increased efficiency or sales resulting from the research.[2]

Notes to Chapter 2

1. The source of this material on planning is Carlton R. Wood, Programa Regional De Capacitación En Desarollo, Vol. 4: Necesidades Funcionales Y Requisitos De Organización En El Desarrollo Industrial Del Sur Del Perú (Arequipa, Perú: AID, 1965).

2. For further examples of the work of a research institute in a newly developing country, see Francis Godwin, The Research Institute as a Key Industrial Development Instrument, Vol. IV, of United States Papers Prepared for the United Nations Conference on the Application of Science and Technology for the Benefit of the Less Developed Areas: Industrial Development (Washington: U.S. Government Printing Office, 1964).

CHAPTER 3 FINANCING

Financing is a highly diversified field that takes different patterns from country to country.[1] When a regional development corporation tries to determine whether it should engage in industrial financing, it should first analyze the various financial needs of industry in the area to ascertain whether or not these needs are being met by existing firms and institutions. The findings of such a study can be used as the basis for a financial program supported or even carried out by the development corporation.

The financial needs are different for every newly developing country. Nevertheless, certain needs are common to them all, especially those of small and medium manufacturing firms. It is these common needs and general problems that will be analyzed. Because small and medium manufacturing firms are predominant in many newly developing countries and because large firms are able to meet most of their financial needs, either from their own resources or from financial institutions, the discussion of financing is directed to small and medium industries and handicraft enterprises.

The principal need for manufacturing concerns is equity capital and long-term loans. Most beginning small- and medium-sized enterprises do not have adequate financial resources and are not able to obtain funds by selling shares to the general public. Often they have little to offer as collateral for loans. Existing firms face similar problems in attempting to expand their business operations.

The second need is working capital. The main costs of many small firms, particularly of artisans, are for the purchase of raw materials and for operating expenses. Small firms and artisans frequently have insufficient resources of their own. Operations are often on a "buy-and-sell" basis--purchasing the raw materials, processing them, and then selling them. The period prior to recovery of expenditures through sales must be covered by working capital loans or equity financing.

In many cases, if more long-term loans were available at reasonable rates and terms, more of the firms' capital could be released for use as working capital.

MEANS OF MEETING FINANCIAL NEEDS

Once the financial needs of industry, and especially of smaller and medium-sized industry, have been clearly identified, the development corporation can try to meet their needs. First, it can try to point out to existing institutions those needs they are not meeting adequately and then it can try to convince them of the necessity of filling the existing gaps. If the director of a development corporation is respected by the private business community and if its staff of technical experts can, by virtue of their knowledge and experience, command the confidence of businessmen, this itself might be enough.

If existing financing institutions are unable to meet these needs, either because they lack the experience of the personnel or because certain types of financial operations may not be sufficiently profitable to them, the development corporation may sponsor or support the creation of new financial institutions. At first such institutions might need government support in the form of subsidies or special exemptions.

One type of financial institution that might be formed is an industrial development finance corporation to aid the development of small, medium, and artisan enterprises. Such corporations have been successfully organized in a number of countries. These corporations make equity investments, long-term loans, and guarantee loans from other investment sources. The most successful have provided management, engineering, accounting, and legal assistance to borrowers: They have sponsored economic studies and surveys, and they have stimulated and promoted promising new investment opportunities. The objective of such banks is development and not pure banking. Terms and conditions of their loans are more lenient than those of other banking organizations. More reliance is placed on the character of the entrepreneur and business prospects than on collateral. They are usually set up as autonomous corporations, with government financial assistance, but not under government or public agency controls. They have private investment funds.

Various financial agencies have assisted in the establishment of such corporations: the World Bank, the International Finance Corporation, private financial groups, and the foreign-aid programs of a number of industrial countries. If it is desirable, the development corporations could promote the establishment of autonomous regional development corporations, providing funds for part of the initial investment. In this way, the corporation, which is a public institution, could be kept out of the banking business and could concentrate on development activities. Other investors could include the international financial agencies, foreign banks and investment companies, the regional and commercial banks, the Industrial Bank, and private investors.

A second type of financing institution is the private equity investment company. As pointed out earlier, one of the major needs, particularly of smaller firms, is equity capital. Another major shortage is that of entrepreneurs and experienced industrial managers. Some countries have met both of these needs by forming private investment companies or venture capital companies that promote industrial enterprises and assist them in their initial stages with equity funds and management assistance. Their profits are derived from the growth of the profits and worth of the companies in which they invest and from certain fees and interest charges on loans and debentures.

These companies serve as an efficient means of harnessing available private capital in the community. Investors who might otherwise hesitate to invest directly in specific industries are often willing to invest in a well-managed company to promote various local industries.

A major feature of such company operations is the attention given to assisting with the management of firms receiving funds. An equity investment company may have a small staff including an experienced manager, an industrial engineer, a business management specialist, and an accountant.

It is quite possible that such a company could obtain long-term loans from international financial agencies and from foreign equity investment companies and banks. An equity investment company would be the logical institution through which private foreign funds could be channeled.

In the special field of export financing, a financial agency similar to those established in many countries is needed to stimulate and support exports, particularly for small and medium enterprises and artisans. Such an institution provides short-term loans to cover the periods before payment is made for products exported, credit insurance on exports, and management services in the export field.

The export financing corporation can use its own funds to support existing financial institutions provided that their programs are adequate and realistic and that they follow certain principles and policies outlined by the development corporation.

It can use its funds to help create new needed financial institutions. Private investors in newly developing countries are often not yet willing or prepared to take the risks connected with new financial ventures; possibly the short-term profitability of such ventures is not attractive to them. Thus, a development corporation could, for instance, put up the initial capital for an industrial development finance corporation which would serve as a basis for attracting additional funds from such institutions as the World Bank, IFC, or the foreign-aid programs of industrial countries. It could be the promotor and key shareholder in a private equity investment company which could then attract private shareholders from the region, from other regions of the country, or from abroad.

If the needed new financial institutions already exist elsewhere in the country, the development corporation could use its influence, leadership, and money to induce these institutions to open branch offices or subsidiaries in the region.

As a last alternative, a development corporation can set up its own loan and investment program in an area where private initiative is badly lacking or where no financial institutions exist.

However, a corporation loan program should always be the last alternative since it is costly to operate, special personnel has to be found and trained to manage it efficiently, and a great deal of financial experience has to be gained by the development corporation which a private existing institution may already have developed. There is also the danger that personal or political factors may have an influence upon loan or investment decisions.

If private initiative in a region is lacking, a development corporation may have to take the initiative to establish industries in its own name and use its funds for this purpose. Again, this should only be a last resort. Such industries established by the development corporation in its name should be sold to private investors as soon as possible. Usually this is possible when their success has been demonstrated. The industries to be established by the development corporation should be key industries which are likely to open a maximum of investment opportunities in related industries. To help assure the commercial success for the corporation industries, separate management corporations should be formed that are free from the political or personal influences which can infringe upon their competitiveness and make them less attractive to investors. In financing corporation industries, a development corporation can often obtain longer-term financing for the entire project, not only for machinery and equipment, from the equipment suppliers in the form of a "turn-key proposal" if the development corporation can obtain a guarantee from its government to the foreign equipment suppliers. Most industrial firms in the highly developed countries today provide this form of financing for industrial projects for which a guarantee from the national government can be obtained.

Often institutions are willing to lend to industry in sufficient amounts and at reasonable interest rates, but their collateral requirements may be high--as high as 25 per cent of the amount of the loan--since they are unfamiliar with industrial lending or unable to make the economic analyses necessary to determine whether an industrial venture is likely to be successful. In this case, a development corporation can use its funds only as guarantee funds with which a larger amount of funds from other institutions can be mobilized. For example, if a financial institution requires a collateral on industrial loans of 25 per cent of the amount of the loan on the basis of the buildings, equipment or raw materials, the individual borrower might put up 10 per cent and the development corporation could put up the remaining 15 per cent collateral through its own guarantee fund. In this operation the guarantee fund of the corporation need only be a certain percentage of the total amount of the collaterals given, provided that enough different industries were financed so as to spread the risks.

Depending on the spread and other risk factors involved, the guarantee might reasonably be as low as one tenth of the total monies invested. This means that with a guarantee fund of $100,000, for instance, a development corporation can mobilize $1 million from other institutions.

In some cases, a development corporation may not want to immobilize its funds in a guarantee fund. If it possesses land or real estate, this can be used as collateral. If it does not possess any real estate, it can use its influence to persuade the municipalities or other public-spirited institutions to pledge some of their land for this purpose. Thus, the resources of the whole community would be made available for industrial development; the resulting public interest and participation in the work of the development corporation and its programs cannot be underestimated.

PRINCIPLES AND POLICIES FOR A DEVELOPMENT-ORIENTED LOAN PROGRAM

Whether the development corporation carries out its own loan program or turns over its funds to an existing financial institution, certain principles should be adhered to in order to assure the most effective use of the funds.

Effective organization and operation of industrial financing programs require: measures to establish a firm public reputation as a businesslike development financing agency; policies and procedures essential to effective development financing; measures for building up information relevant to lending operations; and measures for acquiring and training a staff competent to administer development financing programs.

The general public reputation of an organization has an important bearing on its ability to engage in development lending. It determines the types of borrowers who apply; it influences the responsiveness of loan recipients to controls on the use and repayment of funds; and it influences the ability of the agency to raise funds for its lending operations from other sources.

Nothing is more damaging to an organization's reputation for efficiency than a high rate of delinquency or default among loan recipients, whether it arises from slack or unsound administration or from policies shaped by social or political considerations. If a development corporation accumulates a large number of credit delinquencies due to inadequate selection and supervision procedures, its capability for attracting applications of high development priority and for inducing loan recipients to maintain high development standards in using and repaying funds is greatly weakened.

Four basic factors in a development corporation's policies and procedures[2] facilitate a selection of applicants suitable to the objectives of a development financing program for small and medium industrial enterprises.

First, the interest rates charged should be reasonably close to the commercial interest rates prevailing in the region in order that the corporation does not become too cheap a source of money and that borrowers cannot use the corporation to repay more expensive loans from commercial entities. The higher the interest rate, the greater will be the risk the corporation can assume, and it is the specific function of a development-oriented loan program to assume risks which cannot be assumed by existing commercial institutions. A relatively high interest rate also allows the development corporation to obtain sufficient revenue to cover the costs of a careful selection of loan recipients, of supervision, and of technical and management advisory services. The cost of a development-oriented loan program to smaller and medium industries is usually greater than that of ordinary loan programs. The higher cost results from giving guidance to applicants in formulating acceptable loan requests and in meeting accounting and other requirements of development financing; from making a prompt, efficient, and reasonably accurate evaluation of needs and potentialities in circumstances where required information is not easily obtained or evaluated; and from carrying out more complex control and supervision procedures than are involved in well-secured business loans.

On the other hand, advisory services to the borrower coupled with good supervision represents risk insurance which enables the development corporation to take greater risks than usual.

A relatively high interest rate to cover risks and provide risk-reducing advisory services and supervision services also enables the development corporation to set low collateral requirements. Low collateral requirements are far more important to many industrialists than low interest rates, since interest charges, if kept within reasonable limits, do not usually represent a major cost to a firm. High collateral requirements, however, can virtually bar many small and medium-sized manufacturing firms from receiving a loan.

It can also be argued that in capital-scarce newly developing countries, a relatively high interest rate will assure that only those projects are financed which will make the greatest contribution to economic progress or which are the most profitable to the entrepreneur. There may be many exceptions to the general rule that the most profitable ventures to the entrepreneur are those which contribute most to the progress of the economy as a whole. If this general rule is to apply, the over-all economic policy of the country involved is such that microeconomic profitability and macroeconomic desirability coincide.

The second factor in the selection of suitable applicants is that financing should be directed toward clients with a clear capacity to enlarge their efficiency and output with additional credit facilities. In other words, growth potential of an industry or an entrepreneur is essential. Growth industries are those which benefit from a growing existing or potential market where competition is not yet too strong and where raw materials are available at reasonable cost and in sufficient quantity. Industry outlook surveys serve to determine which industries are likely to be growth industries. Also, the ability of the entrepreneur, as judged by his past experience, is an important selection criterion.

In the case of small industries, only those that can grow should be considered. It may be advisable to deal with artisans, workshops, and very small enterprises in a special way, and even to have separate funds for such development loans. From a development point of view, a much higher standard of selectivity is important, yet more difficult to apply, because of the nature and number of such enterprises. Also, much more simplified and generally different financing procedures and policies are required to make such financing reasonable and practical. Such financing, particularly where social and political considerations modify substantially development financing objectives, is more likely to require special subsidies which should be separated from other operating costs so that they can be accurately determined and clearly provided for.

The third factor in selection of applicants is that evaluation procedures should not be haphazard.[3] Five types of analyses should be made in evaluating loan applications: management, financial, technical, economic, and control. The depth of the analyses will depend upon the availability of information and the amount of credit involved. However, a reasonable basis for judging each of these five elements must be established even in cases where only very rudimentary information is available and only rudimentary procedures can be employed.

Management analysis is one of the most important aspects of the evaluation. This includes a careful check on the applicant's record by use of the various standard sources of information on delinquent and defaulting creditors. For this purpose, it is necessary to establish relationships with commercial banks and other creditors for an informal exchange of such credit information. Management analysis should also provide an appraisal of the manager's character: His drive to learn, his flexibility and ingenuity in coping with unexpected difficulties, and his willingness to accept advice and to use other sources of finance are relevant data. It is equally essential to assess his general business ability and his grasp of the specialized knowledge involved in his particular kind of enterprise.

To carry out such evaluations, a staff must be regularly in contact with the industrial and business community and have a practical knowledge of industrial operations. It is relatively easy to evaluate an entrepreneur when the staff of the lending institution are well informed.

Financial analysis is essential to ascertain the level and trend of costs, profits, and cash flow in order to determine the applicant's potential earnings and his capacity to meet scheduled repayments. Comparison of such data with those of other similar enterprises is of great assistance in evaluation. Information on the applicant's financial status and the sources of his finance is necessary to determine the extent of his need for development financing.

Technical analysis may vary greatly in its degree of detail. In dealing with smaller enterprises, particularly when the staff engaged in loan evaluation has limited practical experience in industrial operations or little specialized knowledge of the applicants' lines of industry, the analysis should be kept as simple as possible. If staff members have participated in surveys of a wide variety of industries involving some comparative plant analysis in the lines surveyed, they will be more able to make quick evaluations of whether the applicant enterprises have adequate production facilities, methods, and plans, as compared with likely competition.

Economic analysis involves an evaluation of the economic outlook of the industry in which the applicant is operating, the extent of the market accessible to the applicant, and the extent of the market which the applicant is likely to capture in view of his competition. Up-to-date industrial survey information can greatly facilitate such evaluations.

The means available to the lender to control the use and repayment of a loan and the earnings which arise from it ensure that the borrower makes the maximum effort to employ the funds productively, and to repay them. Means of control may include: evaluating the applicant's collateral and ascertaining any legal or other problems that may be involved in enforcing claims against collateral; determining to what extent operational restrictions and requirements may prove effective in encouraging efficient management; determining to what extent supervision can be given by means of financial reports or plant visits; and assessing the extent to which the outlook of the enterprise enlarges or diminishes the need for normal controls.

Fairly prompt evaluation of applications is important. Evaluation should not take longer than two to three months as the amounts normally involved in small and medium industry financing clearly limit the costs that are worth incurring to administer a loan. Such costs should normally be much less than the amount of interest due.

In employing evaluation techniques, it should be recognized that the limitations of time and cost preclude complete certainty as to capacity to repay, financial needs, or development priority. For new and relatively small enterprises in particular, it is necessary to accept some degree of uncertainty. Loss reserves should be established with the expectation that they will be required to cover losses that arise from the desirable policy of preferring to take a small risk to rejecting loan applications that may be sound and important to development.

Losses up to 5-10 per cent of the amount of loans issued are not excessive for a development financing organization concentrating on small and medium industry, provided that loan decisions have been based on economic analysis which is reasonable in terms of the information, staff, and time available.

In cases where a limited analysis can be made at best, the risk of loss can be reduced by making loans that are relatively small, short term, and subject to close supervision or control. It should be borne in mind, however, that excessively short-term loans could tend to contribute to the failure of what might otherwise be a successful venture. Once experience has demonstrated the capacity of the client, it is possible to graduate to larger loans made on less restricted terms.

Increasing the availability of information relevant to decision-making can improve the complex judgments involved in loan administration. It is equally important to place decision-making in the hands of credit managers, whose specialized professional knowledge and practical experience in industrial loan analysis equip them to weigh and combine the diverse elements of information which are relevant to loan decisions.

Placing the operational responsibility for loan decisions and related matters in the hands of a professional manager also has other advantages, particularly in public or quasi-public institutions. His professional stature tends to protect him from the kind of pressure often brought to bear on political or business leaders to temper development objectives with political, social, or personal considerations in individual loan decisions. The importance of strengthening the corporation's capacity to maintain strictly impartial loan administration has been stressed already. Policies and procedures can be improved not only with respect to collection and control. A program of regular plant visits to loan recipients by the technical staff can provide regular evaluation and counseling assistance throughout the duration of loans. The value of these measures will be further enhanced if the technical staff acquires an understanding of practical aspects of operating the kind of industrial enterprises they supervise, based on an intimate knowledge of a variety of similar plants.

Control and collection procedures can also be improved if the disbursement and collection of funds is left to a regular banking agency. Banks usually have the staff and facilities to carry out these functions efficiently, whereas a corporation is not as well equipped to perform them.

For loan evaluation and supervision procedures to be effective and economical, certain kinds of relevant information should be readily available.

First, accurate accounts from loan applicants and loan recipients indicating the level and trend of the major elements of profits and liquidity are needed. Satisfactory accounting information is unlikely to be available, particularly from smaller enterprises, unless free or low-cost assistance for establishing appropriate accounts is provided to promising loan applicants and loan recipients.

Also, current information on conditions and trends in particular lines of industry is needed. Such data should indicate particularly the nature, extent, and trends of markets; marketing methods; and other major elements determining the outlook for the industry and the competitive position of enterprises within it. This type of information can be available only if a qualified staff is regularly engaged in conducting field surveys and in preparing analytic reports of their findings.

A development financing program also has some fairly exacting staffing requirements. These arise in part from the fact that this work tends to require several types of specialists, all usually in short supply in developing countries. The staffing problem is further complicated by the fact that only experienced specialists are capable of making the astute judgments needed in this work. Besides specialized professional skills, staff members must also have the personal qualities that facilitate frank interchanges with businessmen on confidential matters.

In view of the general scarcity of required personnel, the most reasonable way for a corporation or other financial institution to begin to cope with these staffing requirements is to try to obtain a permanent head of the industrial credit program who is experienced in term lending. If this is possible, a temporary manager or advisor should be sought from abroad. Lending operations should be kept at a level that allows the manager to devote enough time to provide on-the-job training in development lending to his professional staff. During at least the first two years of operations, a substantial proportion of staff time should be spent in assembling an inventory of information relevant to development lending by conducting an industrial survey involving a brief diagnosis of a large sample of plants. This work would serve not only to build up information, but also to provide the staff with an increased understanding of industrial operations and with a wide range of industrial experience.

FIGURE 3

SAMPLE REGULATIONS OF A DEVELOPMENT CORPORATION LOAN PROGRAM

(Serving an Area of About 50,000 People With an Average Annual Per Capita Income of $200)

Purposes and Fields of Application of the Loan Program

Art. 1. These regulations apply only to loans to handicrafts and small and medium industry as defined by the United Nations. Loans to larger industry will be studied separately and under different viewpoints.

Art. 2. The handicraft and industry development and promotion plan of the corporation includes: economic support to artisans in the form of loans to allow them to develop into small industrialists; eco-

Figure 3 (continued)

nomic support in the form of loans to small and medium industrialists; guarantees to equipment suppliers, banks, and other financial institutions; underwriting of equity investments made by private smaller and medium investors; participation of the corporation in industrial ventures as a shareholder in cases where private investors are not willing to assume the risk; and advisory services to artisans and small and medium industrialists, even those who are not borrowers of the corporation.

Art. 3. Loans will be made to: smaller and medium-sized manufacturing establishments and artisans; mechanical service and repair establishments; fishing companies and other ocean-oriented enterprises; wineries and distilleries; mining companies; community development organizations engaged in the construction of industrial parks, storage facilities, cold storage plants, or electrification projects; and industrial investment cooperatives and finance companies.

Art. 4. Artisans, small industrialists, and medium industrialists are defined as follows:

An artisan is a person working with a maximum capital of $4,000 and employing at least one worker outside his family.

A small industry is a firm with assets from $4,000 to a maximum of $40,000 and employing several workers or employees.

A medium-sized industry is a firm working with assets of from $40,000 to $200,000.

Art. 5. Preference will be given to the following enterprises:

(a) in manufacturing industries: agricultural processing industries; light metalworking industries; chemical and pharmaceutical industries; industries using local raw materials for which substantial

Figure 3 (continued)

and growing markets exist; industries saving transportation costs on locally consumed products which have previously had to be transported over large distances; import substitution industries; industries that develop the natural and human resources of the region enjoying a specific competitive advantage; industries producing basic consumer goods for which there is a large demand, even in a low-income area; industries offering employment to a large number of persons.

(b) in service industries: mechanical repair and service shops, especially for vehicles and agricultural machinery.

(c) in the artisan field: artisans making special products which can compete with industrially made goods; artisans making handicraft products that can be sold domestically, to tourists, or abroad; and general service artisans, particularly those whose shops offer possibilities for development and can grow into small industries.

Amounts and Objectives of the Loans

Art. 6. For small industries and artisans, the corporation can make loans of up to 50 per cent of the total capital invested in the enterprise.

For loans to medium industry the upper limit is also 50 per cent of total investment. In the special cases, of industries whose development is of particular importance to the region, this can be raised to 75 per cent.

Art. 7. Loans can be made for: raw materials and other working capital; machinery and equipment; land and buildings; training of workers and employees and employment of consultants; programs designed to raise productivity and improve marketing; and general purposes of industrial community development. Guarantees will only be given for the purposes stated above.

Figure 3 (continued)

Loans can be made both to new industries and for the expansion, improvement or rehabilitation of existing industries.

Art. 8. Loans can be made for one or more of the above purposes.

Credit Terms

Art. 9. The following interest rates will be charged: 5.5 per cent for loans to artisans, 7 per cent for loans to small industry, and 8.5 per cent for loans to medium industry.

Art. 10. The loans have to be repaid through monthly, bimonthly, or semiannual payments including the principal and interest payments.

Art. 11. Repayment periods are as follows: up to 2 years for working capital; up to 10 years for machinery and equipment; and up to 12 years for land and buildings.

The above periods are maximum periods and can be reduced by the credit department of the corporation if feasibility studies and other financial analyses show that the loans can be returned in a shorter period.

Art. 12. Each loan has to be covered by a sufficient collateral or guarantee. Such collateral or guarantee can take the following forms: liens on machinery and equipment, including those which have been purchased with the loan; mortgages on industrial or residential buildings; and a personal guarantee from somebody recognized by the corporation for his moral integrity and economic solvency.

The amount of the loan can go up to 80 per cent of the value of the collateral pledged. In special cases this percentage can be exceeded.

Figure 3 (continued)

Art. 13. The corporation will normally give guarantees only if sufficient counterguarantees can be given or collateral can be pledged. In cases of industries whose development is of special importance, this requirement can be waived.

Art. 14. All expenses connected with the loan will be assumed by the borrower.

Art. 15. All Corporation loans are supervised loans; acceptance of the loan by the borrower implies acceptance of the corporation's supervisory procedures.

Applications and Loan-Processing Procedures

Art. 16. The loan applications must be accompanied by a sworn declaration on the economic condition of the applicant.

Art. 17. Applicants for artisan and small industry loans will present a memorandum explaining the purpose of the loan, the need for the loan, and the circumstances which have led to the application. Applicants for medium industry loans will present the feasibility study for their project. The personnel of the corporation will help applicants in making the necessary feasibility studies which have to preceed any loan application.

Art. 18. Every loan application must be accompanied by the following papers: invoices for machinery and equipment; certificates to prove that machinery and equipment pledged for collateral is free from other liens; title to the land or buildings to be mortgaged; a letter of guarantee from the guarantor; and bank and commercial references for the applicant and the guarantor, if applicable.

For loans above $4,000, the following papers have to be submitted in addition to the above: a copy of

Figure 3 (continued)

the balance sheets and profit and loss statements of the last four years, certified by a registered accountant; operating licenses of the enterprise; projections of the balance sheets and profit and loss statement for future years; and all papers and documents that may be necessary to check the feasibility study presented.

Art. 19. After all necessary papers have been presented, the credit department of the corporation will make a report on the application within two weeks covering the past and anticipated profitability of the enterprise, data and observations made during plant visits, and other relevant factors. Within another week, the legal advisor will make his report. Within one more week the board of directors of the corporation will then make a decision on the loan application, which will be communicated to the applicant within one day. If the loan application is for less than $4,000, the approval of the manager of the corporation is sufficient.

Art. 20. To its loan investigation, the credit department of the corporation collects the following information on the applicant and his enterprise:

(a) organization of the company: name of the existing company, mailing address, type of business organization, historical background, office and plant location, company officials, capital structure, necessary documents such as copies of charters, partnership or trust agreements, and articles of association or incorporation.

(b) data on existing firms: reorganization plans explaining any contemplated changes in management, recapitalization, reorganization of operations, mergers, etc.; products manufactured; pending litigation; financial statements; comparative balance sheets and profit and loss statements for the last four years; and any available financial reports, financial statements and records of annual meetings.

Figure 3 (continued)

(c) data on new companies and existing companies: summary of the proposal; plant location; industrial buildings and warehouses needed; machinery and equipment needed and criteria that led to their selection; raw and operating material requirements and their availability; labor requirements and available manpower; technicians, and managers; engineering survey explaining the methods and processes of production; the various stages of processing the materials; by-products, and waste materials and how these will be used, sold, or otherwise disposed of; for service industries, an explanation of the service to be rendered and the methods and organizational procedures to be used; total investment in the project broken down into: engineering and planning, land, buildings, machinery and equipment, supplies and spare parts, net working capital, patents and licenses, good will and other intangibles, start-up costs, interest during construction and funds for contingencies; detailed market study; estimated profit and loss statements, for the next five years, if possible; estimated balance sheets, for the next five years, if possible; and estimated return on the investment and schedule for the return of the loan.

(d) legal papers: legalized invoices for machinery, if pledged as collateral; relevant papers for all other objects pledged as collateral; and references on the solvency and integrity of the guarantor, if personal guarantee is given.

(e) additional information to be compiled by the staff of the corporation: long-term outlook for the industry concerned; compatibility with regional or national development plans; and evaluation of the managerial ability of the owner-manager.

It is evident that in most cases it will be impossible to compile complete information. The scheme serves only as a guideline and goal for the personnel of the corporation in analyzing a loan application. In the majority of the cases, therefore, decisions will have to be made on the basis of incomplete information. This is a risk that can be reduced through intensive research but which any development financing institution has to assume. Especially in the case of small industries and artisans, an elaborate analysis is not warranted because of the small sums involved. In such cases, past performance of the applicant, his managerial abilities, and his personal integrity are the overriding considerations.

SUPERVISION OF LOANS

All loans made by a development corporation are supervised loans. Supervision assures that the loans are used for the purpose agreed upon. As soon as a loan has been negotiated, a supervisory plan is worked out with the borrower. In addition, supervision serves to identify needs for advice and assistance that the borrower may require in order to successfully launch, expand, or improve his business.

An official of the credit department of the corporation is assigned to each loan. He may consult other specialists in the corporation for specific problems that may arise.

The borrower is asked to present periodical reports on the progress of his project with respect to construction, the purchase of machinery and equipment, and on the operation's financial situation. Although each project will, of course, require a somewhat different advisory approach, the corporation should have a general supervision procedure.

Construction Period

If the project requires that land be purchased, that buildings be erected, and that machinery and equipment be purchased, the corporation makes periodic checks on the progress of these operations. In many cases, the disbursement of funds is geared to the progress made. The corporation checks that the different stages of the construction of buildings and acquisition of machinery take place in accordance with the plan submitted with the loan application and with the periodic reports presented by the borrower. Specifically, the corporation ascertains that all costs agree with the original plan; that equipment is delivered and installed on the agreed-upon dates; that raw materials are purchased in accordance with the plans; and that all other programs necessary before operations can start, such as training workers, hiring managers and technical administrative personnel, organizing sales and publicity campaigns, etc., are carried out as required.

At the end of the construction period, the responsible corporation official presents a detailed report on this phase.

Operating Period

While the firm is operating and until the loan has been completely repaid to the corporation, the responsible corporation official makes monthly visits to the plant in case a problem requiring technical or managerial assistance has arisen. About a year after the plant has been operating successfully, these visits are made less frequently; and the borrower is then required only to present his annual balance sheets and his profit and loss statements.

During supervisory visits particular attention is paid to the following aspects of a company: the physical and production engineering aspects of the plant, such as plant layout, organization of work flow, maintenance of quality standards, maintenance of machinery and equipment, etc.; management and cost accounting; marketing methods; and financial planning and management.

If defects or problems are discovered, the corporation's advisory staff is called in immediately before the problems can seriously threaten the success of the company. In some cases the terms of the loan may be renegotiated to help the entrepreneur overcome temporary difficulties. This particular procedure is typical of development financing, whereas it would be an unusual one in conventional commercial financing.

The following sample checklist can serve as a guideline to the corporation's supervisory officer during every visit:

(1) Fulfillment of the contract.

(2) Fulfillment of the work plan: technical aspects, administrative and accounting aspects, and economic and financial aspects.

(3) Production Control: output, machinery, raw materials, quality, labor force, and inventory control.

(4) Administrative and accounting control: analysis of balance sheets, profit and loss statements, accounts receivable, accounts payable, loan equity ration, liquidity, reserves for contingencies; cost accounting systems; cost comparisons with similar companies; fulfillment of tax and social security obligations; administrative organization of the company--organization chart, distribution of functions and responsibilities, internal work regulation, and promotion policies; and training and incentives to employees and pay scales; labor relations; safety and sanitation.

(5) Economic and financial control: comparative economic and financial situation of the company--before and after the loan and since previous supervisory visit; situation of the company's markets and its share of the total available market; perspectives for opening up new markets; ability of the company to meet its short and longer-term obligations; and profits.

Before the periodic visits of the supervisory officer of the corporation, the owners or managers of the firms concerned are given a questionnaire to facilitate a quicker assessment of their situation: A sample questionnaire is shown in Figure 4.

FIGURE 4

SAMPLE QUESTIONNAIRE
FOR LOAN APPLICANT

1) Production

   a) What was your production when the loan was made?
   b) What is your actual production?
   c) What will be your future production?

2) Machinery and Equipment

   a) Is your machinery and equipment in good condition?
   b) Are your machines working properly?
   c) Is the capacity of your plant utilized fully?

3) Raw Materials and Services

   a) Are there problems with the supply of raw materials and other inputs?
   b) Do you experience any difficulties with respect to the services your plant requires?

4) Quality Control

   a) Do you have a quality control system and do you follow it?
   b) How has the quality of your finished product varied?
   c) What are the major defects of your finished product?
   d) What causes these defects?
   e) How could these defects be solved?

5) Labor Force

   a) Is the capacity of your employees fully utilized?
   b) Are your workers sufficiently trained for their jobs?

Figure 4 (continued)

c) Do your personnel need more training?
d) How are your labor relations?
e) Are all your employees insured?

6) Administration and Accounting

a) Do you experience any difficulties in the administration of your firm?
b) Is your cost accounting and inventory control system working efficiently and satisfactorily?
c) Do you meet all your tax obligations?

7) Economic and Financial Situation

a) How are your sales developing? Do you experience any difficulties in this respect? Why?
b) Have the prices for your raw materials varied?
c) Have the prices for your finished products varied?
d) How is competition for your products?
e) Do you consider your profits satisfactory?
f) Do you think you have an inflated inventory?
g) Do you think your fixed assets are excessive?
h) Are your accounts receivable excessive?
i) Is your capital insufficient?
j) What financial changes in your business have been brought about by the loan from the corporation?
k) What future sales and profit opportunities do you envision for your company?

It is evident that many artisans or small industrialists will not be able to answer all the questions in a questionnaire. Some of the answers will necessarily be superficial or based on rough estimates. Nevertheless, these questions stimulate the small or large entrepreneur to think about the problems of his business and to try to find solutions for them before the supervisory officer's visit.

International lending agencies and the economic assistance organizations of a number of industrial countries or private foreign banks can be important sources of additional funds to supplement the financing institution's own funds. A well-structured loan application can serve as an important tool in obtaining funds from such institutions.

LOAN APPLICATIONS FROM DEVELOPMENT CORPORATIONS OR INVESTMENT CORPORATIONS TO LENDING INSTITUTIONS

While each lending institution, such as the World Bank, AID, private banks, or investment corporations, requires somewhat different data on the borrower and his financial programs, certain basic information should be provided in any loan application. The more carefully such information has been selected, compiled, and presented, the greater are the chances of positive decision on the loan application.

Each application should include a covering letter which states the amount requested; the purpose of the loan; the terms, including method of disbursement, maturity, interest rate, grace period, and the terms and use of the subloans; and the collateral. A sample letter is presented in Figure 5.

Accompanying the letter should be supporting information which includes the official name and address of the development corporation, the geographic area of its operations, its legal basis, a brief history, a description of its general objectives and functions, and a description of its organization. The description of the organization should include the different organs of the development corporations and their responsibilities, its sources of income, its budgets in the previous three years, and its research and advisory services. An example of a description of research and advisory services is shown in Figure 6.

FIGURE 5

SAMPLE LETTER ACCOMPANYING LOAN APPLICATION
FROM DEVELOPMENT CORPORATION
TO LENDING INSTITUTION

This is to request your consideration of this application for a loan from the bank* to the development corporation for the purpose of developing small and medium industry. Detailed supporting information of this application is attached.

The loan request is for an amount of $1.5 million divided into two interrelated portions:

(1) $1.2 million for subloans to small and medium industries, and

(2) $300,000 for a portion of the costs of the establishment and operation of an industrial park for artisans and small industries and a Crafts and Small Industries Development Center which would serve the entire region.

The purpose of the loan is to supplement the funds of the development corporation to promote an integrated program of industrial development for artisans and small and medium industries, including financial assistance, technical and management advisory services, and physical facilities. The program would be accomplished by making loans to deserving and economically sound smaller industries, and by establishing small factory buildings and a development center for crafts and small industries located on an industrial park now owned by the development corporation. It should be noted that this park is distinct from the industrial park for larger industries.

---

*The term "bank" here refers to any lending institution.

Figure 5 (continued)

As for the terms of the loan, disbursement of bank funds for subloans to small and medium industries would take place within two years from the date of the loan, upon the basis of reimbursement after disbursement of the development corporation's own funds in a ratio of approximately one of development corporation fund to three of bank funds.

Maturity of the loan would be fifteen years after receipt of funds. A grace period of three years is requested for repayment of principal.

The development corporation hopes that the interest rate may be as low as possible, preferably two per cent or less on the outstanding balance. The difference between the rate received and the rates charged will be utilized for such development purposes as advisory services and the costs of investigations and supervised credit operations.* Repayment of the principal would be in thirty-one equal semiannual payments, to begin in the fourth year. Realistically, the development corporation must recognize the potential repayment problems inherent with dollar loans. Income to the development corporation is normally in local currency which may depreciate in value relative to the dollar, thus making interest and principal payments quite burdensome. The development corporation would be well advised to have their government support for such eventualities.

Subloans would be made for specific purposes in accordance with current regulations of the development corporation or requirements of the agency. The main terms of the subloans would be:

---

*In the case of a privately owned investment corporation, it might also be mentioned that the difference will be used to put the corporation on a more profitable footing, thus making it more attractive to private investors of the region.

Figure 5 (continued)

(1) Subloans would be made to industries to be established or for expansion and modernization of existing industries in the small and medium categories, with a capitalization of less than $200,000. Approval for subloans of $60,000 or more would be requested from the agency.

(2) Each subloan application will be carefully examined by the industrial development department to determine the techno-economic feasibility of the project and its compliance with development criteria and priorities established by the development corporation and national and regional plans.

(3) Subloans will be made by the development corporation only if alternative sources of financing are not available on reasonable terms and consistent with development needs of the area.

(4) Amounts of the subloans will normally not be more than 50 per cent of the firm's capital requirements, including working capital, with more liberal terms possible for small firms.

(5) Subloan funds may be utilized for the purchase of raw materials, machinery and equipment, fixed facilities, initial operating costs, and training costs.

(6) Interest rates will vary from 8.25-10.5 per cent in accordance with the size of the firm and the risk involved.

(7) Periods of subloan may be from two to fifteen years, but will usually be up to ten years.

(8) Collateral required will usually be 125 per cent of the amount of the loan, with more liberal terms possible for small firms.

(9) The subloans will be made under the provisions of a supervised credit program.

Figure 5 (continued)

(10) Disbursement of the funds is expected within two years from the date of loan, in accordance with present demand estimates.

Collateral for the loan funds will be: securities from those receiving subloans; a guarantee from the development corporation; and a guarantee from the national government.

The development corporation will be most grateful for favorable consideration of this request. We shall be glad to furnish any additional information needed and to discuss with you any suggested modifications and special terms required.

FIGURE 6

SUPPORTING INFORMATION TO LOAN APPLICATION

The research and advisory services of the development corporation are the responsibility of the industrial development department and the planning department. The industrial development department is divided into a medium industry development section and a small industry and artisan development section. The functions of the medium industry development section are as follows:

1. Industrial Studies

Identification of investment opportunities

Preliminary evaluation of ideas for industrial projects

Prefeasibility studies for industrial projects or selection of outside specialists to make feasibility studies

Studies of plant locations, including industrial parks or developed industrial land

Cost studies and financial estimates of various types

Preparation of investment prospectuses for specific projects for potential investors

Figure 6 (continued)

2. Industrial Promotion and Investment Promotion

Identification of potential investors

Preparation of promotional materials to be distributed to potential investors

Correspondence and direct contact or visits with investors

3. Assistance to Investors and Businessmen

Obtaining technical, financial, economic, market or other types of data for investors or businessmen in general

Rendering technical and managerial advisory services to borrowers under the development corporation's supervised loan program

Maintaining constant contact with industrialists and businessmen of the region to give advice on their technical and managerial problems and to learn about new industrial investment opportunities

Helping new investors, especially investors from abroad, in overcoming any obstacles that might stand between them and their planned investment

Helping industrial entrepreneurs prepare loan applications to the development corporation or to other financial institutions

4. Evaluation and Screening of Loan Applications

Checking the desirability of promoting the industry or trade under question

Checking the technical, economic, and financial feasibility of the proposition

Making recommendations to the industrial promotion committee, the president, and the executive committee of the development corporation

Supervising loans

5. Functions of the Artisan and Small Industry Development Section

Making surveys of existing artisan and small industry products

Studying the markets within the country and abroad for existing or possible new products and trying to open up new markets

Figure 6 (Continued)

Studying the feasibility of new productions

Designing and redesigning products to adapt them to prevailing demand patterns

Studying and recommending improvements in production methods, and technology and quality control

Arranging technical training

Giving advice on the best methods of transportation and distribution of products within the country and especially abroad

Giving accounting and management advice to artisans and small industries

Encouraging producers from abroad to set up branch operations in the region

Recommending loans or other forms of financial assistance to artisans and small industries

Giving financial and technical help in the organization of production and sales cooperatives

The description of functions should be followed by a listing of the personnel of the industrial development department. This should be followed by a description of the industrial credit program of the development corporation, the amounts available for industrial development out of the corporation's own funds, the loans that have already been made, the types of industries that have benefited from them, the development corporation's repayment record, a brief description of the loan regulations, and a listing of the loan applications received which could not be satisfied out of the corporation's own funds and for which the funds to be received are to be used.

JUSTIFICATION FOR THE DEVELOPMENT CORPORATION'S FINANCIAL ASSISTANCE TO SMALL AND MEDIUM INDUSTRY AND FOR THE FINANCIAL ASSISTANCE FROM THE AGENCY

Some background excerpts from an actual loan application from a development corporation are presented in Figure 7.

FIGURE 7

BACKGROUND EXCERPTS FROM A LOAN APPLICATION TO A DEVELOPMENT CORPORATION

Industrial Situation in the Region

The industrial scene of the region is characterized by small and medium industries. Of the region's 160 industrial establishments (excluding a large number of family-operated establishments), only ten firms have more than 100 employees. None of the ten firms has more than 400 employees. One hundred and eight firms (about 75 per cent of the total) have from one to twenty-four employees, and approximately one hundred and twenty-seven firms (about 87 per cent of the total) have from one to forty-nine employees.*

Importance of Industrial Development

Although only six per cent of the active population of the region are employed in industry, industry contributes about 19 per cent of the total income of the region. The share of industry in the total income of the region is, however, below that of industry in the capital city of the country, where it is between 25-30 per cent. Industry will therefore have to be developed further so that it can draw people out of the less-productive activities. Since industry will probably continue to develop around certain centers rather than become dispersed over the countryside, and since the region's principal city may be expected to continue to be the major industrial center of the region, the industry of the agricultural population from the whole region, which has a population of 2.5 million.

---

*A table should be enclosed showing the numbers, sizes, and types of industries in the area.

Figure 7 (Continued)

In accordance with the small size of the regional market and the limited technical experience and training of the local entrepreneurs, many of the industrial growth possibilities will probably be found in the small and medium industry sectors. The development of all types of industries will have to be promoted, but emphasis will be given to those sectors with the greatest possibilities and opportunities: industries based on existing natural resources; industries that supply essential goods and services needed in the region, mainly essential consumer goods that have a wide market even in a low-income area; and industries that can economically replace imported goods or process those export articles that have previously left the area unprocessed or only partially processed and which contribute to earning foreign exchange.

The development corporation conceives its role as that of stimulating, encouraging, guiding, and helping private entrepreneurs who want to take advantage of these industrial opportunities, either by establishing new enterprises or by expanding or diversifying already existing enterprises.

Climate for Industrial Development

Industrial development in the region has been hampered in the past for many reasons: lack of identified industrial investment opportunities; lack of adequate prefeasibility and feasibility studies for identified opportunities; lack of effort to find outside investors for those opportunities for which studies have been undertaken; reluctance of local investors to risk their money in industry; lack of specific incentives for industrial investment in the region rather than in the capital city; and lack of managerial and technical guidance to local investors which led to the failure of some industrial projects that were started.

The development corporation is trying to avoid such deficiencies through its industrial development

Figure 7 (continued)

program. This program involves: identifying industrial investment opportunities; making prefeasibility and feasibility studies; searching actively for investors, regionally, in the country's capital city, and abroad; and giving technical and managerial advice to investors or receivers of loans.

The development corporation has already obtained from the central government far-reaching tax exemptions for newly established industries in the region which will be an incentive to investors to come into the region. It is also planning to build industrial parks where cheap developed land as well as the necessary services and facilities will be available as an additional incentive to investment.

Investment Funds from Other Sources

Savings deposits in the banks of the region approximate $8 million. However, it has been difficult to channel this money into industrial investment in the area. In most cases these accounts belong to small savers who are not accustomed to industrial investment and who would probably not invest even if an attractive opportunity were offered to them. Wealthy individuals whose money is invested in other forms are reluctant to invest it in industry because they are unfamiliar with industry and prefer commerce, apartment houses, or agriculture, or because they have had losses in connection with industrial ventures in the region. Nevertheless, a limited amount of investment funds may be expected to be forthcoming from this source, especially if the development corporation can present thoroughly studied projects for which competent management can be obtained. In some cases this group can be induced to invest if an institution like the development corporation would be willing to share the risk with them. Recently, as a result of various promotional efforts, there has been considerable interest shown in industrial ventures by local capital.

The development corporation is also making efforts to encourage and sponsor a private or semi-

Figure 7 (continued)

private regional investment bank which will channel the funds of smaller investors and reluctant larger investors into investments in regional industry, select suitable investments, and possibly guide or supply management.

Other sources of private industrial investment capital are private foreign investors for equity capital and equipment financing for loan capital. The inflow of private foreign investment capital will depend on the over-all investment climate of the country and the corporation's success in attracting investors to the region, equipment financing is an important source of loan capital, but it is usually available only for larger firms.

Investment Policies and Programs of Other Financial Institutions

Commercial banks make only short-term loans of ninety to a hundred days, or, in some cases, up to a year. Established firms have a more or less continuing account. The interest rate is at least 13 per cent, and it is considerably higher in accordance with the particular credit risks involved. If special fees and charges are included, the cost of an average commercial bank loan is 18 per cent; it may be as high as 30 per cent. Commercial bank loans can be used in industrial financing only for working capital financing.

The industrial bank usually makes loans to industries for five years and, in special cases, for as long as ten years, at interest rates varying from 6-10 per cent plus 1-2 per cent fees. However, the collateral requirements are high: usually a collateral of 200 per cent of the amount of the loan is necessary if real estate is given as collateral, and 250 per cent if machinery or equipment is given as collateral. Although the industrial bank has a branch office in the principal town of the region, loans exceeding $2000 can be approved only in the capital city. The executives of the industrial bank

Figure 7 (continued)

located in the capital of the country cannot have the necessary personal contact and acquaintance with the applicant from this region, nor any direct acquaintance with the project. As a result, applicants from the region find it much more difficult to obtain loans from the industrial bank than applicants in the capital city. The development corporation can be more effective in the region because of its direct, daily contacts with local industries and loan applicants and its ability to supervise borrowers regularly and closely.

The industrial bank also has a special loan program for small industry and artisans for loans up to $8,000 with more liberal guarantee requirements and an interest rate of 6 per cent plus 1 per cent fee. Decisions about these loans can be made by their regional branch office. However, the supervision and technical advice the industrial bank can give to these borrowers is rudimentary. Although the development corporation's loan program for small industries and artisans generally coincides with that of the industrial bank, the development corporation is able to give stronger supervision and technical advice to borrowers and is thus able to make loans in cases where the collateral is insufficient for the industrial bank.

PRIVATE EQUITY INVESTMENT AND LOAN COMPANIES

Private equity investment companies can contribute significantly toward involving private capital in industrial financing, especially in countries where no capital market exists or where the capital market is rudimentary or allows access to only a few firms.

The formation of a private equity investment company begins when the development corporation or a group of citizens concerned with industrial development draws up the initial plan and promotes it among a large segment of the business and financial community of the region. As a result of this promotional effort, a group of founders is formed who put up the initial capital.

The founders or the promoters contact similar companies in other regions of the country or abroad to obtain all available information about operating procedures, organizational structure investment and lending policies, staffing, and operating costs.

An experienced manager is brought in from outside who organizes the company and hires and trains a local staff that will eventually be able to take over the management of the company.

The initial success of the company attracts other investors, either large investors or small investors who are wage earners unaccustomed to investing in industry. The success and good reputation of the company then also attracts foreign investors. Today more capital is available in the industrial countries than can be invested in developing countries. The reasons for this inability of available capital to be invested is the lack of well-studied projects in the newly developing countries, lack of entrepreneurial initiative, and a lack of retail mechanisms for larger foreign loans and equity capital. A larger foreign bank or investment company has little interest in investing in a large number of small projects, each requiring perhaps $40,000 since the administrative costs and the initial costs of making a feasibility analysis for so many projects abroad would be too high. However, they are much more likely to consider an investment of $1 million in an investment company that handles the retailing of this money among many smaller and medium companies in the region. It is for this reason that investment companies get special support from international financial institutions and the foreign-aid programs of some industrial countries.

Eventually the prestige of the company may allow it to float bonds or stocks among the general public, of which it absorbs only a small portion. In this way the company becomes a small capital market of its own.

If, in its initial stages, the investment company has difficulties in gaining the confidence of a public unaccustomed to industrial investments, a public or semipublic entity such as the development corporation may want to subsidize the operation so that a minimum dividend can be guaranteed to the investors. Figure 8 shows a sample organizational structure for a private industrial investment company.

The general manager should be a person of high moral and professional integrity with wide experience in the administration of investment companies. The auditor should have wide banking experience. The financial analysis department should be in the charge of a man with experience in financial analysis. The technical department should be in the charge of an industrial engineer with wide industry experience.

Often it is not possible to find qualified personnel in the developing region or even in the country. In this case foreign personnel must be hired. The World Bank and similar organizations, as well as private banks and investment companies in the major industrial countries, will be helpful in arranging contacts with suitable candidates.

The operating expenses of an organization with this structure, including salaries, rent for office space, legal expenses, depreciation of equipment, and special advisors and consultants would be at least $50,000, taking into account the lower salary levels in newly developing countries. If foreign personnel are hired, this cost may be considerably higher.

To gain a better idea of the possible earnings of such a corporation, consider the hypothetical case of an investment corporation with an initial capital of U.S. $500,000. Suppose that this money is invested in the first year with 55 per cent going into loans, 40 per cent into equity investment, and 5 per cent put aside as reserve against bad debts and losses. As the corporation gains more experience, a larger percentage will probably be invested in equity investments, but initially this percentage will be hardly more than 40 per cent. Assume that the corporation lends money at 12 per cent and earns an average of 18 per cent on equity investments, for these percentages are typical for many newly developing countries. The first year will then yield the following results:

Capital	Earnings on Loans	Earnings on Investments	Total Gross Earnings
$500,000	$31,500	$36,000	$67,500

Minus Operating Costs	Net Earnings	% of Capital
$50,000	$17,500	3.5

Thus the earnings in the first year would be quite low, too low to make the investment attractive to investors in most newly developing countries.

If the capital were doubled or tripled--and administrative costs would probably not rise significantly--earnings would rise to 7 per cent or 10.5 per cent respectively. But even then the enterprise would interest only investors with established business interests in the region who recognize that the stimulation of industrial activity would mean increased business for their own firms--such as banks, electricity companies, department stores, hotels, and restaurants.

The capital would probably have to be raised still further or the investment corporation would have to enter actively into the business of retailing to local industries loans received from foreign banks or governmental agencies, such as the Agency for International Development (AID), at relatively low rates of interest. For instance, it is the policy of AID to lend up to three times the capital of the investment corporation--in some cases even up to five times--at an interest rate of about 3 per cent. Private banks and investment companies from the industrial countries are likely to make loans, too, but at interest rates of about 6 per cent, depending on the financial and political stability of the country concerned. In each case, the guarantee for the loan would be a guarantee from the government of the country in which the loan is placed in addition to the normal guarantees from the final borrowers to the investment corporation, such as mortgages. Grace periods can be from five to ten years.

If this hypothetical investment corporation with a capital of $500,000 receives a loan from AID in the amount of $1.5 million at 3 per cent and then lends it to industries in the area at 12 per cent, the difference would be 9 per cent. Based on the capital of $500,000, this would mean annual earnings of 27 per cent provided the money can be placed within one year. If 5 per cent is deducted as a reserve against losses, and 3.5 per cent earned on the original $500,000 is added, total net earnings would be 25.5 per cent. In the case of a loan from a private bank at 6 per cent, the total net earnings would be 16.5 per cent. Even considering that operating expenses for a company handling $2 million will have risen considerably beyond the $50,000 mark, the resulting earnings can be considered high enough in most newly developing countries to attract a considerable number of private investors.

One of the limitations of AID loans and loans from similar governmental organizations of other industrial countries is that they normally must be used for purchases only in the country of origin; a small percentage is often allowed for local purchases and usually no purchases are allowed in any other countries. This may be too severe a restriction unless such loans can be obtained from several countries. Loans from private banks, the World Bank, and other international institutions do not usually carry with them such limitations, although their interest rates are, of course, higher. Ordinarily such loans are in dollars or other hard currencies. If the currency of the borrowing country is not stable and there is danger of a devaluation, the investment corporation must accumulate sufficient reserves to compensate for currency devaluation in addition to normal reserves for losses and bad debts.

FIGURE 8

SUGGESTED ORGANIZATIONAL STRUCTURE FOR PRIVATE INDUSTRIAL INVESTMENT COMPANY

GENERAL ASSEMBLY OF STOCKHOLDERS

SECRETARY

BOARD OF DIRECTORS

OUTSIDE AUDITORS

EXECUTIVE COMMITTEE

LOAN COMMITTEE

GENERAL MANAGER

TECHNICAL MANAGER

AUDITOR OR COMPTROLLER

HEAD FINANCIAL ANALYSIS SECTION

HEAD ECONOMICS AND STATISTICS SECTION

HEAD ENGINEERING AND MARKETING SECTION

ADMINISTRATION AND ACCOUNTING

SUPERVISORY SERVICES

PERSONNEL

ISSUING OF STOCKS AND BONDS

Thus the first few years of the investment corporation's existence will be difficult ones because capital may still be small, operating expenses high, and lack of experience may initially cause some losses on loans or equity investments which could have been avoided. By the time capital is increased or a low interest rate loan has been obtained from a foreign or international institution, the profit situation will have improved considerably. It should, therefore, be the policy of the investment corporation to increase its capital or obtain an outside low interest rate loan as soon as possible.

In countries or regions where investors have little experience with industrial investment or where real estate investment or investment in other non-industrial fields offers attractive returns, it may be difficult for the investment corporation to raise enough capital during its initial years. In many countries, governments or development corporations, recognizing the importance of mobilizing private capital for industrial investment, have guaranteed a minimum return to the shareholders of an industrial investment corporation, granted a guarantee on the whole investment, or have guaranteed both a minimum return as well as the investment itself, until the investment corporation has become financially sound enough to stand alone. If the development corporation has a steady and secure income, such as a certain percentage of the sales tax revenue of the country or of the import duty revenue, such a guarantee from the government or development corporation can serve a very useful function. The cost to the corporation is relatively low considering the benefits of mobilizing private capital for industry and establishing a new institution that can attract foreign funds to the region. If the hypothetical investment corporation has losses of 10 per cent of its capital during the first year of its operation--which is an extreme situation--and if a minimum dividend of 8 per cent is guaranteed to the shareholders, total losses to the development corporation would amount to $90,000. The investment corporation would probably be able to repay this sum when its operations will have become more profitable.

The loan regulations of an industrial investment corporation should emphasize the economic and technical soundness and the ability and integrity of the entrepreneur, rather than any tangible guarantees the entrepreneur can give. The interest rates should be high enough to cover possible losses due to more liberal, development-oriented lending policies and to attract investors with sound projects that have good profit potentials. On the other hand, the interest rate should not be prohibitively high so as to discourage many types of investments that may not initially have a great profit potential but that can develop into industries that contribute to the region's income and employment. As a rough rule of thumb, interest rates should be about 2/3-3/4 of the rates charged by the commercial banks.

Interest charges are only one of many industrial costs. More important are the terms of the loan, such as lending periods, grace periods, and collateral requirements, and the red tape and time involved in getting the loan. If these latter factors are favorable to the industrialist, he will find it worthwhile to pay a somewhat higher interest rate.

Suppose that a new firm finances 50 per cent of its total investment with its own equity capital and 50 per cent with a loan at 6 per cent payable over eight years. Its yearly earnings on total investment are normally 25 per cent. Its yearly deductions from earnings would then be 6.25 per cent of the total investment for the repayment of the principal and an average of approximately 1.5 per cent of its total investment for interest payments during the eight years; total payments would then amount to 7.75 per cent of the total investment. This cost of financing is not prohibitive if the interest rate is doubled from 6 to 12 per cent. Yearly deductions from earnings would still be 6.25 per cent of total investment for the repayment of principal and an average of approximately 3 per cent of total investment for interest payments during the eight years; total yearly payments would amount to 9.25 per cent of the total investment. The difference between the two figures for total yearly payments or the cost of financing per year is only 1.5 per cent of the total investment. However, no healthy industrial enterprise will be very much affected by a 1.5 per cent higher deduction from profits for the repayment of principal and payment of interest charges, especially in newly developing countries where profits tend to be rather high. Only the marginal firm would be affected by such a small difference, and it is questionable whether the marginal firm should be benefited by money from the investment corporation in view of the fact that capital is scarce in newly developing countries and it should be appropriated only to the most promising ventures.

Frank Coffin[4] has stated that the success of development banks of investment companies seems to be due chiefly, though not exclusively, to the specific factors that follow.

(1) A financial subsidy, usually in the form of a local currency loan from the government with low or no interest rate. Subsidies have also been provided in the form of tax benefits, government sharing of administrative costs, a high debt-equity ratio, and dividend guarantees during the initial years. Such a loan can also come from AID, from other governments, or from private banks.

(2) Outside managerial and technical assistance that enable the bank to get organized and to begin operations on a sound basis.

(3) Local management that is both competent and imaginative.

(4) Management's willingness to promote new projects and new industries, to work with applicants in setting up a sound project for a loan, and to provide technical and managerial services for their clients.

(5) The ability to amass local funds for small and medium-sized businesses.

(6) The attitude that project development is equally important to straightforward lending operations.

(7) Successful investments in equities.

(8) Promotion of foreign private capital investment, not only within the development banks themselves but also in other local enterprises.

(9) The ability to join with other local financial institutions, including insurance companies, to create a location for the exchange of securities which would be the beginnings of a local stock exchange.

(10) Private managership. While ownership can be important, Coffin believes that managership resting in private hands is more important.

(11) Establishment of a "modus operandi" with the respective governments whereby general sectors of industrial activity are identified as priority by the governments and individual projects within those sectors are selected by the development bank for economic rather than political reasons.

(12) A relatively favorable local climate for private investment.

(13) An entrepreneurial class sufficiently vigorous to be able to put available credit to sound economic use.

Notes to Chapter 3

1. The source of this material is Carlton R. Wood, Programa Regional De Capacitación En Desarrollo, Vol. 4: Necesidades Funcionales Y Requisitos De Organización En El Desarrollo Industrial Del Sur Del Perú (Arequipa, Peru: AID, 1965).

2. For further reference see Robert W. Davenport and Peter Duncan, Requirements for the Organization of Industrial Financing Programs by Development Corporations, a Report to Instituto Nacional de Promoción Industrial (Lima, Perú, 1964).

3. The following material on organized methods of applicant evaluation, delegating operational responsibilities to professional management, measures for building up information relevant to lending operations, and measures for acquiring and training staff competent to administer development financing programs consists of excerpts from a Report to the Instituto Nacional de Promoción Industrial in Lima, Perú, by Robert W. Davenport and Peter Duncan.

4. Frank Coffin, Witness for AID (Boston: 1964), Houghton Mifflin Company, Chapter 16, p. 221.

CHAPTER 4 INDUSTRIAL ADVISORY SERVICES

Any industrial development corporation must provide industrial advisory services. This function is particularly important for medium and smaller industries which are unable to pay for such services or are unaware of their need for such services provided by private consulting firms.

However, in many newly developing areas, small and medium industries form the bulk of the existing industries, so that a development corporation must aim at helping small and medium industries to become large, modern, and efficient. Most of the larger, modern concerns in industrialized nations started as small industries. But even where market or other factors prevent an industry from becoming a large concern, smaller and medium industries must be stimulated since they can contribute significantly to the output and employment of a region. Size alone does not prevent small and medium firms from being modern, efficient producers of a variety of products, provided that the products are properly selected. Eugene Staley points out that:

> . . . most of small or medium industry in newly developing countries today is still unprogressive. Much of it produces low-quality, badly designed goods at unnecessarily high cost and provides unstable employment at low wages, often in disregard of labor and social laws. But in many newly developing countries we find exceptional small firms emerging managed by people who can be de-

> scribed as ambitious, hard-working, intelligent, and potentially progressive entrepreneurs. Often they are struggling against great odds but they are capable of responding to the right kinds of developmental help. They often lack basic education, managerial and technical skill, or all three, they are chronically short of capital, they are unfamiliar with modern notions of management in such important fields as cost accounting, production management, marketing, and labor relations. They lack access to management advice, to technical information, and to information on potential markets. But these are deficiencies that, to a considerable extent, can be overcome by developmental techniques that are already being applied with success in a number of countries. The key element in these techniques is an industrial extension service to be provided by a development corporation.[1]

Advisory services are needed in two main fields: economic and business management problems, and technical production and productivity problems.

Management involves many problems. Among those that are noted particularly in newly developing areas are: marketing, including export marketing; purchasing; financial management; inventory control; maintenance of records; cost accounting and analysis; labor and personnel relations; labor training; wages rate determination; ways of meeting the need for technical and craft skills; plant layout; production scheduling and controls; quality control; long-range planning; collection of accounts; business organization; and pricing problems.[2]

Purely technical production problems do not loom large so long as there is an assured market and little competition. At present, however, firms in many newly developing regions are faced with increasing competition from large firms and from foreign products. They must therefore adjust to new technological developments. In order to keep abreast of new developments, greater assistance will be required in technical research leading to new products and techniques of production.

ADVISORY SERVICES NEEDED IN THE FIELD OF BUSINESS MANAGEMENT

Choice of Promising Lines of Manufacture

Small businessmen often inquire about promising lines of manufacture which they could engage in, either by opening a new business or by adding new items to their present manufacturing lines. The initial type of advice needed concerns the kinds of products that appear to have good prospects. This information is obtained from the research and investigations by corporation personnel on industrial opportunities. The individual entrepreneur is usually unable to do all the market, product, and production research needed to enable him to make a decision as to whether to initiate a business.

Location of Enterprise

The entrepreneur may also need advice on the best location for his enterprise in terms of various factors of production and sales. The type of business determines whether it is better to locate near the raw materials, near the market, near transportation facilities, or near sources of auxiliary help, such as machine shops.

Form of Organization

Once a product line has been decided and the entrepreneur has decided to undertake production, he may need advice about the form of organization of his enterprise. Organizational form depends on a number of factors, but principally that of funds that are available or needed to finance the enterprise. His alternatives may be an individual proprietorship, partnership, a stock company, or a joint enterprise with a foreign firm. Very small enterprises interested in jointly manufacturing a product such as shoes may be interested in forming a cooperative association.

Financial Problems

One of the main advisory services needed is to aid the entrepreneur in determining the types of loans and credit he needs, how he can organize his financial accounting, and how and where he can obtain external financial assistance.

Usually the entrepreneur does not have sufficient personal funds to finance his new business or, if the business already exists, to expand production. An important form of advice has to do with sources of funds for various types of needs, such as capital equipment and working capital. Some of the funds will probably be obtained from commercial banks, and some from industrial development financial institutions or the development corporation. Risk funds may have to be obtained from special investment corporations willing to provide equity capital.

Government and commercial banks can provide valuable financial advisory services.

Purchase of Machinery and Materials

Particularly in areas away from capital cities, it is difficult for the smaller entrepreneur to know where to obtain information regarding sources and types of machinery needed for his enterprise. The choice in sources of supplies is wide. Salesmen of equipment are usually more interested in making sales than in providing objective information on the variety of equipment available from other suppliers.

Similarly, for some enterprises, advice may be needed about the best source of materials used in the manufacturing process, prices, methods of transportation, and the like.

Marketing

The failure of most businesses is due to inadequate investigation of market conditions prior to initiating the business. Consequently, a potential entrepreneur must determine methods of marketing a product--whether directly by the firm, through special distributors, or through wholesalers. Often the persons who start a business are experienced in production but not in marketing. Market investigation is a continuing activity in the case of many products because consumer demand may change quickly. Smaller firms in particular need a great deal of assistance in marketing their products.

Sales to Public Agencies

In many countries, government departments, the military services, and public hospitals and schools constitute one of the largest markets for industrial products. Special assistance and provisions may be needed to ensure that the smaller and medium-sized industries, especially those outside of capital cities, get a fair opportunity to bid and supply government agencies. As in the United States, some special privileges may have to be given to smaller industries to help them to compete against large firms. Advisory services in this field would include providing information to the local firms about government-purchasing requirements, methods of making bids, and about the quality, standards, and performance times required by the government. An analysis of items that might be produced locally by manufacturing firms for sale to the government may provide ideas for new industries or production lines.

Accounting and Costing

Modern business management depends on financial controls to determine short-range and long-range production programs, to lower costs of products, and to determine exact costs of each element in the production and sales process. Many concepts of financial controls are new to business firms in developing areas. Advisory services are needed, both on an individual basis and through group training, to bring the latest methods to the attention of business firms. Such financial controls are essential in obtaining loans and credit.

More fundamental for many small businesses is the need for simple accounting procedures. Advisory services in this field can be undertaken at the least cost by conducting group classes. Often universities and associations of accountants can help with this type of advice and training.

ADVISORY SERVICES NEEDED IN THE FIELD OF PRODUCTION AND PRODUCTIVITY

General Production Engineering

Production engineering covers a wide variety of activities including plant layout, timing of inflow of raw materials, flow of materials through the plant, scheduling of use of machines, maintenance of machinery, training of workers, labor relations, quality controls, and shipping. Large firms have foremen in charge of various departments but smaller firms with an owner-manager and a small number of workers have difficulties coordinating all the jobs involved. Advisory services are needed to improve general productivity.

Product Design

Today, product design is extremely important for sales, whether the product is handcrafted or machine-made. Special advice, often beyond the financial ability of the entrepreneur, may be required. Effective design of the product is, to a large extent, determined by the market so that market research is required.

Maintenance of Machinery and Equipment

Many small firms and some larger ones require advisory services with respect to maintenance of machinery, utilization of machinery, tooling, and supply of spare parts. In some smaller firms, machinery is often used beyond its capacity and not properly maintained, so that production costs are greatly increased by the necessity of early replacement of parts or the whole machine. If a firm is not in a position to afford a general mechanic or maintenance man, it may be possible to obtain such services from small firms specializing in undertaking these services for a number of firms on a contract basis.

Quality and Standards

As competition for sales increases and the consuming public becomes more aware of quality, controls over quality in the factory become very important at all stages of production, from the processing of raw materials to the final product.

Maintaining standards is an essential aspect of modern industry. Considerable progress has been made in many countries toward establishing national standards for certain products and toward conforming to international standards. Advisory services at the regional and local level are needed to help individual factories establish their own standards and conform to national and international standards.

Labor Relations

Good labor relations within a plant are important to productivity. Principles of labor and personnel relations are usually known but frequently not applied. In many countries, national productivity agencies have done much to improve this aspect of productivity through training-within-industry programs and special classes. A development corporation should do everything possible to be of assistance in these programs and to advise the industrial firms in the area of their availability and usefulness.

Training

Development corporations can undertake general advisory services to schools, universities, and special institutes with regard to the needs for manpower training in the area. Educational institutions of all types tend to adhere to established curricula without regard to current needs of development. Representatives of all educational institutions and agencies should be kept fully informed of the planning for industrial development and both present and future needs for skilled, semiskilled, and management personnel.

Similarly, the industrial community should be kept informed of the training programs presently available for management and workers through international and national agencies, the universities, and the technical schools.

SOME SUGGESTED METHODS OF MEETING ADVISORY SERVICES NEEDS

Analysis of Advisory Needs

As a first step in planning and programming for advisory services, an analysis of the needs of each industry in the region should be undertaken to determine the main problems in business management and production. In a number of countries national productivity agencies have already undertaken such analyses, and regional development corporations can draw on their results.

Industrial Extension Services

Many developing countries pattern their industrial extension services after the successful agricultural extension services. Similar to the work of agricultural extension officers, industrial (or business) extension officers counsel groups and individuals in general management problems, accounting costing, marketing, financing, personnel management, technical production problems, product design and improvement, location of industry of business, sources of financial assistance, and sources and costs of equipment. The extension officer cannot possibly know all the answers, but he should know where to get the answers.

In supervised credit programs, industrial extension officers provide supervision, advising firms just starting out and obtaining credit, and counseling them until the debt has been paid.

It is advisable that a development corporation have at least one person responsible for providing advisory services. This person should be an experienced businessman who has the confidence of individual firms and who can coordinate the various sources of advisory assistance. He would be the corporation's chief industrial extension officer, assisted by the entire staff of the industrial development department. In addition to their regular business experience, extension officers need special training in extension techniques, such as how to approach industrialists and how to organize and train group classes.

"Self-Diagnosis" and "Group Diagnosis"

Countries whose personnel for advisory services are too limited to permit much assistance to firms on an individual basis have experimented with "self-diagnosis" and "group diagnosis." The Japanese, for example, have encouraged these methods. Small business firms are supplied with pertinent questions and taught to examine their own enterprises critically and to compare them with others. The Copenhagen Technological Institute brings together a group of owner-managers from similar enterprises for a series of seminars under expert guidance to examine their problems collectively.

Private Management Consulting Services

Modern industries are turning more and more to management consultant firms for assistance with their special problems. Management consulting firms are usually located in capital cities; they should be encouraged by the development corporation to open branches in the region concerned.

Industrial Parks and Advisory Services

It is much easier to provide advisory services to smaller industries when they are grouped in the same location. Thus one of the advantages of industrial parks is that they facilitate advisory services. In some industrial parks, advisory services undertake research, training, and advisory services not only for the industries located on the park, but for others in the region.

Technical Inquiry Services

Today a large number of technical publications, films, and other training and advisory aids are available from the technical-aid organization of various industrial countries. Development corporations should have themselves put on the mailing list of all these organizations.

Joint Services

Smaller manufacturers in particular often cannot afford machinery or services necessary to reduce costs or to improve the quality of goods. Textile finishing, leather glazing, and electroplating of metal products are examples of enterprises with machinery that is often beyond the capacities of any one firm to maintain and which would be used only infrequently by that firm. Machinery and equipment maintenance, repairs, and servicing are examples of services for which one firm might not have sufficient experienced personnel.

Through the advisory services of the development corporation, it may be possible to suggest and help initiate means by which several smaller firms can co-operate to establish special services which they need, either by themselves or by encouraging entrepreneurs to establish them as a business.

An excellent example of this kind of cooperation was suggested by a leather expert who worked for several months in a Latin American country. He found that improvement was needed in the preservation of hides and skins in general and in the tanning of alpacas and llama skins. He worked out detailed instruction sheets with regard to these matters. He further suggested a mobile laboratory for demonstration and research work. In addition he advised that for the purpose of keeping the alpaca-llama tanning and dressing business in the region where the skins originate a separate corporation or cooperative be formed with the backing of the development corporation. This cooperative would function, through numerous branches, to provide directions and salt for preservation of hides and skins, to provide directions and the necessary chemicals for tanning, and to purchase tanned furskins of acceptable quality at established prices. In these ways, use of correct materials and efficient procedures could be established. Grading, with higher prices for better quality, should ensure improvement in the product. Tanned skins of good quality would be sold to the skilled fabricators in the area.

Notes to Chapter 4

1. Eugene Staley, *Methods of Industrial Development* (Paris: OECD, 1962), pp. 201-34.

2. The source for this material is Carlton R. Wood, *Programa Regional De Capacitación En Desarrollo*, Vol. 4: *Necesidades Funcionales Y Requisitos De Organización En El Desarrollo Industrial Del Sur Del Perú* (Arequipa, Peru: AID, 1965).

CHAPTER 5 DEVELOPMENT CORPORATIONS AND SMALL INDUSTRY DEVELOPMENT

THE DEVELOPMENT CORPORATION AND SMALL INDUSTRY DEVELOPMENT[1]

There is much confusion about the term "small industry." The definition used here will be the one given by Dr. Eugene Staley: Roughly speaking, small industries are those with fewer than 100 employees. But rather than using a statistical definition, Dr. Staley defines it

> . . . In terms of certain functional characteristics which make its problems and opportunities somewhat different from those of medium and large industry. These functional characteristics include relatively little specialization in management ("one-man" management), lack of access to capital through the organized securities market, no special bargaining strength in buying or selling in major market, and often, though not always, a relatively close integration with the local community through local ownership and management and dependence on nearby markets and sources of supply. These characteristics give small industry certain disadvantages, and certain special needs for types of advice and aid which are not so much needed by large manufacturing firms. They also confer some advantages, chief of which is flexibility. The close personal contact which one-man management makes possible between the top manager and production workers, customers,

> suppliers, and owners can be, if the manager is a good one, a source of strength in many ways. This characteristic goes far to explain why, and in what kinds of manufacturing, modern small industry can compete successfully with large industry.[2]

The type of small industry discussed here is not traditional small industry working with antiquated methods and paying subsistence salaries, but rather modern, efficient, small industry. Even in highly industrialized countries like the United States, Germany, and Great Britain small industry continues to occupy a very important place. According to statistics from 1953 and 1954, manufacturing establishments having fewer than 100 employees account for 91-95 per cent of all manufacturing establishments, 26-33 per cent of all manufacturing employees, and 22-23 per cent of all manufacturing output.[3] These statistics have probably not changed significantly since then.

To gain a better understanding of the role small industry can play in newly developing countries or regions, the types of small industries that have been able to prosper in the already industrial countries in spite of the rise of industrial giants should be examined. The first category of small industry is the artisan. As Dr. Staley points out,[4] if such artisans as the weaver, potter, blacksmith, shoemaker, or low-quality tailor try to compete with industry, they are likely to be replaced by manufacturing establishments. The types of artisans that have been able to prosper in a modern economy are those that have not tried to compete with industry but have rather supplemented factory production. These are either service artisans such as plumbers, electricians, and automobile mechanics who service, install, and repair industrially made goods or artisans making goods that have a special artistic or fashion appeal or that require special characteristics of design. The latter are, for instance, high-quality tailors, artistic ceramists, and craftsmen making articles with a primitive or folklore appeal. It should be the goal of development policy to help artisans transform their business into the type that can still exist under modern conditions.

The second category of small industry is small industry in the narrower sense of the term. Small factories can exist in a modern economy, and in many cases they exist rather comfortably if they make use of the specific competitive advantages that small industry has over large industry. The industrial structure of a country with only larger industries has many "cracks," as Dr. Staley puts it, which larger industry cannot fill. In many cases these cracks can be substantial, and in a country with a small total market or with many markets separated from each other by high transportation costs, it is only small industries that can fit the small markets. In many newly developing countries, the "cracks" are filled insufficiently. It is often characteristic of such countries that the only modern industries are large industries in the coastal cities or major cities, often owned by foreigners, by wealthy native families, or by governments expecting great effects on development of large industrial complexes. Contrasted to these large, modern factories that are often owned and managed by foreigners are the great number of antiquated artisan shops and inefficiently run small industries trying to compete with large industries on grounds where they should not try to compete.

What are the specific competitive advantages of small industry? Dr. Staley lists five factors:

First, economies of scale are less important in some lines of production than in others. In blast furnaces and cement kilns, for example, there are great engineering advantages in using big pieces of equipment to handle large amounts of materials, so that these are not undertakings suitable for small units. But in the manufacture of garments or certain kinds of machine tools, the advantages of scale are much less significant, and a moderate-sized plant may be at least as efficient as a large one.

Second, small units have an advantage in meeting local demands where shipping costs are high or the product is perishable. Thus, bricks and tiles, fresh baked goods, or soft drinks can be produced more economically by relatively small local establishments than by great central factories. Obviously the prospects for regional development of small-medium factories to meet local demands are linked to the growth of local incomes, which means that they are linked to improvements in agriculture and animal husbandry, mineral development, the growth of tourism, or the development of larger industries that bring more income to the locality.

Third, small manufacturing establishments have an advantage in meeting highly specialized or individualized demands or in catering to a small volume market or one requiring frequent quick adjustments because of such factors as style changes. They compete very well in women's wear, some types of specialized machinery, surgical equipment, and other fields where the small firm's flexibility stands it in good stead. Large enterprises are handicapped by their bureaucratic procedures and their relatively large overhead expenses. It is uneconomical for them to produce short "runs" of a nonstandard item, but the small factory can often do so at a profit. Often, the small factory does not even compete directly with the large factory. Instead it produces different sizes, different styles, or slightly different products for which the demand is not great enough to justify large-scale production, but is still sufficiently great to interest the small firm.

Fourth, small and medium factories often produce components and supplies for large factories. Much Japanese small industry works on contract for large industry. One of the reasons for the efficiency of small industry in the United States and Europe is that large plants characteristically buy parts and subassemblies from hundreds of other plants, both large and small. Also, small firms often perform job shop operations for large ones.

Finally, the small-medium factory often serves to initiate new products and sometimes grows large with the growth of the market for the product. Some of the world's great firms started this way. Henry Ford began very small. Soichiro Honda launched the Honda Motor Company in 1948 in Japan with capital equivalent to about U. S. $3,000; now Honda produces 30 per cent of the motorcycles made in the world and has assets of more than U. S. $140 million. Today the electronics industry is bursting with small firms as well as large ones hopefully exploiting new ideas.

Figure 9 is a list of types of products that are usually suitable for small-scale manufacture. Of course circumstances vary in each country and within each region of a country, so that the suitability of a product for small-scale manufacture has to be investigated anew in each case. Moreover, this list is not exhaustive. It is divided into two parts: The first part is for areas that are just beginning their economic development, and the second part is for regions that have already made great development progress.

FIGURE 9

PRODUCTS SUITABLE FOR SMALL-SCALE MANUFACTURE

<u>For Regions of Low to Moderate Industrialization</u>

Processing of agricultural, animal and forest products:
rice, flour, lumber, seed oil, canned and preserved fruit and vegetables, rice-bran oil, starch products, kiln-dried lumber, charcoal, tanning extracts, tanned leather, glue, gelatine, canned fish, sausage, ham, bacon, tea, coffee and cocoa.

Agricultural and animal husbandry supplies:
fertilizers, bone meal, pesticides, poultry and cat-

Figure 9 (continued)

tle feed, barbed wire and wire mesh, fishing nets, rope and twine, boxes and crates, catgut.

Agricultural and transport equipment:
repair and service shops may make simple parts for mill, transport, and farm equipment, perhaps installing foundry and machine sections; from this they may go on to more complex items such as plows, harrows, cultivators, wheelbarrows, chaff cutters, cane crushers, insecticide sprayers, irrigation piping and equipment, pipe fittings, valves, hand pumps, and eventually diesel engine pumps, hammers, screwdrivers, chisels.

Construction Materials and builders' hardware:
bricks, clay pipe, concrete blocks, pipes, posts, poles; floor roofing and wall tiles; wood fittings such as window frames and doors; metal fittings such as window frames and grill work; furniture of wood or metal; wire nails, wood screws; paint, varnish, and lacquer; electric insulators and switches, lampholders, copper wire drawing and insulation; venetian blinds; simple sanitary ware and bathroom fixtures; decorative plastic items.

Consumer goods:
bakery products, laundry soap, soft drinks, knitwear, garments, brushes, metal utensils, kerosene lamps, oil stoves, bicycle assembly, sewing machine assembly, radio assembly, umbrellas, flashlights, buttons, wallets, book satchels, watch straps, plastic items, toys, sport goods, writing paper and envelopes, stationary supplies and office supplies, cartons, simple tin cans and similar containers.

Institutional supplies:
hospital, school, and office metal furniture, surgical cotton, adhesive tape; educational aids, school scientific equipment, printed and published materials, printed stamps.

Figure 9 (continued)

Products Suitable for Localities With a Higher Level of Industrial Sophistication and Income

Metal products and machinery:
bolts, nuts, rivets, screw machine products, springs, bicycle and sewing machine components, components for the automobile industry (starters, springs, coils, batteries, seat covers, radiators), parts and accessories for textile and other industrial machinery, naval supplies, cutlery, surgical and scientific instruments, woodworking machinery, light machine tools, light foundry products, precision gauges.

Service industries:
electroplating, galvanizing, tool and die shops, steel heat treatment, precision die casting.

Electrical equipment:
motors of fractional up to 10 horsepower, starters, switchgear, service meters, heating and cooling appliances (stoves, water heaters, irons, toasters, refrigerator assembly).

Industrial rubber and leather goods:
hoses, bushings, fan belts, V-belts, belting gloves, aprons, leather gears for the textile industry.

Wood products:
millwork, quality furniture, hardwood parquet flooring, wooden barrels.

Glass products:
pharmaceutical glass tubing, decorative glass items, mirror manufacture and resilvering, lens grinding, vials and ampules.

Nonmetallic products:
abrasive wheels, refractories, chalk whiting, concrete slabs and tiles.

Figure 9 (continued)

Chemical products:
printing ink, cleaning and polishing preparations, industrial acids and salts, alcoholic beverages.

Consumer goods:
food preparations (mayonnaise, mustard, sauces, spices, butter, cheese, pasteurized milk, jams, fruit juices), paper bags, paper towels and napkins, spectacle frames, fountain pens, draperies, specialty fabrics.

Excellent information on minimum economic size and other requirements for manufacturing plants of different sizes is contained in "Industry Fact Sheets," put out by the United States Agency for International Development. Any development corporation should have this book in its library.

Comprehensive Development Assistance to Small Industry and Handicrafts

Figure 10 illustrates a special approach to small industry and artisan development which was worked out by Ramy Alexander, formerly of Stanford Research Institute, specifically for design-oriented small industries and artisan shops. Under the direction of Alexander, this approach has been applied successfully in Sardinia, Peru, and other areas.

This comprehensive plan of assistance should include education of owner-managers in making use of available assistance from existing institutions and organizations, in organizing themselves into self-help groups or associations, and in becoming as self-sufficient as possible. In addition, talented owner-managers or potential entrepreneurs should be given every possible encouragement and help to improve their businesses or to set up new enterprises.

FIGURE 10

PLAN FOR DEVELOPMENT ASSISTANCE TO SMALL INDUSTRY AND HANDICRAFTS

Research

Production Research Projects	Market Research Projects
Investigating products, qualities, and quantities	Investigating present markets, distribution methods and costs, competition
Investigating location and organization of shops	Determining the most suitable levels and types of buyers for the types and sizes of products being studied
Investigating sources of raw materials and accessories	Undertaking studies of methods for increasing sales of products as they are, without any changes or redesigning
Investigating skills and equipment	Analyzing market trends
Investigating capital, incomes, and wages	Ascertaining market possibilities for improved, modified, or new products that could be made in the
Investigating sales, present markets	
Investigating present sources of financing	

Figure 10 (cont'd)

<u>Production Research Projects</u> (cont'd)	<u>Market Research Projects</u> (cont'd)
Investigating existing training and technical advisory services	region; technical, functional, esthetic, and commercial requirements that new or modified products should meet; studying the most adequate packaging, distribution channels, and promotional methods.
Investigating capability of small entrepreneurs to intensify and expand their operations	
Evaluating development potential of firms, designs, skills, and various types of cooperation	

Planning

<u>Products That Do Not Require Changes</u>

Selecting producers and buyers

Choosing the best system of establishing contacts between producers and buyers and assisting in the establishment of such contacts

Planning for financing the production-sales cycle

If necessary, planning for the improvement of raw material supplies and workshop organization

Promotional planning

Projecting Time Required for the Above Steps

For Products Requiring Changes or Improvements and New Products Which Could Be Developed in the Region

Determining changes in the various products of the region necessary to obtain or increase sales in view of previous market and production research

Considering projects for new products--new lines of production for existing or new enterprises

If necessary, planning for the introduction of new machinery, training, organization and management, and possibly the organization of cooperatives

Promotional and marketing planning

Projecting a synchronized sequence of the above steps

Testing Analysis

Development assistance begins during the study and research phase and, even more actively, during the planning phase. Development is beginning if all

Figure 10 (cont'd)

Testing Analysis (cont'd)

types of tests are made to check the results of previous analyses and to formulate reasonably safe and realistic plans.

Tests in the Production Field	Tests in the Marketing Field
Productivity and productivity improvement tests	Tests of the reaction of buyers to samples of new products and designs; subsequent suggestions for specific changes
Preparation of new designs and new models	
Testing of raw materials and determination of the best sources of supply	Eventual inclusion of the new, redesigned or improved products in the sales and promotional programs of distribution firms
Preliminary arrangements for financing	
Evaluation of the organizational and managerial capacity of enterprises by introducing the owner-managers to the problems of cost accounting, production planning, cooperatives, etc.	

Beginning of Development

Development begins when definitive plans are made on the basis of positive test results and individual small entrepreneurs or groups of small entrepreneurs begin to execute them.

Improvements in the organization of firms and organization of new firms

Introduction of better methods and tools and training in their use

Preparation of definite samples

Financial arrangements

Organization of packing and shipping

Planning for specific productions, executing plans, and making the first deliveries of final products in accordance with orders

Offering final samples to selected customers and in selected markets

Accepting orders

Organizing various types of promotional campaigns

Continuing market research and study of foreseeable market trends

The process presented schematically in Figure 10 is a combination of feasibility studies and complete assistance for the development of small industry. This process has already been proven to produce positive results when it was applied systematically. Emphasis is put on guiding small entrepreneurs toward self-sufficiency as quickly as possible while they are being given help to improve their production methods, their designs, and their knowledge of new markets and of new marketing methods. Hopefully, a comprehensive assistance plan of this type can bring about a simultaneous development of human and material resources. This means a relatively rapid approach to the point where a rapid, automatic economic growth and accumulation of capital can start.

Research

The study of all aspects of production methods and products as well as market research have to be continuous activities. It is clear that the initial stages of such research into a specific area of marketing or production require intensive efforts. After initial research is completed, it is necessary only to maintain up-to-date information. Also, special attention should always be paid to new types of products and new sectors of existing or potential markets.

Studies of products and their possible sales should be action-oriented. It is suggested that both types of studies be carried out simultaneously and in relation to each other because this synchronization helps to direct such studies toward development action.

A complete, detailed census of existing small industries may be necessary. Unfortunately, however, since it may require many months or years to compile, it may become outdated so that much of the information thus obtained would be of more interest for general economic studies than for planning and programming the development of small industry. This is to say that if limited funds require a choice between an over-all census and a more limited, action-oriented survey, the latter deserves priority. Although a clear idea of the quantitative potential of small industry is indispensable for appropriate, action-oriented research, exact statistical data are not indispensable.

The availability of resources as well as the very nature of the developmental process usually make it impossible to develop a whole sector simultaneously. Therefore a development plan must start with selective studies of trends and potentials. For all practical purposes, such investigations can be undertaken within a relatively short time through action-oriented studies.

The kind of research needed requires neither hundreds of research assistants working for several months, complicated sets of questionnaires, extensive sampling techniques, nor electronic computers. What is needed is a trained, efficient, and experienced research team. The interviewers must be trained in asking questions and they must be able to formulate questions appropriate to the situation and to the mentality of the small entrepreneur being interviewed. All information, even the most direct information, must be checked and verified.

It is apparent that even though an action-oriented survey in the small industry field is likely to be a less complex and detailed operation than a systematic census, it is nevertheless difficult. Before starting their survey, the interviewers must study all possible aspects of small industries and the possibilities for development. Participation in a survey thus becomes a significant part of training in field work.

Planning

The distinction between products that do not require changes and those that do is applicable only to products and only in rare cases to enterprises. To supply new and additional markets, some reorganization of production is almost always necessary. The problem may be one of standardizing sizes, of additional financing, of new business administration methods, or of new packaging or shipping methods, even though the product itself may be acceptable in its original form. Therefore, it is not advisable to promote the sale of such products before various reorganizational measures have been adopted to assure a regular and constant supply. Mere delivery promises from producers or intermediaries should not be relied upon.

More often, however, a product must be modified in various ways before it can seriously be launched upon the market. Many times completely new products or lines of products possess the greatest future potential.

Synchronized Programs

The term "synchronized programs" refers to a projection of coordinated estimates of time needed to carry out a development program for small productions, from its present status to the point where the entrepreneur is self-sufficient and his markets have been established. Such projections are useful as the basis of careful planning, for they help to avoid losses of time and setbacks. Without previous coordination and time and cost estimates, marketing may take a long time, and this may jeopardize the whole project. Such projections must be discussed with the small entrepreneur; in this connection, it will be useful to accustom him to the practice of planning and to explain the usefulness of each sequential step.

The agencies that contribute financially to development programs need such projections not only to facilitate planning, but even more to be able to evaluate progress. Obviously projections are not rigid rules; they are subject to revisions and improvements like any other plan.

Marketing and Choice of the Right Distribution Channels

While conducting market research, the development corporation personnel should already begin choosing channels of distribution for each given product. Production volume, costs, and styles are not equally important to all distributors. Each distributor normally works within a given price range, and many deal in only one specific geographical area or specialize in one type of product.

It is obviously expected that those distributors who help producers will serve their own interests first. A small industry development program would not be effective if small producers were not given assistance in the sale of their products, and in order to do this, development personnel must consider the requirements of buyers. Therefore, the special needs of each distribution channel must be given special attention. Because these needs vary from one buyer to another, it is important that for each product a distributor is chosen who can pay the highest price because of the type of his business, who is willing to sell the articles over a longer period and not only during one season, and who is seriously interested in the production volume that can be supplied to him.

All these factors must be evaluated before collections or samples are offered and sales promotion arrangements made. It is, of course, impossible to examine in detail the best sales channels for each article. However, some general indications can be given for the United States market. The most important distribution channels in the United States are wholesale importers; large department stores, buyers unions and mail order firms; specialty and exclusive shops; manufacturers of fashion articles and interior decorators; gift clubs; and publicity item specialists.

The latter two are generally interested in large quantities of cheap articles. It cannot be expected that they will continue to sell these articles over a long period of time. However, these buyers are usually willing to cooperate in the development of new articles which could be of interest to them.

Among the other types of distributors, there exists a great variety of possibilities as far as price levels and qualities are concerned.

As a general rule, wholesale importers "protect" their lines, carrying them for many years. They may ask a somewhat lower price or require some type of exclusivity. If an exclusive distributorship is granted, it must be qualified as much as possible with respect to its duration, its geographical extent, and with respect to types of products, models, and designs.

Large department stores generally have a tendency to change from year to year any articles that are not important in terms of their over-all sales, such as small industry products and handicraft products. They are always interested in finding new items and new suppliers each new year for such products, for yearly variety helps their sales promotion and publicity. This is only a general tendency; there are many and frequent exceptions to the rule, especially if consumer demand is greater than expected.

Specialty stores can pay higher prices than other types of distributors. But apart from the fact that they only buy smaller quantities per order, not many of them are prepared or equipped to import directly. For small, high-quality productions, specialty stores can nevertheless be very important because they can be satisfied with small shipments and because the best of them contribute to the prestige of the product being sold.

As much as possible, attempts should be made to introduce novelty items through prestige outlets. In this way, the producers can obtain higher prices and the product can become better known to the most influential and the choosiest consumers. Moreover, a new line of products is not usually produced in large quantities. Large department stores, however, will require large quantities during one season, and after that they may no longer want to carry the article at all.

Notes to Chapter 5

1. This section reflects the thinking of two outstanding small industry specialists, Dr. Eugene Staley of Stanford Research Institute and Ramey Alexander, formerly of Stanford Research Institute.

2. Eugene Staley, *Methods of Industrial Development* (Paris: OECD, 1962), pp. 201-34.

3. *Ibid*.

4. *Ibid*.

PART II

THE IDENTIFICATION OF INDUSTRIAL INVESTMENT OPPORTUNITIES

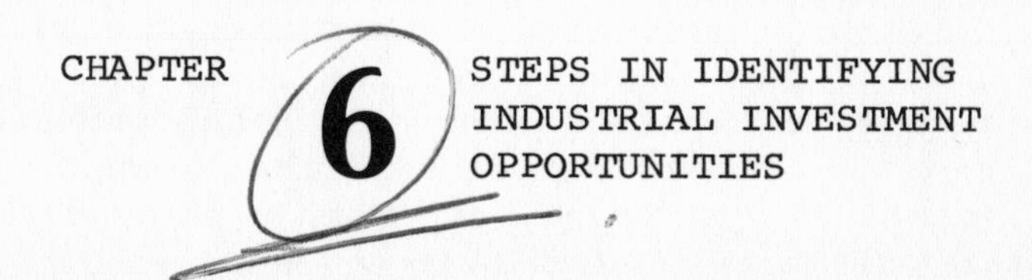

CHAPTER 6 STEPS IN IDENTIFYING INDUSTRIAL INVESTMENT OPPORTUNITIES

In practically every country businessmen, banks, investment companies, and investors in general are constantly looking for new investment opportunities. Even many governments or governmental development agencies charged with stimulating and creating industries are seeking industrial possibilities in which they can invest their funds. For many countries today, foreign investors, in addition to investors from within the country, are becoming an increasingly important source of investment funds. Not only are more industrial giants trying to expand their operations to other countries, but medium and smaller-sized firms are looking abroad more and more for opportunities for expansion and growth, either through direct investments or through participation in joint ventures with foreign companies. The internationalization of business can be expected to become one of the most significant features of the international economic scene in the next two decades. This process is likely to be aided greatly by the creation of common markets or free trade areas which are now becoming realities in Europe and Latin America.

Firms in the more industrialized countries find it increasingly difficult to expand at home because of the limitation of markets, raw materials, labor, space, or technology. Yet it is very often difficult for these firms to obtain information about investment opportunities in other less-industrialized countries. This separation between the potential investor and the investment opportunity has to be bridged by a systematic program of investment opportunity identification. In many developing countries one of the major obstacles to industrial expansion is the lack of identified investment opportunities. The considerable outflow of private savings from many developing countries is certainly due partly to actual or feared political instability, but it is also due to the fact that many local investors are ignorant of possibilities in their own countries or regions. In addition, experience shows that the disproportionately large sums invested in developing countries in real estate or purely commercial activities is due partly to ignorance of industrial possibilities.

Eager and shrewd businessmen and investors will always find investment opportunities. However, in countries where businessmen, entrepreneurs, industrialists and governmental development officials are not yet sophisticated, investors may be slow and painstaking in finding investment opportunities. Thus out of ignorance, investments are made in projects that have little promise for success and only minor significance for the development of the country. This trial-and-error method is likely to be ineffective and wasteful of frequently limited resources.

Any practical industrial development program must, therefore, identify industrial investment opportunities as a means of accelerating investment and directing it into desirable channels. Identification must not be limited to those opportunities predominately suited to foreign investors alone. Foreign investors today are likely to be well-established, large firms that will not consider smaller projects. Therefore, many smaller projects can only be developed by local investors. A fruit, vegetable, or fish cannery, a fish-processing and distribution company, a chocolate and candy factory, a small sugar mill, a mechanical workshop or modern brickyard may be as important to an area's economy as a whole as a foreign-owned and-operated steel mill, automobile assembly plant, cement or fertilizer factory, or a petrochemical complex. Many industrial development programs have overlooked the significance of smaller industries in creating employment, raising incomes, creating a more equitable distribution of wealth, and channeling local funds to productive investment.

In trying to identify investment opportunities, the following steps can be taken: (1) make a list of all industries that seem to be feasible on the basis of preliminary information; (2) select from this list those projects that seem to be the best candidates for prefeasibility studies; (3) make the prefeasibility studies; and (4) promote the studies. Any private, semigovernmental, or governmental development agency undertaking these steps should realize that only meager results can be achieved if this work is carried out entirely from behind a desk. The development agency must be in constant contact with businessmen, wholesalers, importers, exporters, public agencies, engineers, research institutes, productivity institutes, equipment suppliers, and, simply, "people with ideas" both within the country and abroad. A broad knowledge of industrial activities and processes is needed. It is necessary to keep abreast of new developments and discoveries in industrial technology, distribution techniques, domestic and world markets, public works projects, and the opening up of new areas for settlement. Toward this end, those undertaking this work should try to become known to business communities, academic institutions, and governmental agencies. They should try to gain the reputation of maintaining an "open house" for anyone with ideas for industrial possibilities. Periodic informal or formal discussions with all types of businessmen should be arranged to get suggestions and ideas. The staff should keep informed of new commercial, financial, and technological advances through systematic reading and evaluation. Valuable information can be found in regular business reviews, technological publications, prospectives from equipment suppliers, financial résumés, and many governmental publications. Also important are informational trips to other regions or other countries to study different types of industries and new industrial developments on the spot.

After taking all these preparatory steps, then, armed with the necessary background information, it is possible to proceed with the list of candidate industrial possibilities.

There are many simple methods of identifying investment opportunities as well as more complicated, sophisticated techniques which have been recently developed. The choice of approach depends mainly on the financial and personnel resources and the amount of reliable statistical data available.

The simplest approach for agencies with limited staff and finances is to consider those industries with which they are most familiar, both technically and economically. These are most likely to be already existing industries. The next step is to try to determine whether the existing plants can be expanded or whether new plants of the same type should be added. The advantage of this method is that factual information about such industries is easy to secure and managerial skills are more likely to exist for them than for new ones. In addition, local investors are often more inclined to invest in enterprises known to them, especially enterprises with good earning records.

This method can be particularly effective for a country whose industries are centralized in one area and do not require some particular location. The entrepreneurs running such industries will have to be induced to locate new plants in less-developed regions rather than merely to expand their existing plants. Possibly local investors can be induced to open up similar firms independently. These "foot loose" industries are characterized by low-weight, high-value products that require small quantities of raw materials and, usually, a greater amount of labor and processing. Such industries include telecommunications manufacturers; publishing firms; plastic goods plants; shoe factories; pharmaceutical, optical, and watch factories; several types of food industries; some kinds of textile mills; and apparel industries.

Another kind of industry to be considered is the kind which can exist profitably only on a local or regional basis because it needs to be close to the market or because the weight of the product makes transportation over great distances impractical. Figure 11 is a list of industries which could be included in this category.

Many of the industries listed in Figure 11 are those in which the economies of large-scale production are not significant. This means that a number of identical enterprises can exist independently in one country, each of them catering to a relatively small market.

The third type of industry to be considered is one that is highly profitable in a given country. The assumption for this approach is that the profitable fields are likely to be those which offer room for other industries of the same type. In this way, they represent attractive investment opportunities. However, profitable industries may also be those that make use of new technological findings or those that are receptive to innovation and invention. Particularly in less-developed countries, knowledge of current technology and personnel for industries active in innovation and invention are scarce. Typical examples of such industries are the electronics, optical, and chemical industries. Although such industries are difficult to create in countries on the threshold of industrialization, there are exceptions to this rule. For instance, food processing through freeze-drying is a new procedure whose application is possible in such countries and may result in considerable profits. A limitation to this approach is that profits today do not necessarily mean profits tomorrow. It is therefore necessary to ascertain whether a new, profitable field is one in which other investments are already planned elsewhere in the country or abroad, a situation which could result in overcrowding the field and markets.

Another way of finding possible high-profit areas is to consider industrial projects that have been successful in other industrializing countries. For this purpose, development agencies should study and evaluate the industrialization of similar countries. The countries should be similar in terms of the level of industrial development, the size of markets, the availability of raw materials, and the goegraphical and political conditions. Study trips and publications of the development agencies of other countries and other business reviews can provide this information. However, each project has to be considered in terms of the specific circumstances of each country.

Often the first step toward industrialization of a country is processing the raw materials it produces for its own consumption or for export. Therefore, each development agency should make a systematic list of the raw materials produced in the different areas of the country, undertake a study of the latest processing possibilities that technology has created for them, and then check whether these possibilities are being employed.

Processing industries are usually the easiest to create, for capital and manpower requirements are generally moderate and available. They represent the first logical step in the transition from a purely agricultural, raw materials-producing economy to an industrial economy. In agricultural and raw materials-producing countries, wealth has often been accumulated by growing crops and exploiting natural resources. Once the entrepreneurs in those fields become aware of the need for industrialization and the benefits it can produce for them, they will naturally look for investment in industries that can process their products. Since they are familiar with the production of the raw materials for these industries and with the markets for their products, they will more readily invest their funds there than in areas with which they are less familiar. Even in countries or regions at the very beginning of the industrialization process, there can always be found some possibilities in the processing field and entrepreneurs willing to invest in them. Development agencies in such countries should concentrate on the identification of investment opportunities in this field.

Processing industries generally create an increased supply of raw materials. In many countries, fruit and vegetable canneries have expanded the quantity and improved the quality of fruits and vegetables. Milk-processing plants have virtually created dairy farming where there was hardly any before, even though natural conditions were favorable to its development. Fish processing, freezing, salting, and distributing not only stimulate fisheries but, in many instances, create or increase the demand for fish in areas where the demand was previously limited by an irregular supply or by spoilage by the time the product reached the centers of consumption. Processing industries can thus create or enlarge their raw materials supplies and markets and can increase and stabilize incomes in the agricultural and raw materials producing sectors, thus creating more savings and bigger markets for existing and new industries. A development agency should, therefore, not limit its identification program only to existing supplies or raw materials.

In many industrializing countries another important source of investment opportunity lies in the substitution of imports. These countries usually import the majority of the manufactured goods they require. They do this partly because it would be uneconomical to make the imported goods in the country, but also because they have not yet taken advantage of opportunities where domestic manufacture would be at least as economical as imports. The question of protective tariff arises here, but it is beyond the scope of this study to consider the extent to which a country should protect its industries by tariffs. However, the practical development officer should bear in mind the possibility of lowering trade barriers. This could occur in the formation of common markets, free trade areas, or simple trade agreements with other countries that could affect the industry in question.

As in the case of processing industries, import substitution industries can represent a natural step toward further industrialization. In the developing countries, wealth and management skills can be developed in the import-export business. With their knowledge of the markets and of marketing of imported goods, entrepreneurs in these fields will regard import substitution industries as a natural extension of their commercial activities. In countries with foreign-exchange difficulties, this even becomes a necessity for them.

Another advantage of this type of investment opportunity is that potential markets can be estimated easily on the basis of the import statistics which practically every country keeps. However, if high import duties are charged in the country, potential consumption could be much higher than actual consumption if it is expected that the product could be produced domestically at lower cost and with comparable quality. The expansion of demand will take place only if the domestic producers and distributors are forced by a strong enough competition to pass on the lower cost to the consumers in the form of lower prices.

Today, great surpluses of cheap electric power are available in many developing areas as a by-product of important irrigation projects or as a result of utilizing existing water resources for hydroelectric energy. The use of electric energy therefore becomes another criterion for industry selection.

In countries where manpower is relatively cheap, labor-intensive industries may represent profitable investment opportunities. In addition to such labor-intensive industries as artistic industries and handicrafts, industries for the assembly of imported products such as automobiles and electrical appliances should be considered. These may represent good investment opportunities if the market in the importing country is large enough to justify an economically sized assembly operation, if labor is cheaper than in the country of the product's origin, and if transportation costs are lower for the disassembled than for the assembled product.

Carefully following the planning and installation of larger industrial plants and determining the kinds of materials, equipment, and services they will need often gives a clue to a good investment opportunity. For instance, cement and fertilizer plants will require bags, fish-processing plants will require fishing vessels and repair facilities, the electrical industry will need copper wire, and so forth. All that is needed is reliable information on newly planned industries and a knowledge of their imports.

After applying all the above methods, a final check is made by identifying those industries in which employment and net value of production are low in relation to those of other countries with similar economic and geographical conditions. This approach assumes a proportionality between consumption patterns and population patterns.

All these methods take into account only the identification of direct industrial investment opportunities. However, creation of a basic industry or industrial exploitation of a natural resource creates employment in service industries that will, in some cases, double or triple that of the basic industry. The establishment of an automobile plant could give rise to the establishment of manufacturers of parts and accessories, tires, mechanical work and repair shops, gas stations, restaurants, banks, transportation companies, and wholesalers and retailers of many types. The additional incomes earned in these service industries can then create additional demand that may justify another basic industry. This means that an industry that does not seem feasible today may become so tomorrow. Consequently, any program for the identification of industrial investment opportunities must be a constant, dynamic effort directed toward future as well as present possibilities. The need to examine the secondary effects of existing industries and into future possibilities involves the more sophisticated methods of identifying investment opportunities.

There are other, more sophisticated methods of identifying industrial opportunities. The first is the "gross national product method." There are various methods of forecasting the growth of national income or national product. They involve projection of past growth rates to predict the growth of the national product through increases in the productivity of labor due to investment in machinery, improvements in the efficiency of labor, changes in the number of hours worked per year or per week, changes in investment, population increase, and such other factors as new irrigation projects or the opening up of new lands for cultivation. It is not the purpose of this study to deal with these methods in detail. Once the over-all growth of national product has been estimated, it can be broken down into its components and their respective growth rates--personal consumption, government expenditures, investment, and foreign trade. The national product can then be broken down still further into expected growth rates for the different sectors of the economy (such as the iron and steel industry, mining, agriculture, etc.) using all available economic relationships, statistical series on past correlations, and tendencies of over-all economic growth in relation to the growth of different sectors. In particular, family budgets at different income levels can be analyzed, statistics on the production and import of investment goods can be consulted, and foreign trade statistics can be analyzed to arrive at a detailed projection of the composition of future demand in the national economy.[1] Thus a bank of economic indicators is formed which can serve as the independent variables for demand projections for the products of different industries. For instance, a relationship can be established between the volume of construction or investment in buildings and the consumption of cement, or the increase of per capita income for a population and its demand for basic products. Such demand projections can then serve as a basis for determining industrial investment opportunities.

The second method consists of the use of input-output tables. Estimates of gross national product, total consumption, per capita income, the rate of investment, and similar indexes are collected in a great many countries nowadays. However, such figures alone do not explain the differences in the degree of development among different countries, so that they do not suggest any means of accelerating economic development. However, they can be used for analyzing and forecasting. An input-output table is not just a tool for collecting and storing information. According to the specific objective and the availability of trustworthy information, an economy can be conceptually divided into almost any number of industries or sectors. A table for the United States prepared by the U. S. Government in 1947 shows 450 sectors. To illustrate what an input-output table is, consider an economy divided into only two sectors: agriculture and manufactures as illustrated in Figure 12.

In this input-output table for a highly simplified economy, the figures in the horizontal column titled "Agriculture" show that this sector supplies fifty-five production units in the form of finished products to "Final Demand" and twenty units as raw materials to the manufacturing sector (for instance, cotton), and that it delivers twenty-five units to itself (for instance, cattle feed cakes). Here, "final demand" includes goods and services for consumption, investment, and export by the households of the economy. Therefore, the production of 100 units by the agricultural sector satisfies both "direct" final demand for its finished products and "indirect" demand for its intermediary products. On the input aid, the figures in the "Agriculture" column show that in order to produce 100 units of total product, this sector absorbs not only twenty-five units of its own product, but also fourteen input units from the manufacturing sector (such as agricultural implements) and eighty units in the form of labor, capital, and other primary factors of production from the sector generally called "household services." The more developed an economy is, the more interrelated are its sectors, and the more the sectors buy from and sell to each other. An underdeveloped economy is characterized by large gaps in the interrelationships among the different sectors.[2]

FIGURE 11

REGIONALLY ORIENTED INDUSTRIES

	Standard Industrial Classification Number
Food and Kindred Products	20
Meat products: sausage, hams, bacon	201
Dairy products: pasteurized milk, cheese	202
Bakery products	205
Confectionery and related products	207
Beverages: beer, liquors, soft drinks	208
Lumber and Wood Products (excluding furniture)	24
Saw mills and planing mills	242
Millwork: plywood and prefabricated structural wood products	243
Wooden containers	244
Furniture and Fixtures	25
Household furniture	251
Office furniture	252
Public building and professional furniture	253
Partitions, shelving, lockers, office and store fixtures	254
Window and door screens, shades, venetian blinds	256

Industry	Code
Printing, Publishing, and Allied Industries	27
Newspapers	271
Miscellaneous publishing	274
Commercial printing	275
Lithography	276
Bookbinding and related industries	278
Service industries for the printing trade	279
Chemicals and Allied Products	28
Paints, varnishes, lacquers	285
Miscellaneous chemicals: industrial gases (oxygen, acetylene), artificial ice	289
Rubber Products	30
Reclaimed rubber	303
Leather and Leather Products	31
Leather gloves and mittens	315
Luggage	316
Handbags and small leather goods	317
Stone, Clay, and Glass Products	32
Glass, glassware, pressed or blown	322
Glass products made of purchased glass	323
Cement	324
Pottery and related products	326

Figure 11 (cont'd)

	SIC Number (cont'd)
Stone, Clay, and Glass Products (cont'd)	
Concrete, gypsum, and plaster products	327
Cut stone and stone products	328
Abrasive, asbestos, and miscellaneous nonmetallic mineral products	329
Fabricated Metal Products	34
Tin cans and other tin ware	341
Metal stamping, coating, and engraving	346
Lighting fixtures	347
Miscellaneous fabricated metal products: bus and truck bodies, trailers and wheelbarrows, bolts, nuts, and rivets	349
Transportation Equipment	37
Ship and boat building and repairing	373
Miscellaneous Manufacturing Industries	39
Jewelry, silverware, and plated ware	391
Brooms and brushes	3981
Candles	3984
Jewelry cases and instrument cases	3986
Lamp shades	3987
Signs and advertising displays	3993

FIGURE 12

SAMPLE INPUT-OUTPUT TABLE

Outputs \ Inputs	Sector I Agriculture	Sector II Manufactures	Final Demand	Total Output
Sector I Agriculture	25	20	55	100 units
Sector II Manufactures	14	6	30	50 units
Household Services	80	180	40	300 units

Those industries that need many inputs from other sectors or other industries and thereby stimulate the creation of other connected industries are more advantageous to a country or a region than isolated industries that either need few inputs or depend on imports for their inputs. Examples of industries needing many inputs from other industries are the automobile or machine tool industries. Examples of industries generally needing few inputs from within the country are mines or other extractive industries. The first conclusion that can be drawn from analyzing input-output tables is that newly developing regions should try to develop input-intensive industries which will in turn stimulate the creation of other new industries to supply them. If a country or region does not have an input-output table, it can consult those of other countries with a similar economic structure and a comparable degree of economic development.

Each sector of the economy has its own procedure which is determined primarily by technological factors that change only slowly. For any composition of final demand, the input-output table indicates which inputs each industry must absorb from all the other industries or sectors in order to satisfy direct final demand for its products as well as the indirect demands for its products coming from those sectors or industries from which it buys inputs and which in return require inputs from the sector concerned. For example, if an increase in the final demand for agricultural products occurs, agriculture has to buy more inputs from industry (such as implements and insecticides). In order to satisfy this demand for its products, industry will have to buy more inputs from agriculture (such as hides and lumber). This in turn will increase the demand for agricultural products; the demand for agricultural products will raise the demand for industrial products, which will in turn raise the demand for agricultural products, and so forth. Each increase in output will produce higher incomes which will increase demand for industrial and agricultural products. The relationships between the sectors can be expressed in the form of equations. The calculation of final demand for each sector implies the iterative solution of a series of simultaneous linear equations. Since the number of equations increases with the square of the number of sectors included in the table, the calculation of final demand in each sector for a table that is detailed enough to provide meaningful information is a job for electronic computers.[3]

This aspect of input-output tables permits a highly accurate forecast of the demand for the products of all the sectors produced by an autonomous increase of demand in any one sector. Autonomous demand changes are due to factors coming from outside the economic system itself, such as changes in consumers' tastes, technological innovations, the opening up of new lands for cultivation, population increases, and political events. In this way opportunities for new industries can be identified. This method is particularly useful if it is combined with projections of the gross national product and its components, and of different sectors and basic industries of the economy. If, for instance, a considerable increase in the demand for the products of the chemical industries is expected, input-output tables can be consulted to determine the repercussions this will have on all other industries in the economy. If present capacities are then compared with the expected demand increases, opportunities for expanding existing industries or creating new ones can be identified.

However, considerable problems are involved in applying this method. First, very good statistics are needed. Second, the compilation of reliable statistics is a long and costly process. Third, highly experienced specialists are needed for setting up input-output tables and for interpreting them. Fourth, the cost of making all necessary calculations by means of electronic computers may be high. Finally, since this is a highly technical method, highly skilled specialists are required who can interpret the results of input-output analyses and communicate them clearly to businessmen and government officials. This combination of common sense, business knowledge, and the statistical and mathematical abilities required for input-output analysis is very rare, especially in newly industrializing countries.

In conclusion, although it may be useful for a country as a whole to work out input-output tables for its economy, this may be too complicated an undertaking for regional development corporations.

After having identified all industrial investment opportunities that seem feasible and having compiled a list of candidate industries, each project has to be checked more carefully before deciding to make a prefeasibility or feasibility study for it. To determine which of the candidate industries deserve to be studied further, a number of factors must be analyzed.[4]

An estimate needs to be made of the total amount of investment required. It is necessary to ascertain whether the size of the investment will deter or attract private domestic investors, or whether it is more likely to be a project for foreign investors with large sums at their disposal or with knowledge of the specific technology needed. In some cases, a joint venture between local and foreign investors may represent the best solution.

The size of the market needs to be estimated, for it is the key factor in determining the size of the factory, its short-term profitability, and its longer-range prospects. For each industrial process there is usually a minimum economical size, although minimum economical size is a flexible concept and technological changes are constantly at work to move minimum economical size upward or downward. The requirements of newly industrializing countries with their small markets, on one hand, but the need to industrialize, on the other, are inducing equipment manufacturers to develop processes and to build equipment that are economical even for small plants. Thus, minimum economical size in cement manufacturing and spaghetti and noodle manufacturing has decreased. The modest management requirements of small industries and their greater flexibility can give them a competitive advantage and can thus move the minimum economical size downward.

After determining the probable market and minimum economical size, it remains to determine what percentage of total demand for a product (or series of products) the new plant will meet, and approximately at what price. This estimate can be made by judging the production capacities and production costs (including transportation costs) of other competitive plants in the country or abroad, and estimating what percentage of the total market, preferably a growing total market, to which the new plant can hope to cater.

All factors which determine or influence operating costs have to be given a preliminary evaluation: raw materials, operating materials, fuel, water, electricity, skilled and nonskilled labor, depreciation, administrative costs, sales and distribution costs, and unforeseen expenses.

Longer-range profitability must also be estimated. The most dynamic and most profitable industrial projects are generally those that tie into the longer-range growth of the country's or region's economy. In addition to short-term profitability, long-term profitability is an important factor in making an investment decision. To obtain a clear picture of the long-range perspectives, developments, and tendencies of an economy, estimates and projections of the major economic constants and variables that determine the direction of development are needed. Projection of gross national product, of its different components, and of the different sectors of the economy, as well as analysis of input-output tables to project future demand for specific products can be useful.

If national or regional development plans or priorities exist, care should be taken that the project is in accordance with such plans. This is to assure that scarce resources are channeled into those fields which have been given priority from the point of view of over-all development objectives.

The determination of whether an industry should be located in the region is of utmost importance, especially in regions removed from the major markets and centers of consumption or production.

The location of an industry is relevant to three aspects of its operations: obtaining raw materials and transporting them to the plant; processing raw materials into finished or semifinished goods; and transporting and distributing end products from the factory to the markets and consumers.

If transportation costs represent an important percentage of total manufacturing costs, the factory should be located where transportation costs can be minimized. If the cost of transporting raw materials to the plant is substantially higher than the cost of transporting the finished product from the plant to the consumers, the plant has to be located near the raw materials source. This applies to all industries whose product weighs less than the raw materials. Examples are the leather industry, the iron and steel industry, any dehydrating, concentrating, or refining industries, the paper industry, and many chemical industries. The same considerations apply to industries whose raw materials spoil rapidly, such as fish canneries and fruit and vegetable canneries. When raw materials have to be imported from abroad, the plants have to be located near the ports of importation of the raw materials in order to reduce inland transportation costs to a minimum.

If, however, the cost of transportation and distribution of the finished product is higher than the transportation costs of the raw materials, the plant has to be located close to the consumer. This is generally true of products that spoil easily and products whose weight or volume increases considerably during processing, such as soft drinks, perfumes, medicines, or furniture. This category also includes such industries as packaging or assembly plants.

As a general rule, it is cheaper to transport finished or processed products than raw materials, since transportation costs of finished products constitute a smaller percentage of total costs than transportation costs of raw materials. The higher the value of a product, the higher are the transportation costs that can be absorbed by the manufacturer or customer, so that industries based on such products are better suited to regions far from major markets.

Most factories are located somewhere between the two extremes of proximity to raw materials and proximity to markets. This is so partly because an intermediate location between the raw materials source and the markets, minimizes all transportation and distribution costs, partly because of personal, political, or accidental factors, and also because of other factors that influence the choice of an industrial location. These factors include the availability of basic services such as water, electrical energy, gas, transportation facilities, sanitary facilities, and waste disposal facilities. They also include the cost of buying and developing land, the cost and availability of factory buildings and storage facilities, and the cost and availability of banking, insurance services, and other industrial services such as repair shops and foundries. Other factors influencing industrial location are the existence of adequate roads, railroads, ports, and transportation companies to assure transportation of raw materials and finished products without delays, interruptions, or damages. Of special importance are the availability and cost of skilled workers, technicians, and management personnel, as well as the sanitary, educational, recreational, and cultural facilities a location has to offer to the employees of an industry. Decisions about location are no longer made only on the basis of technical or economical considerations. Scotland's industrial promotion program, for example, is based entirely on the great variety of recreational facilities it has to offer, not on any specific economic factors. Scotland has found this approach to be highly successful.

Finally, such factors as the incidence of taxes, political and social stability, labor relations and the attitude of labor unions, and the entire investment climate are relevant to industrial location.

Although it is difficult to change the purely geographical or physical location factors, practically all other location factors can be changed by industrial parks: the training of skilled workers; the building of roads, railroads, ports, electricity plants, water supply systems and airports; the development of recreational facilities; and tax concessions and incentives.

Special tax concessions and tax incentives are important for areas suffering from a disadvantageous location. It is true that a certain concentration of industrial and related activities could be made economical for industrial and commercial development by effecting reductions in transportation costs and distributing such social overhead costs as housing, schools, hospitals, streets, water and sewage systems, and cultural facilities. But when concentration becomes excessive, these economies of concentration may turn into diseconomies. Indicative of such diseconomies of concentration are traffic congestions in many capital cities, even of newly developing countries, that cause workers to spend several hours in traveling from their homes to their places of work. In such cases large investments are necessary to widen streets and build passes and elevated streets. Other diseconomies of concentration are the contamination of air and water, overcrowding and inadequate housing which make costly new housing developments necessary. If growth were more evenly distributed over medium and smaller towns as well as larger cities, it could be more easily accommodated since it would occur gradually.

In spite of the undesirable effects of overcrowding, big cities continue to grow and the majority of industries continue to establish themselves there in many countries. This is largely due to the fact that municipal and national tax systems are not usually designed to charge industries with all the social overhead costs they cause. As a result, traffic continues to be chaotic, the air contaminated, and land values inflated. If new firms had to pay for the social overhead costs they create, or if new migrants to the cities had to contribute toward such costs, industries probably would stop establishing themselves in big cities and people would be reluctant to migrate there. Since it would be difficult to reform tax systems in accordance with the need to decongest cities, one way of achieving a more economical distribution of industry would be to grant industries tax incentives or reductions for locating outside of the big cities. The government does not lose any actual revenue. The best system of tax incentives would be one granting incentives to all new industries, regardless of their location, but with larger incentives in those areas which could become industrial growth centers.

A number of industries may appear initially to be less feasible because of negative locational factors. The question is then which of these industries might become feasible if the locational disadvantages were lessened through a development program. It has often been found that a combination of tax incentives, infrastructural investments, community improvement work, industrial parks and active industrial promotion work, are most effective in making a region attractive to industry. Tax incentives alone or other isolated efforts usually are not as successful. The exact mixture of measures to be applied varies with each specific situation.

Notes to Chapter 6

1. See *How to Select Dynamic Industrial Projects*, Washington, D.C., Pamphlet, International Cooperation Administration, 1960, p. 52.

2. See Wassily Leontief, "The Structure of Scientific Development," *Scientific American*, Vol. 209, No. 3 (September, 1963), 148.

3. *Ibid*.

4. See *How to Select Dynamic Industrial Projects*, *op. cit*.

PART III

INDUSTRIAL PROMOTION

CHAPTER 7 BENEFITS OF INDUSTRIAL PROMOTION

The benefits to be gained in any given area through attraction of new industry or the expansion of existing industry are well known in the developed and developing countries around the world. New jobs mean more purchasing power and a corresponding increase in the economic level of the region. A multiplier effect normally sets in, and each new industrial job carries with it several new openings in allied service industries. As a general rule of thumb, the developed countries estimate that a new industrial job carries with it between two and three jobs in such diverse fields as trucking, hotels, and restaurants.

While these economic advantages of industrialization have been universally recognized since Huddersfield,* only during the last few years have specific techniques evolved enough to form a scientific approach to the highly competive business of industry attraction and implementation.

In a very real sense, industrial promotion is a job of selling: selling one's country, one's region, one's labor, one's skills, and all the other advantages the area can boast, be they a dry, excellent climate, good port facilities, or tourist attrac-

---

*Huddersfield is a town in northern England where the industrial revolution ostensibly began. The name "Huddersfield" has been made famous by James Morris in his book The Road to Huddersfield (New York City: Random House, 1963).

tions. Industrial promotion may be likened to the manufacturer who advertises his product for sale. He must first assess his product, then improve it to make it desirable and salable, and, finally, when his product is in the best condition possible, he must go to the marketplace and sell against all competition. Today, the stakes are high, the competition fierce and sophisticated, and only the quality product can pass the test of customer acceptance.

The ideal customer or investor is one who brings with him a completely developed product and the necessary capital to launch the venture. Hopefully, this ideal customer will also bring to the new or expanding industry technical and managerial skill which may be in short supply locally. He will also bring along an established market for his product.

This chapter will review the various factors which make up the investment climate, enumerate various sources of investment information available to potential investors, discuss the industrial park as a promotion tool, note the more commonly used promotional aids, and list the better-known services which should be available to investors.

INVESTMENT CLIMATE

As a first and most important step, the developer, be he a representative of a development corporation or a development bank, an entrepreneur, or the representative of a community organization, must take stock of the "investment climate." He must attempt to capitalize on the strong points and eliminate the weak spots, for every region has both its drawbacks and its opportunities for improvement.

The term "investment climate" sums up all the factors--economic, social, and political--which influence an investment decision in a given area. The astute investor will normally make an intensive study of a number of areas. His final decision will be governed by his analysis of the facts plus an intangible "gut reaction" to the people with whom he will have to live and work.

Determining Investment Climate

Economic Factors

The checklist must always begin with the region itself and its natural resources. How available are the raw materials needed? What is the infrastructure for power, fuel, and water? How is the climate? Are there any other natural phenomena that might play upon promotion of industry? Is land available? Are there specific plant sites? At what cost?

A routine check must be made into communication and public services in the area, and their costs.

Transportation must be investigated. Are there good local, regional, and national transportation services? What is the availability of public services, such as bus transportation for employees, and at what cost?

As an added factor in plant location, a market for the productive output of the enterprise is a *sine qua non*. As such, it will receive priority attention from the investor.

As noted elsewhere, the development of export substitution industry in many developing countries has just about ended, and it is therefore of paramount importance that the modern domestic markets be expanded greatly. This will require a high degree of urban-rural integration. Dr. Walter Rostow has noted that "a critical part of the job consists in urgent efforts to get the food in from the countryside to the cities; to expand the next harvest; and to make sure that the wastage of Latin American agricultural products is rapidly diminished by better storage and movement."[1]

In all too many of the developing countries we find a few islands of economic development surrounded by large numbers of people living outside the so-called "money economy." Only to the extent that the investor sees possibilities for a future expanding market for his product will he be interested in making the final investment decision.

Then, too, any final decision will take into account potential export market for the venture. Just as the European Common Market has played an important part in investment decisions in Europe, so the Latin American Free Trade Area (LAFTA) and the Central American Common Market (CACM) will play increasingly important roles in many investment decisions in future years.

The old adage that "industry goes where industry already is" holds true to a large extent. It is also true that an increase in common market possibilities for the sale of a product will serve as a magnet to attract new industry to a given area.

Human Resources

After looking into the economic resources of the area, the strength of human resources for both the labor force and the management force must be ascertained.

Regardless of how labor- or capital-intensive the proposed investment may be, the investor is, of necessity, concerned with manpower--its availability, skills, education, costs; the laws affecting employment of labor; and the positions and attitudes of labor itself.

In considering the human resources available for his investment, an investor will want to look into the general educational level of his prospective employees. Frederick Harbison and Charles A. Myers point out in Education, Manpower and Economic Growth that "there is a high correlation and presumably some causal relation between enrollment in education (and hence, investment in education) and a country's level of economic development as expressed by its GNP per capita."[2] He will be equally interested in the number of technical schools for skilled employees. The need for technical schools is becoming widely recognized in the developing countries. Indeed, in some countries the urgency of this need is being expressed as a "must." To cite an example, Eugenio Steiger notes that "for Venezuela the creation of these technical institutes is of primordial importance because their graduates will form the vertebral column of our industry."[3]

While it is doubtless true that the human resource development institutions of many of the developing countries are not yet producing the numbers and kinds of technicians needed for economic modernization, there are bright spots on the horizon. With the help and assistance of AID, many of the military forces in these countries have commenced basic training programs in such areas as toolmaking and carpentry. Also with help from AID, many unions have set up labor training institutes aimed at worker education in areas such as responsible collective bargaining. The number of regional technical high schools has recently increased, as well as the number of technical courses taught in normal high schools.

No investment will be any more successful than its management and personnel in general. It is continuously pointed out by leaders in the field that the prime requirement for the new challenges in developing countries is to find the necessary men to assume the responsibility for carrying out these challenges. Sooner or later, and by whatever means available, men must be found to think, to see, to plan, and to lead.

Just as managerial competence is important, so are the attitudes of management. Good managers will see the need for modern techniques once their eyes are opened to their value. These needs can be assuaged in part by the growing number of productivity centers in the developing countries.

Productivity centers serve to disseminate technological information, passing along the latest techniques of U.S. and European industry. A common method used by productivity centers is to bring in short-term consultants, for periods of from three to six months, from the developed countries. These consultants conduct seminars, make plant visits, and generally do all they can to pass along the knowledge of their specialty to representatives of the economic sector they represent, be it leather tanning, meat cutting, foundry, metal working, textiles, or whatever.

Sound future planning includes a realization of the part the enterprise can play within the economic framework of the community. A lack of confidence in the nation, the government, or business associates generally results in unwillingness to plan ahead, a desire for a quick turnover, and a disproportionately high yield on the investment. Frequent obstacles to development are the result of a philosophy and a state of mind rather than any lack of technical competence. Accordingly, the wise investor will be justifiably concerned with management attitudes in any given area.

One attitude of management which merits special consideration is its reaction to change. In a world dominated by technological, social, and economic changes which year by year appear to be gathering momentum, the knowledgeable manager must show a willingness to adapt to new innovations and a desire to direct, control, and guide change with wisdom and understanding to maximize the economic and social gains for his community and his company. The truly versatile manager will want to stay abreast of new developments in such varied fields as atomic energy and space technology in order to relate technological advances in these fields to his own products.

Management Education

Through their universities and high schools, the developing countries have been giving limited management training to students in such areas as economics, law, accounting, and marketing, but only recently has there emerged an awareness of the possibilities inherent in graduate business education.

An example of this new awareness is to be found in Lima, Peru, where the first school of graduate business administration in Latin America was started in 1963 by Stanford University under a contract with U.S. AID. The Escuela Superior de Administración de Negocios (ESAN) provides a one-year course in Business Administration patterned along the lines of the Harvard Business School and the Stanford Business School. The case method is used, and a degree of Magister is granted. The school has full-time students and a full-time faculty and does not have "co-gobierno," the Latin system whereby the students have a voice in the running of the school. The success of ESAN and its acceptance by the Peruvians bodes well for the future of this kind of management education. In Central America, a similar institution supported by a group of businessmen is now in the planning stage, under the sponsorship of Harvard University.

Political Climate

While all of the preceding factors will be carefully considered, probably none will receive more attention from a would-be investor, foreign or domestic, than the political climate. The investor, large or small, is most interested in the attitudes of the government toward industry in general and private enterprise in particular. He is also very curious about the government's reaction to foreign technicians and personnel of all categories.

The phrase "favorable political climate" conjures up in the investor's mind a friendly government with a traditional policy of nonexpropriation of foreign interests and a reputation for fair dealing with foreign investors. This same government will have shown by its actions that it recognizes the mutual advantages to be gained by new domestic as well as foreign investment.

A government which threatens confiscation of private investment, either officially, through its leaders and elected representatives, or through the press, scares off the potential investor. In recent years a number of Latin American countries have been "building a case" for expropriation of extractive industries, such as the petroleum industry. This threat of expropriation has put off or canceled many an investment decision. The saying that "there is nothing as timid as a million dollars" is certainly true in this instance. It is equally true that the small investor is also caught up in a fear psychology and postpones his investment or goes elsewhere. While no figures are available, it is a safe assumption that several hundred millions of dollars of investment have not been made by U.S., European, and Asian investors in certain developing countries due to expropriation threats.

The investor also looks for political stability, which to him means strong government, sound public administration, government stability, and freedom from fear of internal coups and revolution.

The human side of an investor's relations with government personnel cannot be overlooked. He likes to deal with friendly, cooperative people, but he also likes to perceive ability, knowledge of their jobs, farsightedness, ambition, imagination, and creative energy.

Special Governmental Inducements

The governments of the developing countries have at their command many special inducements they may extend to the potential investor. Probably the most powerful tool is their use of tax incentives of all kinds. These incentives, where they exist, form an important part of the investment climate for the investor. As it involves the entire economic structure of the country, the tax program must be well thought out and carefully administered. Certainly, it would be extremely foolhardy for a government to adopt the plan of another country without careful study and deliberation.

While tax exemptions are actually nothing more than subsidies by the government, they have advantages over other types of subsidies such as direct cash advances and protective custom duties.

> The most important advantage is that when exemptions are granted a firm that makes no profit and fails, the government has lost nothing. No income taxes would have been paid by the company even if it had been subject to taxation, and whatever property taxes the government would have to forego would be more than compensated by income in the form of excise taxes and taxes on employees' earnings. Further tax exemption requires a very minimum of administration and expense.[4]

In commenting on the success of the tax-exemption program in Puerto Rico, Theodor Moscoso points out that while Puerto Rico is part of the United States,

> it must be remembered that it has few natural resources other than climate and has a very limited internal market necessitating that her effort be concentrated almost solely on the export market . . . Our experience has shown us that the tax exemption program constitutes the most effective means of awakening interest on the part of the industrialist. A recent study shows that 80 per cent of the firms sponsored by the Economic Development Administration (of Puerto Rico) and currently operating began to explore their present projects due to something they heard regarding tax exemption.[5]

It would appear that tax exemptions of various kinds will exist in the foreseeable future. As in the case of Puerto Rico, they have had a stimulating effect in most of the developing countries. They are certainly preferable to subsidies and protective tariffs which tend to protect the weak and encourage monopolistic practices, with all their attendant evils and political maneuvering.

Many towns and regions have experimented with special regional and local tax incentives, but their effectiveness is still open to doubt. Once introduced into one region or locality, it is difficult to keep them from spreading, so that the advantages initially obtained by one area may be nullified. Only time and research will determine the efficacy of this procedure. While an investor may be attracted by tax incentives, he will wish to make a thorough analysis as to the long-run implications for his investment.

The tax chart in Table 1 describes industrial development incentives for the Central American Common Market. These incentives are typical of the types and kinds of incentives offered as tax inducements in many developing countries.

Other special government inducements might include such items as: favorable tariff protection; modest exchange controls allowing for inexpensive repatriation of capital and earnings; favorable immigration regulations affecting the skilled labor and management personnel needed by the enterprise from other countries; favorable policies regarding import duties on machinery, equipment, and raw materials and supplies. Many developing countries have signed treaties with the government of the United States and other countries guaranteeing certain protections against inconvertibility of currency, expropriation, and war risk. It is sufficient to say that they are strong inducements for firms from the industrial countries to invest in the developing countries. Table 2 shows typical incentives for industrial investment in Colombia.

Financial Factors

The lack of capital markets has long been a drawback to development. The opportunity to buy and sell shares and raise equity capital has given tremendous impetus to U.S. and European expansion. In many of the developing countries, there is little or no protection for the minority shareholder, and this has acted as a strong depressant.

However, there is a growing tendency to correct this problem by fair legislation. The emergence of capital markets will certainly provide a strong impetus to development in future years.

Monetary Stability and Flight Capital

A stable of currency and the lack of a history of inflationary tendencies are concrete indications of healthy investment climate factors. On the other hand, an unstable currency and a history of fluctuating inflation are not attractive features for any investor. So, too, the investor is not happy to observe "flight capital" in the country under consideration. While local flight of capital to the safety of a Swiss bank or as an investment to the U.S. stock exchange is understandable in the light of political unrest, it goes a long way in dampening the enthusiasm of the foreign investor. He quite naturally asks, "Why should I invest in a country where the citizenry itself sees no future for its own investment effort?" Economic stability is part objective fact and part psychological mood, but it is always related to confidence in the economy.

The availability of local finances is of great importance and is discussed at length in our chapter on financing.

Social Considerations

An aspect which is sometimes overlooked by those desiring to attract industry involves the personal concerns of the executive management group which must join the community along with the new or expanding industry; as individuals, their reactions to the area are just as important as the economic factors which will contribute to the success or failure of their company.

TABLE 1

CENTRAL AMERICAN COMMON MARKET INDUSTRIAL DEVELOPMENT INCENTIVES

	Import Duties and Counsular Fees		Fuel	Income Tax	Tax on Capital
	Equipment	Raw Materials			
Group 1[A]--New	100% 10 yrs.	100% 5 yrs. 60% 3 yrs. 40% 2 yrs. -- --	100% 5 yrs. -- --	100% 8 yrs.* 100% 2 yrs.*	100% 10 yrs.* 100% 4 yrs.*
Existing	100% 6 yrs.	100% 3 yrs.	100% 3 yrs.	100% 6 yrs.	100% 6 yrs.
Group 2[B]--New	100% 8 yrs.	50% 2 yrs.	50% 2 yrs.		
Existing	100% 5 yrs.	-- --	-- --	-- --	-- --
Group 3[C]	100% 3 yrs.	-- --	-- --	-- --	-- --

*Term extendable for 2 additional years for producers of raw industrial materials or capital goods, if at least 50% by value are local.

A) Those that produce industrial raw materials and capital goods, or consumer goods, containers, or semifinished goods which use at least 50% Central American raw materials by value. B) Those that produce consumer goods, containers, or semifinished goods which use a "high percentage" (but less than 50%) of local materials and realize substantial foreign-exchange savings and C) All the rest. Groups 1 and 2 are further divided into new versus expanding firms.

Country-By-Country Incentives

	Costa Rica[4]	El Salvador	Guatemala	Honduras[5]	Nicaragua[5]	CACM
Income tax	100% 5 yrs.[1]	100% 5 yrs.	100% 5 yrs.	100% 5 yrs.	100% 5 yrs.	100% 8 yrs.
	50% 5 yrs.[1]	50% 5 yrs.	50% 5 yrs.	75% 5 yrs.[2]	50% 5 yrs.	
Tax on capital	100% 5 yrs.[1]	100% 5 yrs.	100% 5 yrs.	100% 5 yrs.	100% 5 yrs.	100% 10 yrs.
	50% 5 yrs.[1]	50% 5 yrs.	50% 5 yrs.			
Tax on installation, production & sales	Subject to waiver by Municipal authorities	100% 5 yrs.	100% 5 yrs.	100% 5 yrs.	90% 5 yrs.	-- --
		50% 5 yrs.	50% 5 yrs.			
Custom duties						
Building materials	99% 10 yrs.	100% 10 yrs.	100% 10 yrs.	100% no limit	100% no limit	-- --
Machinery & equipment	99% 10 yrs.	100% 10 yrs.	100% 10 yrs.	100% no limit	100% no limit	100% 10 yrs.
Maintenance needs	99% 10 yrs.	-- --	100% 10 yrs.	100% 10 yrs.	100% 10 yrs.	-- --
Fuel	99% 10 yrs.[3]	-- --	100% 10 yrs.[3]	100% 10 yrs.	100% 10 yrs.	100% 5 yrs.[3]
Raw materials	99% 10 yrs.	100% 10 yrs.	100% 10 yrs.	100% 10 yrs.	100% 10 yrs.	100% 5 yrs.
						60% 3 yrs.
						40% 2 yrs.

1) The term for incentives depends on the benefits to the economy, but is never more than 10 years.
2) The Honduran Industrial Development Law provides for 5 years of total exemption plus 75% on profits reinvested in fixed assets in the following 5 years.
3) Except gasoline.
4) In addition to the listed benefits, municipal authorities may grant 5-year waiver of land and local taxes; total waiver of export taxes is granted, and import duties on competing products may be trebled.
5) In addition to the listed benefits, total waiver of export taxes is also granted.

Source: Reprinted from "Latin America's Merging Market," published by Business International, New York, January, 1964, with the permission of the publisher.

TABLE 2

TYPICAL INCENTIVES FOR
INDUSTRIAL INVESTMENT IN COLOMBIA

INVESTORS	EXEMPTION
Corporations which (a) exploit basic industries and use at least 60% local raw materials or (b) engage in activities complimentary to iron production and use local producers or their exchange articles as source of more than 50% of their materials.	Up to 100% from income and excess profits tax.
Producers of asbestos, coal and coke, petrochemicals, wood pulp, fertilizer, pesticides, copper, zinc, lead and other nonferrous metals, tools and machinery.	100%
Sulphur-refining producers.	75%
Iron and Steel producers.	50%
Wood pulp and Sulphuric acid producers (using 60% local content).	10%
Additional Incentives: Corporations can set aside tax-free up to 5% of annual net profits as a special fund for increasing production of raw materials and import substitutes. A portion of income (40% of gross export sales) earned by firms exporting products other than coffee, bananas, oil, precious metals and raw hides is also tax exempt.	

Relocating management executives will be concerned with the following items as they affect their personal cost of living: personal income taxes; property taxes; cost of housing rental and purchase; cost of clothing; heating and fuel costs--utilities; cost of commuting to work; laundry and cleaning costs; entertainment available for wives and families, clubs, resorts; insurance costs; and medical facilities and their costs.

Too often, the development-minded community tends to forget that the individual making the feasibility report or company survey may try to picture himself living in the community. Accordingly, anything which can be done to make the community a better place in which to live as well as work is of utmost importance.

Improving Investment Climate

Obviously, different types of industry will give different weights to the various investment climate factors, but it should be emphasized that they are all important. Systematic and intense efforts to improve these factors in any given area are known as investment climate promotion work--an integral part of any industrial development program. If these efforts are successful, the risks to new industries can be curtailed. Their chances of success are thereby increased, along with their subsequent contribution to the economy of the area. It should be emphasized that every factor may be subject to influence by national and state laws, government and state budgets, and the attitudes of the people of the area. But they can all be improved if the need for improvement is recognized.

How can the investment climate be improved? First, the problems encountered by those wishing to start a new plant or expand an old one must be clearly pinpointed. This can be done by analyzing how and why projects have been put off or delayed due to unsatisfactory economic factors. Documented studies will be most helpful, and the action required to correct the problem in each instance should be noted in great detail.

The course of action on each problem then must be clearly thought through in order to generate support for any new stratagem and new laws that may be required. Point by point, the entrepreneur, the industrial development agency, or the development corporation should attempt to have the so-called localization factors improved by every method of persuasion at their command. The work of improvement is not the work of a day, or a week, or a year, but a continuing job requiring continuous follow-up on old problems and minute attention to new problems as they arise. Quite rightfully, the major share of this work falls to the government agencies concerned, but a most important part can and should be played by the community itself, the development corporations, and the entrepreneural innovator.

Notes to Chapter 7

1. Department of State, Agency for International Development, Proceedings of Conference on the Development of National Markets in Latin America . Washington, D.C., October 16-17, 1964, p. 10.

2. Charles A. Meyers and Frederick Harbison, Education, Manpower and Economic Growth (New York: McGraw-Hill, 1964), p. 185.

3. Eugenio Steiger, Educación, Pamphlet, Vol. III, No. 114, (Caracas: Ministry of Education, Feb., 1965), p. 53.

4. Teodoro Moscoso, "Industrial Development in Puerto Rico," Proceedings of the Economic Planning Seminar (Puerto Rico, 1958), Publisher, Regional Technical Aids Center, International Cooperation Administration (ICA); Mexico, 1960, p. 215.

5. Ibid.

CHAPTER 8 SOURCES OF INFORMATION FOR SMALL- AND MEDIUM-SIZED INVESTORS

Many a small investor and entrepreneur has given up on his plan to form a joint venture or make a personnel investment merely because of a lack of information on how best to proceed. Lacking the sophistication and knowledge available to government organizations, large corporations, and the consultant, he simply does not know where to turn for his information.

It is difficult to assess the needs of the small- and medium-sized investor, but one cannot overemphasize his importance in the development scheme of things. In Peru, for example, it has been estimated that about 50 per cent of the gross product of all industries comes from small industry and the artisan sector; significantly, this group provides 80 per cent of all employment in the country.

Today there are numerous sources of information available to the industrial developer, whether he is a representative of a development corporation or a development bank, or an entrepreneur seeking capital and technical assistance.

As a first and most important source of information, the prospective investor should be directed to the office of the Commercial Attaché in the American Embassy in his country. The commercial attaché or economic counselor and the AID industry officer, in those countries where AID missions are maintained, have access to a wealth of information. As a minimum, most embassies maintain a Dun and Bradstreet Service, a _Thomas Register_, and a _Sweets Catalogue_.

These and other services provide useful information on both U. S. and foreign firms. Through the U.S. Commerce Department, the commercial attaché and the industry officer are provided constantly with a wealth of statistical business information. If there is no American Embassy in the vicinity, a visit to the office of the American Consul would be in order. Embassies and consulates of almost every country are very helpful in providing prospective investors with information.

Various divisions of the Department of Commerce of the United States produce a number of guides and reports, which are very helpful to businessmen considering investments overseas.

The Office of International Regional Economics puts out the Overseas Business Reports, a series of pamphlets providing basic and authoritative information on specific countries which can be useful to exporters, importers, manufacturers, and researchers, as well as investors concerned with international trade.

The Commercial Intelligence Division furnishes the World Trade Directory Reports. These reports contain commercial and financial information on specific foreign firms and individuals which is normally reliable and very much to the point.

The Business and Defense Services Administration provides guidance and analysis of economic factors relating to the sale, purchase, or marketing of a specific commodity in foreign countries, or to investments in production facilities for specific commodities.

The Department of Commerce publishes a Check List, a bibliography and handy reference to the hundreds of published reports available to the U.S. business community interested in world trade and overseas investment.

It also publishes a weekly periodical called International Commerce. This periodical, published by the International Affairs Section, contains practical and concise international marketing information information, news and reports of potential advantages to U.S. businessmen in profitable international sales of U.S. products. It regularly lists new investment opportunities around the world.

Any of the above reports and periodicals may be obtained from the commercial attachés of the various overseas embassies, or from the Department of Commerce. Inquiries should be directed to: Bureau of International Commerce, U.S. Department of Commerce, Washington, D.C.

The United States Government, through the Agency for International Development, supports a Regional Technical Aids Center (RTAC) in Mexico, which supplies technical literature and films in Spanish to the United States Missions in Latin America. Most country missions maintain libraries of books and films that are available on loan to the development agencies, both public and private, in Latin American countries. Corporations and individuals may also avail themselves of this service. In recent years, RTAC has translated books and pamphlets into Spanish on such subjects as agriculture, business administration, engineering, community development, economic development, education, industry, industrial relations, and public health. Catalogues of currently available titles are obtainable through the missions. Persons wishing to use RTAC's books and films are cautioned to place their requests through the missions, rather than contact RTAC directly.

Through the country missions, the Communications Resources Division of the Agency for International Development provides answers to individual questions relating to products, processes, machinery and equipment, production operations, work techniques, management practices and concepts, factory engineering, and basic requirements for industrial production. This service is a helpful source of information to the small businessman, although there is the very real problem of delay from the time the particular question is submitted to the mission until it is researched in Washington and the answer is returned to the mission. Efforts are under way to speed up this relatively lengthy process.

The Statistics and Reports Division of the Agency for International Development provides statistical data on virtually every economic aspect of the economies of the developing countries. This data is particularly useful to the market researcher and is usually up to date.

The Agency for International Development maintains an Index of Technical Publications and has put out numerous useful brochures and publications on a continuing basis on such subjects as feasibility studies. Through its Private Enterprise Development Section, it maintains an up-to-date catalogue of opportunities for investment in the developing countries. This list has been translated into Portuguese as well as Spanish.

An AID publication meriting special mention is _A Selected List of U.S. Readings on Development_, prepared for The United Nations Conference on the Application of Science and Technology for the Benefit of the Less Developed Areas. This compilation was prepared by Saul M. Katz and Frank McGowan, of the Graduate School of Public and International Affairs, University of Pittsburgh.

For years, the United Nations has published a wealth of information useful to the individual interested in development. Figure 13 is a list of places where United Nations publications as well as those publications of the International Court of Justice may be purchased.

Local governments in the developing countries provide information through their planning offices, both national and regional, their development agencies, productivity centers, government banks, and fiscal, commercial, and tourist offices. While there is a great lack of good information, and while much of the available data requires careful screening as to sources and compilation, a good researcher will gain much by a study of what is available. Addresses of the above organizations can normally be obtained from the country's embassies and consulates.

Possibly the best source of local information may be obtained from private commercial banks, many of which put out printed information which may be had for the asking. Monthly and quarterly reports of a very comprehensive nature are the rule rather than the exception, and are well worth perusing.

Dr. Lawrence C. Lockley of Santa Clara University, working under an AID contract, recently compiled a marketing guide for the five Common Market countries of Central America. This guide, well thought out and soundly constructed, provides a wealth of information on Central America. Entitled _A Guide to Market Data in Central America_, it was published under the auspices of the Banco Centroamericano de Integración Económica. Copies may be obtained by sending $2 (U.S.) to the bank at Apartado Postal 772, Tegucigalpa, D.C. Honduras. Dr. Lockley has just completed a similar guide to Peru, and AID is contemplating similar guides in a number of other developing countries. For information on Dr. Lockley's work and similar studies for other areas, inquiries should be directed to the Agency for International Development, Private Enterprise Division, New State Department Building, Washington, D.C.

Management organizations of all kinds, both national and foreign, are springing up in most of the developing countries. Almost all of them put out their own reviews, reports, and brochures. These sources should not be overlooked. Often the prospective investor will find kindred souls anxious to be of help in giving background on their own experience within the country.

A source of special interest for those interested in business subjects dealing with Latin America is a bibliography compiled by Dr. Arnulfo Trejo,

Chief Librarian of ESAN, a graduate school of business administration in Lima, Peru. His bibliography entitled Bibliografía Comentada Sobre Administración de Negocios y Disciplinas Conexas brings together for the first time most available titles in Spanish dealing with business administration subjects. It was published by the Regional Technical Aids Center in Mexico, and copies may be obtained through the U.S. missions in Latin America.

In addition to the sources listed above are the World Bank (International Bank for Reconstruction and Development), the Inter-American Development Bank, The National Planning Association, and The Committee for Economic Development, all with headquarters in Washington, D.C.

Many more private organizations are sources of useful information. Two management consulting firms meriting special mention due to their wide experience in development work around the world are the Stanford Research Institute, Menlo Park, California, and Arthur D. Little, Inc., of Cambridge, Massachusetts. The investor today has so much information on which to base his investment decision that he is often faced with the problem of when to stop and make a decision on the facts already assembled. When he starts on his search, he will find innumerable doors and avenues of information opening to him. His determination to stop and make a decision will be a prudent one indeed, for if he continues he may well end up with too much information, which may be worse than none at all.

FIGURE 13

WHERE TO BUY UNITED NATIONS PUBLICATIONS
AND THE PUBLICATIONS OF THE
INTERNATIONAL COURT
OF JUSTICE

A F R I C A

CAMEROON:
LIBRAIRIE DU PEUPLE AFRICAIN
La Gérante, B.P. 1197, Yaoundé.
DIFFUSION INTERNATIONALE CAMEROUNAISE DU LIVRE ET
DE LA PRESSE, Sangmelima.

CONGO (Léopoldville):
INSTITUT POLITIQUE CONGOLAIS
B.P. 2307, Léopoldville.

ETHIOPIA: INTERNATIONAL PRESS AGENCY
P. O. Box 120, Addis Ababa.

GHANA: UNIVERSITY BOOKSHOP
University College of Ghana, Legon, Accra.

KENYA: THE E.S.A. BOOKSHOP, Box 30167, Nairobi.

LIBYA: SUDKI EL JERBI (BOOKSELLERS)
P. O. Box 78, Istikial Street, Benghazi.

MOROCCO: AUX BELLES IMAGES
281 Avenue Mohammed V, Rabat.

NIGERIA: UNIVERSITY BOOKSHOP (NIGERIA) LTD.
University College, Ibadan.

NORTHERN RHODESIA:
J. Belding, P. O. Box 750, Mufulira.

NYASALAND: BOOKERS (NYASALAND) LTD.
Lontyre House, P. O. Box 34, Biantyre.

SOUTH AFRICA:
VAN SCHAIK'S BOOKSTORE (PTY) LTD.
Church Street, Box 724, Pretoria.
TECHNICAL BOOKS (PTY) LTD., Faraday House
P. O. Box 2866, 40 St. George's Street, Cape Town.

Figure 13 (continued)

SOUTHERN RHODESIA:
THE BOOK CENTRE, First Street, Salisbury.

TANGANYIKA: DAR ES SALAAM BOOKSHOP
P. O. Box 9030, Dar es Salaam.

UGANDA: UGANDA BOOKSHOP, P. O. Box 145, Kampala.

UNITED ARAB REPUBLIC:
LIBRAIRIE "LA RENAISSANCE D'ÉGYPTE"
9 Sh. Adly Pasha, Cairo.
AL NAHDA EL ARABIA BOOKSHOP
32 Abd-el-Khalek Sarwart St., Cairo.

A S I A

BURMA: CURATOR, GOVT. BOOK DEPOT, Rangoon.

CAMBODIA: ENTREPRISE KHMÈRE DE LIBRAIRIE
Imprimerie & Papeterie Sarl, Phnom-Penh.

CEYLON: LAKE HOUSE BOOKSHOP
Assoc. Newspapers of Ceylon, P. O. Box 244, Colombo.

CHINA:
THE WORLD BOOK COMPANY, LTD.
99 Chung King Road, 1st Section, Taipeh, Taiwan.
THE COMMERCIAL PRESS, LTD.
211 Honan Road, Shanghai.

HONG KONG: THE SWINDON BOOK COMPANY
25 Nathan Road, Kowloon.

INDIA:
ORIENT LONGMANS
Calcutta, Bombay, Madras, New Delhi, Hyderabad.
OXFORD BOOK & STATIONERY COMPANY
New Delhi and Calcutta.

INDONESIA:
PEMBANGUNAN, LTD., Gunung Sahari 84, Djakarta.

JAPAN: MARUZEN COMPANY, LTD.
6 Tori-Nichome, Nihonbashi, Tokyo.

KOREA, REPUBLIC OF:
EUL-YOO PUBLISHING CO., LTD., 5, 2-KA, Chongno, Seoul.

Figure 13 (continued)

PAKISTAN:
THE PAKISTAN CO-OPERATIVE BOOK SOCIETY
Dacca, East Pakistan.
PUBLISHERS UNITED, LTD., LAHORE.
THOMAS & THOMAS, Karachi.

PHILIPPINES:
PHILIPPINE EDUCATION COMPANY, INC.
1104 Castillejos, P. O. Box 620, Quiapo, Manila.
POPULAR BOOKSTORE, 1573 Doroteo Jose, Manila.

SINGAPORE:
THE CITY BOOK STORE, LTD., Collyer Quay.

THAILAND:
PRAMUAN MIT. LTD.
55 Chakrawat Road, Wat Tuk, Bangkok.
NIBONDH & CO., LTD.
New Road, Sikak Phya Sri, Bangkok.
SUKSAPAN PANIT
Mansion 9, Rajadamnern Avenue, Bangkok.
VIET-NAM, REPUBLIC OF:
LIBRAIRIE-PAPETERIE XUAN THU
185, rue Tu-do, B.P. 283, Saigon.

E U R O P E

AUSTRIA:
GEROLD & COMPANY, Graben 31, Wien, I.
Georg Fromme & Co., Spengergasse 39, Wien, V.

BELGIUM:
AGENCE ET MESSAGERIES DE LA PRESSE, S.A.
14-22, rue du Persil, Bruxelles.

BULGARIA:
RAZNOÏZNOS, 1, Tzar Assen, Sofia.

CYPRUS: PAN PUBLISHING HOUSE
10 Alexander the Great Street, Strovolos.

CZECHOSLOVAKIA:
ARTIA LTD., 30 ve Smečkách, Praha, 2.

DENMARK: EJNAR MUNKSGAARD, LTD.
Nørregade 6, København, K.

Figure 13 (Continued)

FINLAND: AKATEEMINEN KIRJAKAUPPA
2 Keskuskatu, Helsinki.

FRANCE: ÉDITIONS A. PEDONE
13, rue Soufflot, Paris (V).

GERMANY, FEDERAL REPUBLIC OF:
R. EISENSCHMIDT
Schwanthaler Str. 59, Frankfurt/Main.
ELWERT UND MEURER
Hauptstrasse 101, Berlin-Schöneberg.
ALEXANDER HORN, Spiegelgasse 9, Wiesbaden.
W. E. SAARBACH, Gertrudenstrasse 30, Köln (1).

GREECE: KAUFFMANN BOOKSHOP
28 Stadion Street, Athens.

HUNGARY: KULTURA, P. O. Box 149, Budapest 62.

ICELAND: BÓKAVERZLUN SIGFÚSAR
EYMUNDSSONAR H. F., Austurstraeti 18, Reykjavik.

IRELAND: STATIONERY OFFICE, Dublin.

ITALY: LIBRERIA COMMISSIONARIA SANSONI
Via Gino Capponi 26, Firenze,
and Via Paolo Mercuri 19/B, Roma.
AGENZIA E.I.O.U., Via Meravigli 16, Milano.

LUXEMBOURG:
LIBRAIRIE J. TRAUSCHSCHUMMER
Place du Théâtre, Luxembourg.

NETHERLANDS: N.V. MARTINUS NIJHOFF
Lange Voorhout 9, 's-Gravenhage.

NORWAY: JOHAN GRUNDT TANUM
Karl Johansgate, 41, Oslo.

POLAND: PAN, Patac Kultury i Nauki, Warszawa.

PORTUGAL: LIVRARIA RODRIGUES Y CIA.
186 Rua Aurea, Lisboa.

ROMANIA: CARTIMEX, Str. Aristide Briand 14-18.
P. O. Box 135-135, Bucuresti.

SPAIN: AGUILAR S.A. DE EDICIONES
Juan Bravo 38, Madrid 6.
LIBRERIA BOSCH, Ronda Universidad 11, Barcelona.
LIBRERIA MUNDI-PRENSA, Castelló 37, Madrid.

Figure 13 (Continued)

SWEDEN:
C. E. FRITZE'S KUNGL, HOVBOKHANDEL A-B
Fredsgatan 2, Stockholm.

SWITZERLAND:
LIBRAIRIE PAYOT, S. A., Lausanne, Genève.
HANS RAUNHARDT, Kirchgasse 17, Zurick 1.

TURKEY: LIBRAIRIE HACHETTE
469 Istikial Caddesi, Beyoglu, Istanbul.

UNION OF SOVIET SOCIALIST REPUBLICS:
MEZHDUNARODNAYA KNYIGA
Smolenskaya Ploshchad, Moskva.

UNITED KINGDOM:
H. M. STATIONERY OFFICE, P. O. Box 569, London, S.E. 1
(and HMSO branches in Belfast, Birmingham,
Bristol, Cardiff, Edinburgh, Manchester).

YUGOSLAVIA:
CANKARJEVA ZALOŽBA, Ljubljana, Slovenia.
DRŽAVNO PREDUZEĆE
Jugoslovenska Knjiga, Terazije 27/11, Beograd.
PROSVJETA, 5, Trg Bratstva i Jedinstva, Zagreb.
PROSVETA PUBLISHING HOUSE
Import-Export Division, P. O. Box 559.
Terazije 16/1, Beograd.

L A T I N A M E R I C A

ARGENTINA: EDITORIAL SUDAMERICANA, S.A.
Alsina 500, Buenos Aires.

BOLIVIA: LIBRERIA SELECCIONES, Casilla 972, La Paz.
LOS AMIGOS DEL LIBRO
Calle Perú esq. España, Casilla 450, Cochabamba.

BRAZIL:
LIVRARIA AGIR
Rua Mexico 98-B, Caixa Postal 3291, Rio de Janeiro.
LIVRARIA FREITAS BASTOS, S.A.
Caixa Postal 899, Rio de Janeiro.
LIVRARIA KOSMOS EDITORA
Rua Rosario 135/137, Rio de Janeiro.

Figure 13 (Continued)

CHILE:
EDITORIAL DEL PACIFICO, Ahumada 57, Santiago.
LIBRERIA IVENS Casilla 205, Santiago.

COLOMBIA:
LIBRERIA AMERICA, Calle 51 Núm. 49-58, Medellin.
LIBRERIA BUCHHOLZ, Av. Jiménez de Quesada 8-40, Bogotá.

COSTA RICA: IMPRENTA Y LIBRERIA TREJOS
Apartado 1313, San José.

CUBA: CUBARTIMPEX, Apartado Postal 6540, La Habana.

DOMINICAN REPUBLIC: LIBRERIA DOMINICANA
Mercedes 49, Santo Domingo.

ECUADOR:
LIBRERIA CIENTIFICA, Casilla 362, Guayaquil.
LIBRERIA UNIVERSITARIA, Calle Garcia Moreno 739, Quito.

EL SALVADOR:
LIBRERIA CULTURAL SALVADOREÑA
2a. Av. Sur, San Salvador.
MANUEL NAVAS Y CIA.
1a. Avenida Sur 37, San Salvador.

GUATEMALA:
LIBRERIA CERVANTES, 5a. Av. 9 39, Zona 1, Guatemala.
SOCIEDAD ECONOMICA-FINANCIERA
6a. Av. 14-33, Guatemala.

HAITI: LIBRAIRIE "À LA CARAVELLE", Port-au-Prince.

HONDURAS: LIBRERIA PANAMERICANA, Tegucigalpa.

MEXICO: EDITORIAL HERMES, S.A.
Ignacio Mariscal 41, México, D. F.

PANAMA: JOSE MENENDEZ
Agencia Internacional de Publicaciones.
Apartado 2052, Av. 8A Sur 21-58, Panamá.

PARAGUAY:
AGENCIA DE LIBRERIAS DE SALVADOR NIZZA
Calle Pte. Franco No. 39-43, Asunción.

PERU:
LIBRERIA INTERNACIONAL DEL PERU, S.A.
Casilla 1417, Lima.

Figure 13 (Continued)

PERU (Continued):
LIBRERIA STUDIUM S.A.
Amargura 939, Apartado 2139, Lima.

URUGUAY: LIBRERIA RAFAEL BARRETT
Ramón Anador 4030, Montevideo.
REPRESENTACION DE EDITORIALES,
PROF. H. D'ELIA
Plaza Cagancha 1342, 1° piso, Montevideo.

VENEZUELA: LIBRERIA DEL ESTE
Av. Miranda, No. 52, Edf. Galipán, Caracas.

M I D D L E E A S T

IRAN: MEHR AYIN BOOKSHOP
Abbas Abad Avenue, Isfahan.

IRAQ: MACKENZIE'S BOOKSHOP, Baghdad.

ISRAEL: BLUMSTEIN'S BOOKSTORES
35 Allenby Rd. and 48 Nachiat Benjamin St., Tel Aviv.

JORDAN: JOSEPH I. BAHOUS & CO.
Dar-ul-Kutub, Box 66, Amman.

LEBANON: KHAYAT'S COLLEGE BOOK COOPERATIVE
92-94, rue Bliss, Beirut.

N O R T H A M E R I C A

CANADA:
THE QUEEN'S PRINTER/L'IMPRIMEUR DE LA REINE
Ottawa, Ontario.

UNITED STATES OF AMERICA:
SALES SECTION, UNITED NATIONS, New York.

PUERTO RICO:
PAN AMERICAN BOOK CO., P. O. Box 3511, San Juan 17.
BOOKSTORE, UNIVERSITY OF PUERTO RICO, Rio Piedras.

Figure 13 (Continued)

O C E A N I A

AUSTRALIA:
U.N. ASSOCIATION OF AUSTRALIA
McEwan House, 343 Little Collins St., Melbourne C. 1, Vic.
WEA BOOKROOM, University, Adelaide, S.A.
UNIVERSITY BOOKSHOP, St. Lucia, Brisbane, Qld.
THE EDUCATIONAL AND TECHNICAL BOOK AGENCY
Parap Shopping Centre, Darwin, N.T.
COLLINS BOOK DEPOT PTY. LTD.
Monash University, Wellington Road, Clayton, Vic.
COLLINS BOOK DEPOT PTY. LTD.
363 Swanston Street, Melbourne, Vic.
THE UNIVERSITY BOOKSHOP, Nedlands, W.A.
UNIVERSITY BOOKROOM
University of Melbourne, Parkville N.2, Vic.
UNIVERSITY CO-OPERATIVE BOOKSHOP LIMITED
Manning Road, University of Sydney, N.S.W.

NEW ZEALAND:
GOVERNMENT PRINTING OFFICE
Private Bag, Wellington (and Government Bookshops in Auckland, Christchurch and Dunedin).

W E S T I N D I E S

BERMUDA: BERMUDA BOOK STORES
Reid and Burnaby Streets, Hamilton.

BRITISH GUIANA: BOOKERS STORES, LTD.
20-23 Church Street, Georgetown.

CURAÇAO, N.W.I.:
BOEKHANDEL SALAS, P. O. Box 44.

JAMAICA: SANGSTERS BOOK ROOM
91 Harbour Street, Kingston.

TRINIDAD AND TOBAGO:
CAMPBELL BOOKER LTD., Port of Spain.

United Nations publications may be purchased or ordered from booksellers throughout the world and paid

Figure 13 (Continued)

for in local currency. For further information write to United Nations, Sales Section, New York, N.Y. 10017, or to United Nations, Sales Section, Palais des Nations, Geneva, Switzerland.

CHAPTER 9 THE INDUSTRIAL PARK

THE INDUSTRIAL PARK AS A PROMOTION TOOL

An industrial park is today generally conceived to be a parcel of land subdivided into sections in accordance with a master plan to provide sites for small- and medium-sized industrial enterprises. Normally, streets, roads, transportation, and various utilities are provided for the prospective client. In addition, industrial-type buildings of various sizes and shapes are available--on a rental or lease purchase basis--along with a number of community services such as police and fire protection and a post office. Management advisory services will usually be available to the tenants in such fields as accounting and law.

If properly conceived, well planned, and efficiently run, the industrial park is a powerful weapon in the arsenal of the developing country. Not only does the industrial park encourage investment and help create jobs, it can also ease the socio-economic problems of the fast-growing metropolitan areas. If properly located and administered, the industrial park may slow the flow of migrants to the large cities, which is one of the gravest problems of our times.

The concept of the industrial park developed in England in the latter half of the nineteenth century. The English used the term "industrial estate" and originally promoted industrial estates in areas of chronic unemployment. The success of these early experiments resulted in the establishment of industrial parks in the British Commonwealth, especially Canada.

In the United States, the industrial park began to take hold after World War II. During the past ten years, these parks have mushroomed all over the United States. So-called light industry, especially small- and medium-sized electronics firms, have been particular candidates for the new parks. In the United States, the impetus for organizing and running the parks is usually private. This is not the case in the developing countries. In recent years, industrial parks have been established in such widely separated countries as India, Peru, Mexico, Jamaica, Nigeria, Pakistan, Puerto Rico, and Venezuela. The initiative in these countries has usually come from state or regional organizations charged with promoting industry expansion or decentralization of present industry.

One reason that the industrial park has fallen to the lot of the development agencies is that it is not the kind of investment per se that finds favor in the developing countries. In essence, an investment in an industrial park is a long-term investment. Rarely do industrial parks begin to pay off financially until the fifth or sixth year of operation, and then the rate of return would be considered low by most yardsticks. By no stretch of the imagination can the industrial park be considered a high-yield, quick-return investment. It is not unusual in Latin America, for example, for the investor to expect a 100 per cent return on his money during the first year of his investment. Accordingly, for the foreseeable future, development agencies will have to provide the impetus for industrial parks.

In the United States, the great centers of learning in the fields of advanced technology have played an important role in the growth of the industrial park. Numerous small parks have sprouted around such universities as Stanford University, in California, and Massachusetts Institute of Technology, in Massachusetts. Companies specializing in electronics, space science, and technology have much to gain from a proximity to centers of learning. In future years, as technological institutes in the developing countries gain stature and competence, they will undoubtedly give added impetus to the formation of industrial parks.

Steps to be Undertaken in the Establishment of an Industrial Park

When considering the establishment of an industrial park, the first vital consideration is the size of the market. It is all-important that a thorough market analysis be conducted to determine the size and nature of companies that might be willing to locate or relocate to the proposed site. Before conducting the survey, a few general guide lines must be established.

The size of the industrial tenant should be decided. A typical range in the developing countries might be from six to forty employees. Another size limitation might be based on the size of investment. A recently proposed park in Peru set an upper limit of approximately $1 million capitalization.

Before the survey can be conducted, a determination of the size and type of buildings to be offered must be made.

General decisions must be made as to the kinds of industry that will be invited to enter the park. Industries normally considered acceptable might include: processing industries, such as canning, candles, cheese adhesives, etc.; leather-making industries that engage in injection molding, low-pressure molding, compression molding, and blow molding; metal-working industries involving aluminum assembly and light extrusion work; automobile spare parts manufacturing; radiator assembly; battery, springs, and filters manufacturing; kitchen appliances, lamps, ranges, and cabinets manufacturing; electronics firms; drug firms; and book companies engaged in binding and printing.

Industries such as iron foundries and glue factories, which might be objectionable to neighbors from the point of view of safety, noise, odor, etc., have been omitted from this list.

In the course of the survey, it will be imperative to determine the type of lease desired by the client, the size and type of building desired, and possibilities for reasonable expansion of the tenant.

In his book Industrial Estates, Dr. William Bredo has noted the importance of the time element in getting the project "off and running." A most important element in developing a successful industrial park is speed in constructing the project and having it fully occupied by industrial enterprises. Early recovery of development funds sunk into an estate makes it possible to reuse them more quickly. Conversely, comparatively slow development of the estate and slow disposal of sites retards the income stream from the investment and jeopardizes the financial success of the project. If firms are located before the estate is completed, slowness in the installation of utilities may endanger the solvency of these firms and may discourage other industrialists from applying for sites.[1]

Ideally, the initial market survey will be followed quickly by a detailed feasibility study of the location or locations under consideration. The time spent on the detailed study is basic, but it is important to complete the study and begin construction at the earliest moment to keep the momentum gained in the original market study. Businessmen are like most people in that they tend to lose interest in any project that seems to drag on and on.

A good basic study should assemble all the information required for the projected park. Dr. Bredo lists the following features as important to an evaluation of the proposed project: (1) an estimate of what the estate will cost, including fixed and operating costs; the annual expenditures projected during the construction period and thereafter; (2) details on financing, including sources of financing, foreign exchange required, real estate revenues and service charges expected from occupants, long-term net revenue, and the net return on the investment anticipated for the future; (3) a description of the proposed site, including financial, economic, and other aspects. The description should include a tentative layout plan for each site, showing the location of streets, access roads, rail and utility easements, and building lines; (4) a proposal of the kinds of facilities and services to be offered. Will factories be provided? Will they be sold or rented? Or, will only architectural and construction services be offered? Will special services be provided, such as canteens, postal service, banking and credit facilities, and industrial advisory services? (5) presentation of a long-term development plan, showing the phased development of the project. This should include detailed plans for each construction period, showing the land area to be improved, the various utilities to be installed, and the facilities to be constructed for the benefit of the occupants; (6) the proposed organizational structure of the sponsoring agency, and plan of how the estate is to be managed; (7) a proposed method for controlling the estate. This should include specific details on existing and proposed zoning restrictions to be included in the covenants, and proposed ways of dealing with the problems of annexation, if the estate is located outside city limits and annexation is considered necessary; (8) proposed methods for selecting and attracting industry to the estate; (9) a study of the features of the plan which should make it beneficial and acceptable to the community; and (10) finally, accompanying the comprehensive plan, a detailed report on alternative sites, and why the site in question is preferred.[2]

In addition to the detailed technical economic data contained in the study, some guide lines might be suggested as to the type of tenants desired. The individual solicited should obviously be of high moral character and should possess executive and technical qualifications. Also, it should be borne in mind that his financial standing--past, present, and future--will reflect to a marked degree on the other park occupants.

As a final item, the study might also include a brief description of the future prospects of the various companies to be solicited, how they fit into the national economy, and the role they can play in the future in international trade.

INDUSTRIAL PARK STUDIES

Industrial parks can be an effective tool for industrial promotion and to compensate for disadvantages of a locality or region. Once a development organization or private entrepreneur has decided to promote the industrial development of a city or an area in this way, a feasibility study can be made.

> An industrial park is a planned approach to establishing a usable aggregation of industrial enterprises. A tract of land is subdivided and developed with all the basic elements of internal physical infrastructure needed by industrial establishments. These include access roads and streets, water, power, and sanitation utilities to meet projected industrial requirements, and the provision of supplementary or auxiliary services such as rail sidings, warehousing facilities, and fire protection services as required. The rational location of all components of this infrastructure, the orientation of the traffic arteries, the dimensions and location of factory sites of various sizes, and the service facilities are planned to achieve maximum usefulness and effectiveness by being developed according to a well-conceived layout plan. Financial aid and technical assistance in building and equipping factories may also be offered to the

> prospective tenant by the developer; or the developer may construct standardized buildings to provide industrialists with modern and complete facilities.[3]

An industrial park feasibility study should meet the following specific objectives:

(1) Determining the types and sizes of industries for which an industrial park in the area would be a desirable location.

(2) Estimating the number of enterprises that might become occupants of an industrial park, and determining their land area and building size requirements.

(3) Locating a suitable industrial park site within the region or the locality.

(4) Carrying out the economic and engineering analyses necessary to determine cost of the development, with regard to the existing physical features of the site.

(5) Preparing a physical layout drawing in accordance with the formulated advance development plan.

(6) Providing suggestions as to legal and organizational mechanisms for bringing the industrial park into being, and to assure long-range viability and control.

To achieve these objectives, an industrial park feasibility study should cover the following aspects:

(1) A study of the area in question as a location for an industrial park.

(2) Selection of the industrial park site within the locality.

(3) An estimate of the demand for space and services in the future industrial park by existing and new industries.

(4) The physical layout of the park.

(5) The financial feasibility of the park.

(6) The steps to be taken to implement the industrial park plan.

An industrial park can be successful only in areas where there already exists a basic industrial infrastructure of power, transportation, some skilled labor, a progressive attitude on the part of the people, and at least some raw materials and markets on which industries can be based. If these prerequisites do not exist, an industrial park cannot be a panacea for industrial development. Unsuccessful industrial park ventures have usually been due to lack of any incentives for industrial location other than an industrial park. Therefore, the first step in the feasibility study should cover such factors as: the population of the region or town, especially the economically active population; labor characteristics; existing industry, its sizes, types and distribution; existing land planning for industrial development, if applicable; the ports, roads, public transportation, rail service, freight traffic and costs; water supply and sewerage systems; electric power and communications; present factory facilities; hotel and office facilities, fire protection, housing, medical; and educational facilities.

Site requirements differ for different industries, and a site selected to accommodate a number of enterprises is not likely to be the best possible site for any one group. Thus, the advantages of grouping must outweigh the disadvantages accompanying the compromise park site. Fortunately, for a group of small- and medium-sized production-type manufacturing enterprises, the diversity in location requirements is not likely to be very great. Transportation, accessibility, and availability of inexpensive land with adequate water and power are of primary importance.

Of the two fundamental factors--location and size--which must be resolved before a park is established, location is the more important. Once established, a park cannot be moved, although it can be enlarged if future expansion is allowed for at the time of the site selection. Such a consideration would include provisions to control adjacent land use and to prevent the encroachment of undesirable developments by natural barriers, enforceable zoning, or acquisition of a purchase option or title to adjacent land.

For every combination of circumstances, a size range exists within which a park is most likely to be a successful venture. Since size of the park is closely related to physical and cost factors, the minimum size is most easily obtained. Experience in urban areas indicates that separate parks should not be built if the size will be much less than ten hectares in gross area. The economic minimum size for the rural industrial parks is probably considerably less. These parks often provide quarters for blacksmith shops repairing agricultural implements and tools, pump and engine repair shops, and equipment rental services for local agriculture. The size of such a rural park may be two hectares or less. A more realistic upper limitation for the larger parks may be number of enterprises or employees, rather than over-all area. Little guidance on maximum size is available from India or Puerto Rico, where efforts have been made to build a great number of small parks throughout the country. India, for instance, has seventy-one parks in communities with a population of less than 100,000. In England, however, some of the large "new towns" of 60,000 to 100,000 population have industrial areas equivalent to 160 hectares, or over 10 per cent of the total planned town area, which will eventually employ more than 16,000 factory workers.

Criteria utilized in selecting and evaluating alternative sites for an industrial park relate to situational factors, or the general area, and site factors, which pertain to a specific site within the area:

General Situational Factors	Specific Site Factors
Amount of land available	Size
Cost of land	Acquisition cost
Transportation facilities	Slope and drainage
Political jurisdiction	Bearing capacity of soil
Altitude, climate, and attractiveness of area	Accessibility
Availability of labor and management personnel	Shape
Effect of park on community development	Present ownership, pattern

The amount of land available is of prime importance. A site that is too small for the period of industrial development, during which new intra-park locations for factory construction must be provided to create a reservoir of factory accommodations, will be inadequate. Thus, in making the preliminary estimate of park size, upon which a selection of alternative sites is to be based, it is safer to overestimate the size required , for it is always possible to use only a portion of a large site. Care must be taken, however, to avoid a gross overestimation, which would eliminate a substantial number of desirable smaller sites.

The cost of land is an important factor in any large-scale industrial development. There is considerable variety in cost, related to site accessibility and the availability of utilities. It is frequently more economical to develop a private water and power supply and access roads to an outlying area rather than locate in an area of higher priced land served by existing utilities that may become inadequate. High-cost locations due to the attractiveness of the area for housing development are undesirable for an industrial park. Expropriation of land to obtain clear title is often necessary; however, such action should not be used to obtain land below the market price because of unfavorable public reactions to such practice.

Facilities for air, water, rail, and road transportation must be investigated in terms of the requirements of potential park candidates. Truck transportation is often least expensive for most small industries; however, road conditions, the problems of traffic congestion, and access to various parts of the city influence trucking costs.

It is of primary importance to investigate political jurisdictions and the nature and extent of the taxing power that they represent. The location of an attractive site within easy commuting distance of established housing areas from which local labor is available, closeness of adequate quarters for management personnel, and community acceptance of a park project and its site are also important factors.

Essentially, flat sites with good drainage are desirable; however, sites with slopes up to 5 per cent can be used without appreciably increasing costs, if the development follows existing contours. Slope and drainage of the surrounding area are also significant. Run-off resulting from flash floods or historic conditions of flooding in low areas should be carefully investigated. Some knowledge of subsoil conditions is desirable, in that certain types of soil may adversely affect the bearing capacity and thereby increase the cost of building construction.

It is desirable to select a site that conforms to existing property lines and topography. Undesirable encroachments can often be controlled by selecting a site protected by natural or artificial barriers, such as a major highway, or a water-course. All other things being equal, a site comprising a few large parcels of land will be more desirable than one comprising a large number of small parcels, in that undue difficulties in land acquisition will be avoided.

To evaluate the relative importance of the cost of land, site accessibility, transportation facilities, and other criteria, it is necessary to establish the needs of probable park occupants in terms of markets for their products, raw materials, and availability of labor.

Demand for space and services in an industrial park ordinarily comes from three sources:

The first is from existing industries that would have located in an industrial park earlier if such a possibility had been open. This is "pent-up" demand. These enterprises are now occupying inadequate facilities. If such companies can relocate in the industrial park, their growth and efficiency can be stimulated significantly.

The second is from very small or new firms that will become small- or medium-sized firms in the future.

The third is from new firms formed by local or outside entrepreneurs in response to industrial development incentives--including the industrial park itself--under a systematic industrial development program.

Pent-up demand can be estimated easily by making a survey of existing local enterprises to determine their space and services requirements. Such a survey should include as large a variety of industries as possible, since requirements vary considerably from industry to industry, and should categorize industry as to size and type. The following types of questions should be asked in such a survey:

(1) Identification of the enterprise; type of production; how long in existence; a summary of past history of expansion with regard to space and equipment; average growth rate in recent years; opinion of the owner with respect to future expansion and stability of his company.

(2) Location of the enterprise; distance from place of sales, transportation of raw materials and finished products, as well as commuting time for employees.

(3) The importance of financing land and buildings; here it might be asked how many occupants want and need to acquire land or buildings on an installment purchase plan.

(4) Cost of land, buildings, and rent on lots where industries are presently located.

(5) Whether the industrialists would consider locating in the planned industrial park.

(6) Demand for important basic services, such as paved roads, additional storage facilities, bus services, central telephone services, etc.

(7) Incentives that might be needed for firms to locate in the industrial park, if any, as for instance, tax exemption.

(8) Present and expected future use of electric power, the number of horsepower, and other technical data on motors; present and future water requirements; sewage systems and transportation requirements (road, plane, railroad).

(9) Preferred location for the industrial park.

(10) Present size of lot and buildings, and sizes desired in the park.

(11) Whether the occupant prefers to lease or rent land with or without multipurpose ready-to-occupy buildings on it, or prefers to buy land with or without a ready-to-occupy factory building.

It is useful to hold a meeting with groups of industrialists to discuss all aspects of the industrial park, since questionnaires are often a rather inferior means of communication. In this way, they will also have a sense of participation in decision-making which will elicit their cooperation, and thus assure that a maximum number of potential candidates will locate in the park.

The demand from small- to medium-sized enterprises can be estimated by analyzing past growth of this type in the locality and by estimating the possible influence on this past growth rate of small industry development programs by development corporations, self-help programs, or other stimuli such as growing markets and population or governmental measures.

The demand for space and services from new industries is the most difficult component to estimate. Basically, two methods can be suggested:

The first is to select those industries from the list of industrial investment opportunities which the development corporation has studied and found to be feasible, which are expected to become a reality in the near future, and which are likely to locate in the industrial park.

The second is to make a survey among new industries in the planning stage in the country as a whole to determine which of these would consider locating in the industrial park in question. If realistic answers are to be obtained, the questionnaires should include a description of the industrial park projects and any other advantages and incentives which the specific region or town may have to offer. Also, it will be advantageous to concentrate on those new industries which are relatively "foot-loose"; in other words, industries for whom proximity to raw materials or markets is not of prime importance. The quality and intensity of the whole industrial development program of a region will have a strong influence on this demand component. Where a good industrial development and promotion program exists, and where the necessary infrastructural facilities are available, this component of demand tends to be underestimated rather than overestimated. In one specific case, demand for space from this component which was estimated to materialize over a fifteen-year period occurred in a two-year period, because the industrial park was only one part of a carefully planned development program in a locality that could offer the necessary infrastructure for industry, tax incentives, pleasant living conditions, and a good climate.

In estimating demand for space and services in an industrial park, a number of limiting factors should be taken into consideration.

Not all industries can or should locate in an industrial park. Industries causing excessive amounts of noise, smoke, dirt, odors, danger, or other undesirable side effects should be located elsewhere. Examples are slaughter houses, fish meal factories, explosives plants, and some chemical plants. Also, some industries must be located near their raw materials, such as cement plants, steel plants, sugar mills, and saw mills.

Typically, an industrial park is designed for small, medium, or moderately large manufacturing plants. Very small enterprises should be located in a special small industries or artisan park; since these industries are generally rather unstable and often fail, they do not represent good clients for the usual industrial park. For this reason, the minimum lot size in a normal industrial park should be about 1,000 square meters.

On the other hand, very large factories requiring large amounts of land that they do not use intensively, or that would take up most or all of the space in the proposed park, may not be suitable candidates either. From the point of view of development, preference should be given to those industries which produce a maximum of direct or indirect employment or sales per unit of space required. Also the facilities and services required by very large industries may be different from those for medium industries, or they may require special services and installations which the park cannot provide. For such very large enterprises, a special industrial reserve at the outskirts of the city should be set aside by the development corporation or city planning authorities. This reserve could have basic services such as an access road, a railroad spur, water, and sewage.

The location of the park may represent a good solution for the majority of potential occupants, but some potential occupants may be excluded.

The services which the park will provide should be wanted by the majority of occupants; others may not want to pay for them, or may not want to locate in the park at all for that reason.

The price of land and buildings in the park is, without doubt, a strong determinant of demand. Smaller industries may not realize that the large-scale installation of services and facilities makes these less expensive for each user. An information campaign may be required to publicize the advantages an industrial park can offer.

Finally, administrative policies for the park may act as a deterrent to some potential occupants. If strict standards as to the financial stability and economic soundness of an enterprise are set, this may deter some firms.

A good promotional campaign emphasizing the advantages of the park and of the region or city in which it is located can do a great deal to stimulate demand.

Tax incentives offered to park occupants can also act as stimulants.

If longer-term financing at reasonable interest rates is offered for the acquisition of buildings and land, this represents another strong incentive for industries to locate in the park.

In an industrial park, land can either be rented or leased with or without multipurpose buildings on it, or it can be sold to occupants with multipurpose, ready-to-occupy factory buildings, or without any buildings on it. Each of these alternatives has its advantages, and the survey to determine demand for space and services should also determine how many potential occupants prefer each of the different alternatives. The general attitude of a country's businessmen toward owning or renting land or buildings can also serve as a useful guideline. Renting land with ready-to-occupy multipurpose factory buildings on it may represent an incentive for some, because it reduces their total investment requirements, and a deterrent to others, because they need special buildings or they do not want to forego the possible gains from an increase in property values. On the other hand, whether the occupants will reap the benefits of an increase in real estate values depends on the policy adopted by the park's developers. In some cases, the occupant is under obligation to resell the land and buildings to the developers at their original price; in others, no such limitation is imposed; and in still other cases, the gains are split between the developers and the occupants. If the developers are willing to leave the increase of real estate values to the occupants, at least partially, and if real estate prices rise rather rapidly in a country--as for instance in countries plagued by chronic inflation--and if businessmen attach great importance to owning their land and buildings--for instance, in order to use them as collateral for a loan--then it may be wisest to offer most lots for sale with or without buildings, rather than for rent or lease. Lots which already have ready-to-occupy multipurpose industrial buildings on them (either for sale or for rent), may attract some clients who are in a hurry to start their business, to beat a competitor or take advantage of a particularly favorable market or raw materials situation. Careful analysis of the preference of businessmen for one alternative or another must be made, and the park planned accordingly. If it is difficult to evaluate these factors, the safest policy will be to develop the land and install a small number of ready-to-occupy multipurpose factory buildings, either for rent or for purchase. The risk of not selling, renting, or leasing such buildings is probably greater than that of losing potential clients because no such buildings were ready for immediate occupancy when applied for. The better the knowledge about the types of industries that will probably locate in the park, and their building and land size requirements the less risky it will be to put up ready-to-occupy, multipurpose factory buildings.

Orderly and sustained industrial growth can best be achieved by planning as far in advance as possible. As a general rule of thumb, a fifteen- to twenty-year period would be the most desirable. In planning and developing an industrial park to serve over a twenty-year period, the concept of a phased development provides for maximum benefits from invested funds. Changes in industrial production methods, world markets, and political policies and alignments that might occur in twenty-years' time cannot be fully assessed in advance. Since some of these changes greatly affect industrial growth and demand for factory space, it is wise to plan a twenty-year development in phases, so that the direction and rapidity of change can be re-evaluated frequently and appropriate action taken to alter the original plan. A typical division into phases over a twenty-year period might be Phase I for the first five years, Phase II for the following ten years, and Phase III for the final five years.

Phase I is probably the most important period. Projections of industrial demand for space are more reliable for the immediate than for the distant future. Interest in and need for space in an industrial park are acute in the first stages of development. Moreover, initial development will set the tone and pattern of future developments. Successful development during Phase I will create additional interest and demand, while haphazard or spotty development will cause many industrialists to lose interest and to seek alternative locations to meet their needs.

The projected demand for industrial sites within the park dictates the planning parameters for an industrial park layout. It is not necessary to prepare individual industrial sites for occupancy until shortly before they are expected to be utilized. However, major streets, utilities, and auxiliary facilities and services must be designed initially to accommodate later developments. It is often difficult and costly, for example, to replace small water lines with larger ones, or to widen a narrow road after its capacity has been exceeded.

Experience indicates that the following physical facilities and services are needed to assure the long-term desirability and success of a relatively large industrial park development:

Physical Facilities	Services
Paved roads	Bus service
Well-drained sites in sufficient number and dimensions	Public telephone and telegram service
Off-street parking and loading areas	Post office
Adequate water supply	Cafeteria or restaurant
Sanitary and industrial sewage system	Picnic grounds
Adequate electric power	Soccer or football field
Fire hydrants	Police and fire protection services
Telephones	Industrial advisory services
Paved sidewalks	Office building for the administration and maintenance services of the park
Landscaping	Commercial facilities such as essential stores, banks, gas stations or service stations
Street lighting	
Fences (optional)	
Ready-to-occupy buildings (optional)	
Access roads	
Railway spur (if needed)	

The less investment funds are available and the smaller the park, the more limited can be these facilities and services.

In planning the layout of the park, a high degree of flexibility is desirable. If demand for space and the desired lot sizes are known in advance, the layout can be rather detailed and individual lots can be laid out. If demand and lot sizes are uncertain it is advisable to lay only major roads, water and sewerage lines, electrical lines, and substations as well as access roads for the first phase of development.

Adequate provision for an efficient flow of traffic within the park is essential, but it is not desirable for outside traffic to pass through the park. Multiple entrances or exits help to avoid morning or afternoon congestion by commuting workers. Although a park location adjacent to a principal highway access route is ideal, it is virtually mandatory that none of the enterprises have individual entrances from the highway. Such a practice can easily result in highway congestion that destroys the value of the park location for all other occupants. As a corollary of this rule, care must be taken in the street layout of the park to prevent the main thoroughfare from becoming congested by vehicles entering the park from the highway. One way of achieving this is to locate the larger industries near the park entrance; this also improves the appearance of the park.[4]

The amount of street frontage is a most important factor in the cost of developed sites, since it affects the length of required streets and the utilities that follow them. Street frontage is minimized by reducing the ratio of lot width to depth within the limit required for building purposes. A ratio of 1 1/2 to 2 or more is desirable. Likewise, larger lots that reduce the number of streets required also reduce unit development costs. Thus, it is desirable to provide only enough small lots to meet the well-established demand, and to arrange the layout so that certain large lots might be divided later, by a small amount of additional street construction, if future demand materializes for lots in smaller sizes.

> Water, sewer and power-line investment can be minimized by locations that will serve sites on both sides of the lines. Since this is also true of streets (it is a matter of economy to avoid streets that follow the perimeter of the site), all utilities might follow streets. This is mandatory for water lines because fire hydrants must be readily accessible. However, in many cases it is not essential for sewers, and sewers that are built in phases, by running sewers in easements along the rear lot lines and between lots, are often more satisfactory. By following a similar practice for power lines, the unsightly appearance of overhead lines and service drops to individual buildings along the main streets of the park can be avoided. An extra length of overhead power line along the perimeter of the development is much less expensive than underground power distribution, a practice that can rarely be justified in industrial developments.[5]

Like the feasibility study for an industrial enterprise, a feasibility study for an industrial park should cover the following points:

(1) An estimate of the amounts of investment in land, site improvement, drainage and leveling of land, roads, railroad spurs, sidewalks, landscaping, and the installation of services like water, sewage, electricity, and telephones, and the administrative building, if included. If the construction of factory buildings by the park developers is intended, their cost must also be included.

(2) An estimate of the number of lots and buildings to be sold, leased, or rented, as reflected by a reasonable forecast of demand for space and buildings.

(3) An estimate of the cash outflow in the form of personnel costs, maintenance costs, depreciation, taxes, land development costs, and building construction costs.

(4) An estimate of income from the sale, leasing or renting of land and buildings, and administrative charges to park occupants. This estimate, of course, has to be based on an estimate of the expected demand for land and buildings in the park.

(5) The combination of these estimates into a cash flow forecast, showing all cash outflow in the form of investments and operating costs, and all cash inflow in the form of sales, leases, or rent of land and buildings or administrative charges. This cash flow forecast will show the financial needs of the industrial park, both in its initial stages and its later operating periods. It can also be the basis for a possible loan application to a financial institution such as a mortgage bank or the World Bank.

All these estimates should be broken down into the different phases of development projected for the park. The important point is always to see the industrial park as an enterprise which should be able to amortize the funds invested in it. If circumstances indicate that this will not be possible, or that it will be possible only over a very long period because of the need to make far-reaching concessions to occupants in an effort to attract new industries to the locality, then the necessary subsidy should be determined clearly, and should be limited as to the amount and the time period required. This type of thinking will also require the developing entity of the park to set up an efficient and businesslike administration to manage the park.

Figures 14 and 15 show how the different financial estimates can be arranged and presented.

FIGURE 14

DEVELOPMENT COST ESTIMATES, BY PHASES
(in monetary units)

Components	Phase I 5 years	Phase II 10 years	Phase III 5 years	Total
Offsite improvements				
(Extension of water main, access roads)				
Site Improvements				
Preparation and drainage				
Leveling				
Drainage pipes				
Roads				
Railroad spur				
Cement sidewalks				
Landscaping				
Subtotal for site preparation				
Utilities				
Sewage pipes				
Water distribution				
Fire protection (hydrants)				
Booster pumps for increasing water pressure				

Components	Phase I 5 years	Phase II 10 years	Phase III 5 years	Total
Electricity distribution				
Street lighting				
Telephones				
Subtotal for utilities:				
Total for site improvements:				
Total development costs, including offsite improvements:				
Gross area:				
Cost of site improvement per gross hectare:				

FIGURE 15

BUILDING CONSTRUCTION FOR LEASE AND/OR SALE
AND SCHEDULE OF LAND SALES

	Total Number of Lots	Number of Lots	Number and Types of Buildings	Number of Firms	Space Within Buildings in Sq. Meters	Cost of Buildings in Monetary Units
Phase I						
Large lots						
Medium-sized lots						
Small lots						
Total						
Phase II and Phase III						
All phases						
Large lots						
Medium-sized lots						
Small lots						
Total						

Note: Small lots could be classified as having from 1,000 sq. meters to 1,500 sq. meters; medium lots from 1,501 sq. meters to 4,000 sq. meters; and large lots, 4,001 sq. meters and over. According to regulations, buildings on lots would not occupy more than 50 per cent of the lot.

The actual land development costs have not been stated in Figures 14 and 15 since they vary with circumstances and countries, and according to the facilities installed. However, Table 3 may provide some idea as to the cost ranges of developed land in industrial parks of different sizes and in different countries.

TABLE 3

EXAMPLES OF COST RANGES OF DEVELOPED LAND IN INDUSTRIAL PARKS

City	Size of Park in Acres	Development Cost per Acre in U.S. $
Puerto Rico	100 or less	6,000-12,000
United States (70 typical industrial districts)	300 or less	6,320 median 3,800 average
United States (small industrial districts with few facilities)	80	3,900
Greece	188	4,655
India	15-20	3,000-5,000
The Karachi Estate, Pakistan	1,500	4,200
The Gurjanwala Estate, Pakistan	93.7	1,170
Arequipa, Peru	128.0	5,120

Sources: Puerto Rico Development Company; Stanford Research Institute; Urban Land Institute, Washington, D.C.; Government of India Small Scale Industries Board; West Pakistan Small Industries Corporation; and Junta de Rehabilitación y Desarrollo de Arequipa, Arequipa, Peru.

To the horizontal division in Figure 15 into number of lots, number and types of buildings, number of firms, space within buildings, and cost of buildings can be added "Land and Buildings for Sale." As a final column, "Land for Sale" can be added. On the vertical side of this figure would again be the phases and years of park development. The horizontal columns could be arranged as in Figure 16.

FIGURE 16

FORM FOR CASH OUTFLOW TABLE

Purchase of land
Offsite improvements
Site improvements
- Drainage and leveling of land
- Roads
- Railroad spur
- Sidewalks and landscaping
- Utilities

Subtotal

Capital development costs
- Buildings for rental
  - Large
  - Medium
  - Small

Subtotal

Buildings for sale
- Large
- Medium
- Small

Subtotal
Total development costs

Operating costs
- Administration
- Maintaining railroad right-of-way
- Operation of services (street lighting, cleaning, fire protection, etc.)

Total operating costs

Total cost outflow

As a next step, renting, leasing, and selling prices for developed land and buildings should be determined. Such prices should be in line with or lower than prices for developed land or industrial buildings elsewhere in the community, region, or country. The lower they are, of course, the stronger will be the promotional effect of the industrial estate.

One side of a cash inflow table would show the phases and years of development. In the other direction, the columns shown in Figure 17 could be presented.

FIGURE 17

FORM FOR CASH INFLOW TABLE

Income from the sales of assets
    Sale of land
    Sale of buildings
        Subtotal

Rental of unused land for agricultural uses

Charges payable by occupants
    Maintaining railroad right-of-way
    Administrative charges
    Service charges
    Rent
Depreciation

Total cash inflow

As a final step, total cash outflow can be compared with total cash inflow for each year and each phase of development. The resulting difference will show the need for outside funds, that is, funds not generated from the operation of the park itself, to help finance the industrial park development, and the possibilities and time period for repaying such funds.

It will also show the rate of return that could be earned on equity capital invested in the park. If the rate of return is not attractive enough for private investors, a low-interest rate, long-term loan from international financial institutions might be obtained for a considerable portion of the outside funds required. In this case, the same principle for making a development venture attractive to private investors that was discussed in connection with private industrial finance companies would become operative here. This would make it possible for a public entity or development corporation that has pioneered the establishment of an industrial park and has invested its own funds to liquidate its investment and turn the park over to private enterprise.

As a first step in implementing an industrial park plan, an industrial park management corporation should be formed. The formation of a separate management corporation largely independent of the development corporation or other sponsoring entities, firms, or institutions assures that due attention will be paid to the undertaking, and that the regular channels of a development corporation will not become congested with the management of a major undertaking. Other advantages of a separate organization are that it becomes eligible to receive construction loans from certain international lending agencies which restrict funds to entities chartered for specifically defined purposes. It is also easier for a development corporation to liquidate its investment and turn the industrial part over to private enterprise at some future date, provided that it is financially attractive to private investors.

The manager of the industrial park development corporation, as well as his staff, should be carefully selected and trained. For an industrial park of the size that has been considered, one manager with one or two assistants would probably be sufficient. The manager should preferably have a background in law or business administration. His assistants can be trained in technical or civil engineering. If no candidates with experience in industrial park development and management are available, suitable candidates can be sent abroad to serve an internship period with industrial park management corporations. Figure 18 shows a possible organizational structure for an industrial park corporation.

Figure 18 shows that two advisory groups are included in the organizational structure of the park. The advisory group or committee representing the Chamber of Commerce or similar industry organizations is to insure that due attention is paid to the interests of the local industrial community as a whole. The group providing industrial advisory services is to advise the park administration on selection of applicants and assist occupants with the solution of managerial and technical problems, so that they can become permanent, well-established clients of the park, as well as progressive, forward-looking, and efficient industries contributing to the economic advancement of the community, region or country. The concentration of a large number of industries in the park simplifies the rendering of advisory services considerably, since it saves time and distance and fosters a direct and intimate relationship between advisors and industrialists. For the same reason, industrial research institutes and vocational schools also find it advantageous to be located near large industrial agglomerations such as industrial parks.

Proper selection of occupants helps to insure the success of an industrial park in terms of its financial stability and the economic development of the community or region concerned. Only sound, reliable firms should be admitted, whose future seems to be assured by virtue of their markets, the supply of raw materials, the efficiency of their production processes, the quality of their management, and other factors. Any new firm should be required to submit a feasibility study before it is granted admission into the park. Preference should be given to firms that create a maximum of direct or indirect employment per unit of land used, or that maximize other factors important for the development of the community or region, such as training of workers, technicians, and managers, and creating investment opportunities for other related industries. In the case of existing industries desiring to relocate in the industrial park, preference should be given to those that combine their move with an increase in production, productivity, or employment, and to those that can be expected to continue to grow. A special effort should be made by the park management to attract industries which are likely to have the highest future growth rates in terms of production and employment. Economic forecasts can be of value in determining which industries are most likely to meet this qualification. Industries undertaking dangerous or noxious activities should be prohibited, such as explosive plants and fish meal. Very small industries should be located in a special park for small industries or artisans, and industries with very large space requirements should not be admitted into the industrial park, but rather in an area set aside especially for very large industries. A suggested application form for evaluating and screening applicants is given in Figure 20.

"Restrictions on the use of property within the park are valuable instruments in assuring the long-term desirability and control of the development. These restrictions, written into deeds of sale and leasing agreements, serve a number of functions: (1) they prevent occupants from violating planned measures to assure quality control for the installations and industries of the park and aesthetic harmony; (2) they prevent occupants from engaging in disharmonious, dangerous, or undesirable manufacturing or warehousing activities; and (3) they discourage land speculation and other similar practices within the park."[6] They also assure that planning norms are maintained. Specifically, they can serve the following purposes:

They can assure that not more than 50 per cent of a lot is covered with buildings, thus assuring aesthetic appearance and reduction of fire hazards.

FIGURE 18

ORGANIZATION FOR AN INDUSTRIAL PARK CORPORATION

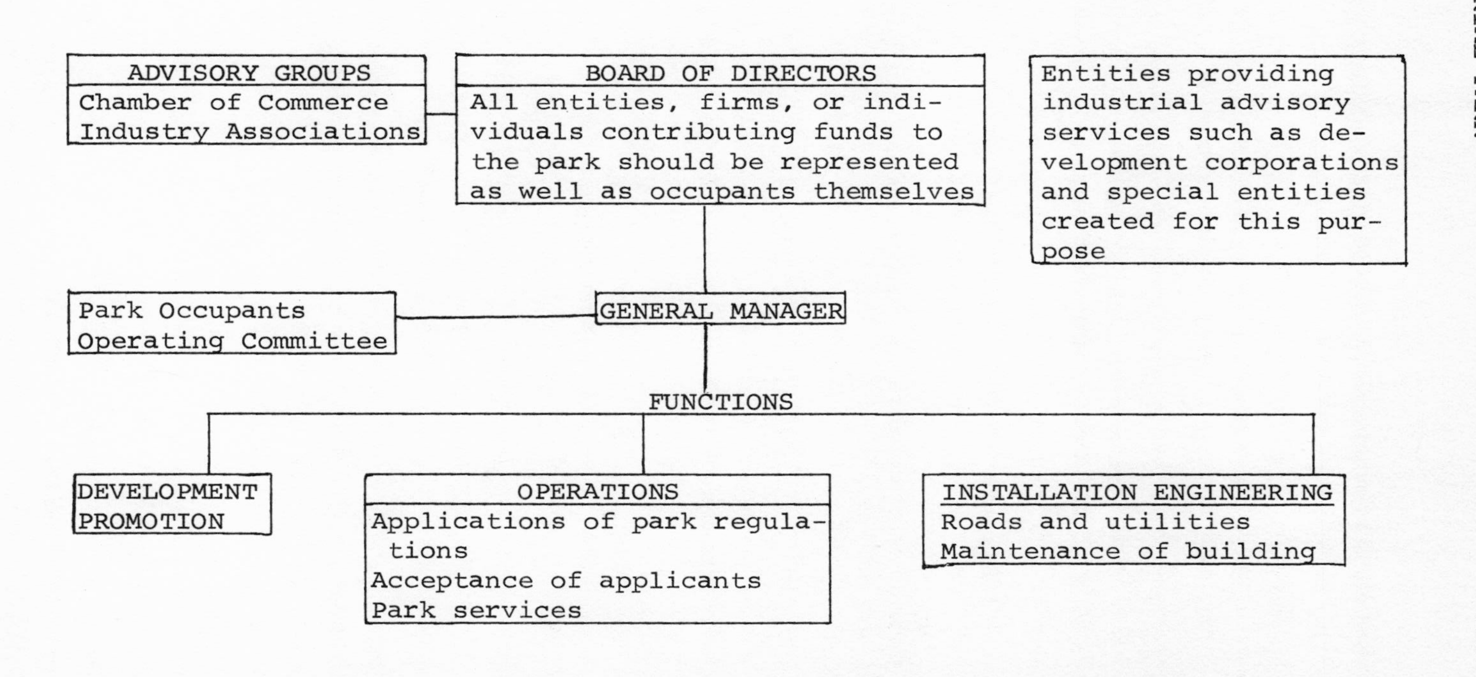

They can permit the enforcement of regulations on setbacks, inside storage, parking and loading space, maintenance of buildings and lots, quality of buildings and installations, and other similar quality controls.

They can be used to prevent industries within the park from undertaking dangerous or noxious activities.

They can also prevent the private resale of property to industries that would be undesirable occupants of the park.

They can prevent speculation and subleasing of property. (In order to prevent speculation, an occupant can be required to start manufacturing operations within a certain time after purchase of the land.)

In Figure 19 are typical regulations which the Puerto Rico Industrial Development Company has introduced, which reflect the quality and other control regulations needed to safeguard the quality standards and objectives of an industrial park.

FIGURE 19

REGULATIONS FOR INDUSTRIAL BUILDINGS CONSTRUCTED IN PRIDCO'S INDUSTRIAL SUBDIVISIONS*

Contents — The purpose of these regulations is to encourage and guide the construction and the use of privately owned buildings within in-

---

*Information pertaining to Puerto Rico's development program may be obtained from the Economic Development Administration of Puerto Rico, 666 Fifth Avenue, New York, New York, 10019.

Figure 19 (continued)

dustrial subdivisions owned by the Puerto Rico Industrial Development Company. The company provides industrial subdivisions equipped with streets, sidewalks, and utilities; lots in these subdivisions will be sold to individuals or corporations for the purpose of constructing manufacturing buildings thereon, as defined on the previous page.

<u>Definitions</u>

a) <u>Industrial Subdivisions</u>. An industrial subdivision for the purpose of these regulations is defined as an improved tract of land owned by the Puerto Rico Development Company, on which buildings are constructed for the purpose of leasing or selling them to manufacturing industries.

b) <u>Manufacturing Industry</u>. A manufacturing industry is defined as an industry whose activity consists primarily of manufacturing, assembling and processing, of the kind which this company is accustomed to aid or finance.

<u>Development of Industrial Subdivisions</u>

The company develops its industrial subdivisions based on standards which are equal to or superior to the standards of the Land Subdivisions Regulation (Regulation No. 3) of the Planning Board. It constructs all streets, sidewalks, and utilities including water supply, drainage system, electric distribution system; these are carried to the front property lines of individual lots. Where a sanitary sewer system is

Figure 19 (continued)

installed, sewer will be included on the same basis; where no sanitary sewers are installed or proposed, individual sewage disposal will have to be provided by the prospective builder. Lots are graded to the street level.

Use of Buildings and Land — The buildings to be erected shall be used exclusively for manufacturing purposes, in either light or heavy industrial classifications, as the case may be; no other uses will be permitted, except that special commercial uses may be allowed for certain designated lots.

Land Coverage — Land coverage for any building shall not exceed 50 per cent of the lot area, so that proper ventilation, space for parking and circulation can be provided.

Yards — Front, rear, and side yards shall be allowed in order to provide space for ventilation, distance from other buildings, and circulation. Minimum yards are as follows: a) front yard--6 meters; b) side yards--3 meters; c) rear yard--10 per cent of lot's depth.

Height and Floor Area — The height of building to be constructed should be limited to two stories, so that the total floor space of building will not exceed an area equal to that of the lot; however, in cases where it is necessary to exceed the above-mentioned height, the lot coverage should be reduced so that the total floor space of building does

Figure 19 (continued)

	not exceed the area of the lot, as has been mentioned.
Construction and Design	No building shall be constructed with a floor area of less than 10,000 square feet, except in such cases where the lot size is considerably larger than one acre; in the latter case, the minimum size of the building may be increased up to a size to be determined by the company. Expansion of any building shall be permitted up to any size provided that the requirements of this Policy Memorandum applicable to maximum land coverage, minimum yards and the maximum heights are complied with. In any case, expansion up to 20,000 feet shall be provided for. Building construction shall be in accordance with the Building Code of Puerto Rico (Planning Board Regulation No. 7). In addition, the company reserves the right to review the construction details and the design of any building, including the structural features, and in particular the front or street elevations.
Signs	No advertising signs will be permitted. Building signs containing the name of the firm or directing attention to the business conducted on the premises will be permitted; these signs shall be placed flat against the wall and shall not exceed 10 per cent of the wall area to which they are attached, including windows and doors.

Figure 19 (continued)

Maintenance and Landscaping	It is proposed that an attractive appearance be maintained at our Industrial Subdivisions and that appropriate maintenance be provided in and around individual factories. The builder shall provide a minimum amount of landscaping in the front yards of lots and within the public area between the curb and the property line; such landscaping should include lawns, shrubbery and trees, planted by the owner and to be subsequently maintained by a tenant.
	The design and layout of landscaping done within the aforementioned public areas will be under the control of PRIDCO. This control will cover the spacing and kind of trees and the design and construction of fences, gates and other architectural features.
Off-Street Parking and Loading Space	Sufficient open area shall be allowed on the lot for off-street parking and loading space for private cars and for trucks and commercial vehicles.
	Paving within the open area shall be provided to the extent necessary to accommodate the cars and trucks of owners who are normally present in the building at any given time.
Applicable Regulations	Existing regulations adopted by the Government of the Commonwealth or any of its agencies, covering the use of land and the construction of buildings, streets, or

Figure 19 (continued)

	utilities, shall be applicable to the industrial subdivisions of this company and any buildings constructed therein; if the government regulations impose more restrictive conditions than those of this company, the requirements of the government regulations shall govern. The following government regulations may directly be applicable: Land Subdivision Regulation (Planning Board Regulation No. 3); Zoning Regulation (Planning Board Regulation No. 4); Construction Code (Planning Board Regulation No. 7). In addition, the rules and regulations of the Department of Health, the Puerto Rico Aqueduct and Sewer Authority, the Puerto Rico Water Resources Authority, and the Insular Fire Service may also be applicable.
<u>Application</u>	Any party interested in purchasing a lot shall make written application to the company giving full information, as required by the company in a form to be designed.
<u>Start of Construction</u>	A term of six months from the date of the deed or sale will be given to the purchaser to start construction of the building. After that term the company may re-acquire the land at the same price it was sold, the purchaser to absorb all expenses incurred in the transaction.
<u>Sales Procedure</u>	The selling price shall be paid in cash. Upon acceptance of the

Figure 19 (continued)

company of the application, the purchaser shall make a deposit equivalent to 5 per cent of the selling price of the lot, which the company will retain if the transaction is not closed within at least 60 days after such acceptance.

FIGURE 20

TYPICAL APPLICATION FORM FOR JOINING AN INDUSTRIAL PARK GROUP

Site Requirement Guide Outline

The information you are to furnish below is needed to provide our Planning Department with an intelligent basis for helping you in the selection of a suitable site for your project, or to help you evaluate a location tentatively selected. It is designed to protect you against any future inconvenience that could arise through faulty location, site, or building, and to protect other firms already established in your vicinity.

Please be specific in your answers. Do not give such answers as "normal for this type of operation," when you could be more specific. Please furnish information in addition to that required whenever you deem necessary. Future needs should be covered when possible.

Please sign this form when it is completed to your satisfaction. Thank you.

I. General Information:

A. Proposed local firm's name:______________

____

B. Parent firm's name and address:__________

____

Figure 20 (continued)

C. Name and address of local representative:
____
____

II. <u>Type and Activity</u>:

A. Basic product:____________________

B. Brief description of operation:________
____
____
____

C. List of machinery with individual weight and area covered by base:

____________________ ____________________
____________________ ____________________
____________________ ____________________
____________________ ____________________

III. <u>Utilities</u>:

A. Electric power requirements:

1. Maximum demand in KVA ____________
2. Total power required in horsepower ____________________________________
3. Voltage ____________
4. Phases ____________
5. Other comments____________________
____

B. Water requirements:

1. Total consumption (GPD)____________
2. Duration of this consumption (hours/day)____________________________
3. Peak rate of use (GPM)____________
4. Duration of peak use______________
5. Pressure required________________
6. Breakdown of water uses:
   a. Industrial process__________ GPD
   __________________% of total
   b. Sanitary uses______________GPD
   __________________% of total
   c. Cooling purposes____________GPD
   __________________% of total
   d. Air conditioning____________GPD
   __________________% of total

Figure 20 (continued)

e. Steam production____________GPD
_______________% of total

f. Other________________________GPD
_______________% of total

7. Special characteristics desired of water supply (purity, chemical content, temperature, salinity, etc.)
____
____
____

C. Sewer facilities:
Will your industrial plant produce any effluent other than the normal sewerage from sanitary facilities: Yes____ No___
If so, give details
1. Total volume of waste (GPD)_________
2. Duration of discharge (hours/day)
____
3. Peak rate of discharge (GPM)________
____
4. Duration of peak discharge_________
____
5. Plans for treatment of waste________
____
____
6. Submit certified copy of physico-chemical analysis of waste originated in similar plant, including:
   a. Temperature
   b. pH (alkalinity or acidity)
   c. BOD (biological oxygen demand)
   d. Total solids concentration
      1. Suspended solids
      2. Volatile solids
      3. Settleable solids
   e. Qualitative and quantitative analysis of waste.

IV. <u>Site</u>
A. Size of lot required___________________
B. Special requirements as to location (community preference, geographic orientation,

Figure 20 (continued)

climatic conditions required, proximity to waterfront, etc.)____________________
____
____

C. Subsoil conditions, indicating soil bearing capacity desired____________________
____

V. <u>Building</u>

A. Floor area____________________________
B. Type (single or multistory, flat roof, semimonitor, full monitor, etc.)________
____
C. Special requirements (floor bearing capacity, air conditioning, etc.)__________
____
D. Projected future expansion:
   1. Size______________________________
   2. Expected date______________________
E. Characteristics desired:________________
____
____

VI. <u>Characteristics of Process</u>:

A. Raw materials:
   1. Itemize materials__________________
   ____
   ____
   2. Expected source____________________
   3. Fire, explosion, or health hazards associated with materials used______
   ____
   4. Plans for storage facilities (raw materials and products)________________
   ____
B. Obnoxious conditions originated in proposed operation (dust, odors, fumes, smoke, noise, vibrations, etc.)_________
____
C. Similarly, describe possible environmental factors to which your operation may be peculiarly sensitive____________________
____

Figure 20 (continued)

D. Proposed special treatment, such as smoke abatement, floor padding, air conditioning, etc.________________

VII. <u>Labor Force</u>

A. Number of employees and sex distribution:
1. At start of operations____________
Male____________ Female__________
2. At full production______________
months after start________________
Male____________ Female__________
3. After anticipated expansion (______
months after start)______________
Male____________ Female__________

B. Number of work shifts anticipated:
1. At start of operation________
2. At full production__________

VIII. <u>Additional Comments</u>:

____
____
____
____

If the information above presents, in your opinion, a true picture of your contemplated Puerto Rican operation, and may be used by our Planning Department to determine the best possible location for your factory, please so signify by signing below.

Signature:______________
Firm:__________________
Title:_________________
Date:__________________

NOTE: This information will be handled in the strictest confidence and will not be unduly disclosed to any personnel not related to the firm or engaged in the selection of the site.

From the viewpoint of the small and medium businessman, perhaps the single greatest asset of the industrial park is that it enables him to conserve his cash position by not buying a building outright. Being able to rent or enter into a lease purchase arrangement over an extended period of time enables him to put the money otherwise required for a building into machinery and inventory. Traditionally, businessmen desire to own their own building and plant, but the formative years of most businesses are a drain on ready cash. The purchase of costly fixed-capital assets can well break the small company. The typical lease-sale arrangement has great appeal for the small- and medium-sized businessman as it enables him to have his cake and eat it too by actually purchasing his building in small payments over an extended period of time.

Readily available advisory services in such areas as law and accounting are considered very important by the small company. Sharing the costs of these and other similar services lowers the net cost to the small business.

Entering an industrial park confers a prestige element which is especially important to a new company. This is especially true if the other tenants selected are "quality companies." An important consideration is the appearance of the park. A good-looking, well-landscaped park can make a considerable impression on visitors and increases the pride of the tenants in being part of the park.

A factor often overlooked is the opportunity for the entrepreneur to exchange ideas and suggestions with other entrepreneurs in a wide variety of different types of businesses. Our small- and medium-sized businessman hopes to gain ideas from his park neighbors which will help him in his own business. In most estates, a certain warm camaraderie exists among the businessmen in the park which is stimulating and quite noticeable.

Finally, there is the feeling of working with other companies that have the same problems. There is a feeling of belonging, and the knowledge that jointly the entrepreneur and his neighbors can face the difficulties of economic life in the developing countries with more confidence than would be possible alone.

Notes to Chapter 9

1. William Bredo, Industrial Estates--Tool for Industrialization, Glencoe, Ill., Free Press, 1960, p. 63.

2. Ibid.

3. The source for much of the material and outline structure for this chapter comes from an AID-sponsored study to determine the feasibility of creating an industrial park in Arequipa, Peru. The study was conducted by Stanford Research Institute under the guidance of Dr. Carlton R. Wood. The study, titled The Arequipa Industrial Park, was done in 1964.

4. Ibid.

5. Ibid.

6. Ibid.

CHAPTER 10 PROMOTIONAL AIDS

A general investment prospectus, sometimes referred to as a country brochure, is a useful reference, containing under one cover all the information which the prospective investor needs. Ideally, the prospectus does not exceed twenty-five or thirty pages; it has an attractive cover, and color pictures. Light in weight, it may also be used as a mailing piece to prospective investors. It also serves as a handy give-away document for any prospective investor or visiting student from abroad wishing to learn more of the country.

While the information contained in the investment prospectus is usually of a general nature, it serves to arouse the curiosity of the investor and serves as "the country's salesman." In most developing countries, such brochures can be very helpful if carefully assembled. Conway Research, Inc., of Atlanta, Georgia, specializes in the preparation of this specific type of prospectus for such countries as Honduras, Guatemala, Nicaragua, El Salvador, Costa Rica, Peru, and Colombia. Conway Research has also done a brochure on Central America as a whole.

The prospectus, which is a basic promotional aid, will generally include the following items:

(1) A picture of the president or chief of state of the country.
(2) A map of the country, along with a brief description of the country, its history, and its people.

(3) A population chart showing population by region within the country.
(4) A map showing geographical location of country in relation to neighboring countries.
(5) A current list of investment opportunities within the country, by type of industry.
(6) An economic profile of the country which includes: area, population, the capital and its population, gross national product, per capita income, principal exports, principal imports, electric output, banking system, and current monetary-exchange rate.
(7) List of hourly wage rates in selected industry.
(8) A list of the better-known companies and/or subsidiaries doing business within the country.
(9) A profile of the common market into which the country falls.
(10) A list of the requirements for doing business in the country.
(11) A tax breakdown showing various exemptions granted by law.
(12) A map showing principal roads, airports, ports, and jet facilities.
(13) The names, addresses, and pictures of the key development personnel in the country, along with a brief history of their organization.
(14) Pictures of typical companies currently operating in the country.
(15) Several pictures showing public buildings, parks, beaches, etc.
(16) Pictures and description of any industrial park.

A regional prospectus deals more specifically with one section of a country. While its structure and outline tends to follow that of the country prospectus, the focus is on the region, and its advantages over other sections of the country are highlighted.

A typical regional prospectus should include:

(1) A general description of the country as a whole.
(2) A general description of the over-all economy of the country.
(3) A description of industrial history in the country.
(4) A brief description of the economic climate for foreign investment in the country.
(5) A brief description of labor and its capabilities.
(6) A description of the tax structure as it pertains to industry.
(7) A specific detailed economic description of the regional area and how it fits into the country as a whole.
(8) A description of transport facilities available.
(9) A list of the specific factors affecting the region or community; i.e., wage rates, labor availability and cost, availability of technical schools, industrial land and building costs, raw material availability, present industry in the area, and service industries.
(10) The geography and climate of the area.
(11) A general description of the community as a place to live, including health conditions, housing, schools and churches, cultural activities, and recreational facilities.
(12) A chart of communication ties to other parts of the country and other important cities throughout the world.
(13) A section on any special tax legislation for the area.
(14) A section on any special labor legislation affecting the area.
(15) A list of investment opportunities in the region.

While all the above items are important, each item will have to be considered separately for each region. No two factors have the same weight in different localities, and the above list is merely a suggested outline.

While the General Country Prospectus and the Regional Prospectus are two main promotional aids to the developer, many communities have had good luck in their developmental efforts through the use of pamphlets and fliers. The Puerto Rican Economic Development Administration has turned out such widely assorted fliers as "A List of Private School Facilities in Puerto Rico," "Recreational Organizations in Puerto Rico," "Labor Availability in Puerto Rico by Municipalities," "Information on Trucking Service and Rates," and "U.S. Firms Operating Plants in Special Incentive Zones." These simple, inexpensive (usually one sheet) giveaways are good eye catchers, and especially appropriate for handouts at airports, railroad stations, and hotel rooms. While their cost is minimal, they tend to focus attention on one aspect of the investor's possible interest. The Puerto Rican Economic Development Commission has also developed attractive brochures to promote specialized industry such as electronics and light metal products. Having succeeded in attracting these industries, they deal from strength, and focus in these brochures on points of special interest to the prospective electronics or metal manufacturer.

In seeking to build up an arsenal of "handouts," banks and utility companies should always be asked to assist. The banks and the utilities have much to gain through industrial development, and they often have the staff and facilities to turn out brochures and pamphlets at little or no cost to the development group.

Even a sign can serve as an effective promotional aid. Every hotel, bus, taxi, airport, and train should have in some conspicuous place a sign with the name and address of the institution within the country responsible for industrial development work. The businessman on vacation may often be interested in combining business with pleasure. Signs cost very little and can be quite effective.

Every promotion budget should have some money earmarked for advertising and press releases. While it is extremely difficult to assess the value of this type of promotion, a limited amount can do no harm. It is good for the morale of the country and personnel of the development institution, if nothing else. A kind of advertising that has become quite popular among the developing countries are advertising supplements in the Sunday issue of The New York Times. In The New York Times of July 25, 1965, the Liberian Development Corporation came out with a sixteen-page supplement in color on the advantages of investing in Liberia. The supplement stressed such factors as a growing market, currency stability, stable government, investment incentives, and establishment of a new industrial park.

The supplement also devoted space to selling Liberia as a tourist attraction. This type of advertising has sometimes been called "general advertising" or "shotgun advertising" as opposed to specific "rifle approach" to a particular prospective investor. Unless the developing country has substantial funds, promotion money might best be spent on the so-called rifle approach of seeking out specific investors for a specific project.

In the final analysis, an investment opportunity must be brought together with the capital necessary to launch the venture. If this fusion does not take place, nothing happens. The world is full of projects that never got off the ground because an appropriate investor could not be found. Once a project has been unearthed, an immediate, intensive search for the "right" investor should be started. Time is of the essence, for the statistics in the pre-feasibility study or the feasibility study that are accurate today may not be accurate tomorrow. Furthermore, a "shopworn" project loses interest for the customer. It is therefore essential that the right customer be found as quickly as possible.

How to go about finding the right investor depends on the project itself and the amount of money required, as well as the technology involved. If a steel mill is involved, obviously it is not a small private investor that is wanted. Similarly, if an investment of $10,000 is needed, the Chase Manhattan

Bank is not the place to apply. As a matter of fact, they would probably prefer not to be troubled with investments of this size, for their interest lies for perfectly good economic reasons in large loans. On the other hand, there are some general guide lines that might well be followed in a search for an investor, large or small.

First, once the project is in salable form, discreet inquiries should be made through local financial circles to determine if local money is available, either on a country or regional basis. It would seem self-evident, and it certainly is within the accepted policy of most governments today, that private investment should come as far as possible from inside the developing countries. If the project is a sound one requiring modest sums of money, such money can usually be found.

A second fruitful approach is through the various economic counselors of embassies in the country who know of nationals of their respective countries who may be looking for good investments.

A third approach may be made through one of a growing group of management consulting firms in the developing countries. The names of these concerns can be obtained from the AID missions and embassies of most countries, or through the chambers of industry and commerce. A word of caution is in order as to the selection of the consultant. While many are highly reputable, having close affiliations with U.S. and foreign European companies with high reputations, it is not unusual to find a number of concerns whose practices might not be considered completely ethical.

Depending on the project, one of the International Banks may be approached.

Many enterprising entrepreneurs seeking technical assistance, joint venture capital, or complete financing, have found it worth their while to come to New York to visit the Chase Bank, the Hanover, or the Morgan Guaranty, which are three U.S. banks interested in the foreign investment field. One advantage to this approach is that it gives the potential investor the chance to meet and talk with able, experienced people in the financial field who may have a customer or contact that would find the proposal interesting, in case his own bank is not interested. There is no substitute for this direct approach when other channels are not available within a developing country.

Another avenue of contact with potential investors is through the large, well-known investment houses. Again, the brokers may not be interested, or for legal reasons they may not be able to invest in the proposition, but they would have numerous contacts that might be interested.

Another channel to be pursued is through one of the growing number of independent private lending sources. A representative list of these institutions is given in Figure 21.

FIGURE 21

TYPICAL PRIVATE LENDING SOURCES

INLAND CREDIT CORPORATION	200 Park Avenue, New York, New York
C. V. STARR & CO., INC.	102 Maiden Lane, New York, New York
EXCHANGE PLACE CORPORATION	20 Exchange Place, New York, New York
AMERICAN UNION TRANSPORT INC.	17 Battery Place, New York, New York
SINGER AND FRIEDLANDER LTD.	20 Cannon Street, London E. C. 4, England

Figure 21 (continued)

ATLANTIC FINANCING LTD.	Othmarstr. 8, Zurich, Switzerland
THE DELTEC BANKING CORP. LTD.	P. O. Box 29, Nassau, Bahamas

Any one or several of these avenues might prove to be appropriate in the search for the right investor. While investors are not hiding under every rock, they are around, and a well-planned, sincere search with a sound project in hand will usually result in success.

CHAPTER 11 SERVICES FOR INVESTORS

In approaching a potential investor, the direct approach is usually more effective than the generalized approach.

For example, when the project has been completely conceived (prefeasibility condition) and the investors have been pinpointed, the president of the country might write a personal letter to the individual selected, inviting him and his family to visit the country as the president's personal guest to inspect the investment directly. Alternatively, a similar letter might be written by the president of a regional development corporation. The main purpose of any tpe of approach is a visit from the potential investor, and letters of this type have had great impact, provided that effective project presentation and appropriate investor selection have been made.

The following specific services should be made available to the potential investor, large or small, by the development or promotion institutions:

(1) Helping to identify industrial investment possibilities.
(2) Preparing prefeasibility studies for these investment opportunities.
(3) Identifying potential local investors and assisting in "selling" the local investors on the possibilities of joint ventures.
(4) Tax exemptions, dealing with government bureaucracy, arranging for meetings, hotel reservations, plane reservations, etc.

(5) Searching out qualified local personnel for the operation.
(6) Recommending competent legal and accounting help. The investor, who is strange to the country and unaware of local legal matters, will usually be particularly appreciative of any help in this area.
(7) Finding suitable land for his plant.
(8) Helping to obtain loans from the commercial and government banks. While the investor may bring his money with him, there will be times when he will have to avail himself of the local money market.
(9) Making contacts with building and construction companies, insurance companies and machinery suppliers.
(10) Assisting socially. A promotion organization would be well advised to make sure that the wife of the visiting prospective investor has all of her questions about schools, hospitals, churches, etc., answered.
(11) Many development organizations in developing countries provide "one-stop-shopping." They offer a "package deal" to the investor, wherein he is provided with the investment opportunity and also the opportunity to borrow money and to obtain equity financing through the same institution. He is also supplied all the other services listed.
(12) In many developing countries, rotating committees of local businessmen operate on an ad hoc basis to serve as guides and suppliers of information to the visiting investors. Members of the local business committees from the banks and utilities, or members of the chambers of commerce can be effective in making the visitor "feel at home with one of his own kind" during his stay in the country.

PROMOTION OFFICES IN THE UNITED STATES

A number of institutions in developing countries have found it worthwhile to establish promotion offices in the United States. Two such offices have been established by Nicaragua and El Salvador in New York City. In both of these offices the investment is modest, and the operation is headed by one carefully selected individual assisted by one or two secretaries. An operation of this nature lends itself to the direct "rifle approach," as "the man on the scene" can appropriately visit any prospective investor on his home ground. This has a double advantage in that while the industrial promoter is presenting his story, he has an opportunity to take a close look at the investor, his company, and its operation.

There are a number of additional advantages in that useful contacts can be made with investment houses, banks, and insurance companies, and it gives the developing countries an opportunity to keep abreast of economic developments in one of the largest potential supply sources of capital and technical skills in today's world.

U.S. Government Services for Investors[1]

The government of the United States, through the Agency for International Development (AID), attempts to encourage overseas investment by U.S. companies in the developing countries of the world as a part of its policy to foster and promote the participation of private enterprise in foreign economic development. Three important services rendered by AID for U.S. investors are the maintenance of a catalogue of investment opportunities, an investment survey program, and the investment guarantee program.

Over the years, AID and other public international and private institutions, including banks, foundations, and firms, have sponsored many industrial and economic feasibility studies in the developing nations. Unfortunately, this information had been scattered so that it is not readily found. AID has brought these studies together, and has abstracted the principal data and printed it on Keysort (R) cards in a catalogue of investment opportunities.

When the catalogue was started in 1964, it had approximately 1,500 cards containing valuable information on such items as capital required, markets, projected sales, production, and finance. Certain data have also been coded so that by a simple mechanical sorting procedure, only those cards of particular interest can be selected. For example, if an investor is interested in opportunities for manufacturing metal-working machinery, Standard Industrial Classification (S.I.C.) Code 354, in Central America, he may select only the relevant cards, or he could refine his selection even further by selecting the same category of opportunities by sales volume.

The catalogue has been criticized as listing only "shopworn" projects with no appeal; this is a valid criticism in some instances. However, some of these projects are "live" ones, and well worth investigating. At best, one may find a "world beater," and at worst he will end up with a wealth of information which may well be invaluable in an investment decision.

Individuals or firms wishing to examine the catalogue may do so in the U.S. Department of Commerce Field Offices or in the Office of Development Finance and Private Enterprises, Agency for International Development, New State Department Building, Washington, D.C.; AID Missions in various developing countries also have partial sets of the catalogue.

An index to the catalogue has been published as a ready reference, which identifies each investment opportunity by country and by industry. Copies of the index may be obtained by writing directly to the Office of Development Finance and Private Enterprise.

Each of the original feasibility and economic studies abstracted in the catalogue has also been reproduced on microfilm. Accordingly, an individual interested in obtaining an original copy of the report may do so by ordering it at the cost listed in the index.

AID has evolved a program to encourage potential investors to investigate specific investment opportunities. Under this plan, if the prospective investor makes the investment, he bears all the expenses of the survey and retains exclusive rights to the information derived from the study. On the other hand, if he does not make the investment, and if he has complied with the participation agreement, he is entitled to payment from AID of 50 per cent of the cost of the survey. The survey then becomes the property of the U.S. Government.

AID participation in an investment survey in no way implies that the U.S. Government will render further financial assistance.

Citizens of the U.S. or any corporation, partnership, or other association substantially owned by U.S. citizens are eligible to participate in the AID investment survey program. The survey may be made by the potential investor or by a qualified independent contractor engaged by him.

AID must assure itself that there are reasonable prospects that an investment will be made and that the proposed investment will be consistent with AID's objective of developing sound private sector enterprise.

The survey will usually include an analysis of the potential market, plant location, raw materials availability, local supply, availability of qualified personnel, financial soundness, capital requirements, potential, and contributions to the host country's economy.

In general, surveys of extraction opportunities (i.e., oil, gas, ore, or other minerals), are not eligible for AID survey help.

If the investment survey is acceptable to AID, it will agree to pay the prospective investor an amount not to exceed 50 per cent of the total allowable costs of the survey. Survey costs may include the normal salaries of survey team personnel while assigned to the survey, travel and subsistence expenses, consultant fees, and other approved expenses directly allowable to the survey. This applies only if the investor does not make the investment. If the investor decides to invest in the project, no payment is made by AID, and the investor maintains all rights to the results of the survey.

Inquiries (there is no special application form) should be addressed to Investment Survey Branch, Office of Development Finance and Private Enterprise, AID, Department of State, Washington, D.C. 20523.

The letter of inquiry-application should be submitted in quadruplicate, at least thirty days prior to the contemplated start of the survey, and should include the following information:

(1) The applicant's full legal name, address, type of organization (corporation or partnership, etc.), and the country in which organized or incorporated, together with a statement as to the percentage of ownership interest and voting rights held by U.S. citizens.

(2) A description of the projected investment that indicates the estimated size and form of the investment and the tentative plan for capitalization, including the anticipated equity to be invested by the applicant.

(3) A statement indicating the ability of the potential investor to finance the investment opportunity to be surveyed.

(4) The names and qualifications of persons who will conduct the survey.

(5) The scope and estimated cost of the survey in the form of a budget identifying the principal elements and costs. The budget should be sufficiently detailed to show the names and titles of persons for whom reimbursement will be sought for personal

services, their current rate of remuneration, the number of days they are to be employed, and an extension of this detail to subtotals and over-all total. Expenses for other than personal services should be listed under a separate heading in the budget and the method of calculation explained. Estimates of per diem costs should also be detailed to show for whom such amounts are estimated, the number of days involved, and the total amount of cost for this category of expenditure.

(6) The proposed time schedule, including the expected start of the survey, expected completion of the survey, and the date by which the investment decision will be made.

(7) Proposed plans for the implementation of the investment project.

(8) To the extent known, relationship of investment project to the over-all economy and development program of the cooperating country.

The U.S. Government through AID seeks to increase investment by United States private enterprise in the economies of friendly developing countries by guaranteeing investors against certain political and business risks.

The purpose of the guarantee program is to encourage and facilitate those private U.S. investments abroad which further the economic development of the developing countries. Accordingly, guarantees are normally available only for new investment. Guarantees are also available for additions to existing investments.

Currently there are three investment guarantee programs: (1) specific political risk guarantees against inconvertibility of foreign currency, expropriation or confiscation, and losses due to war, revolution, or insurrection; (2) extended risk guarantees which cover up to 75 per cent of both political and business risks; and (3) extended risk guarantees covering up to 100 per cent of losses on pilot or demonstration private housing projects.

This study touches only on the more important aspects of each of the three guarantees, but more details can be obtained by writing for the "Investment Guaranty Handbook," which may be obtained without cost from the Office of Development Finance and Private Enterprise, AID.

Specific Political Risk Program

The specific political risk guarantee program has been in operation for approximately seventeen years. Guarantees are now available in more than fifty-five of the developing countries. Some of the countries of the world have one guarantee, some have two, and some cover all three of the following political risks: the inability to convert into dollars foreign currency representing earnings on, sale of, or return of, capital; loss due to expropriation or confiscation; and loss due to war, revolution, or civil insurrection.

Obviously, protection for the American investor in these three areas is quite an inducement for overseas investments. While it is difficult to pinpoint the results of the guarantee program, it is safe to assume that millions of dollars have been invested in the developing countries as a result of the security afforded by the specific political risk program.

The investment guarantees result from an agreement between the United States and a foreign government. This agreement generally governs the administration of the investment guarantee program for projects approved by the host government. The United States is attempting to arrange for all three parts of the risk program included in all its contracts with other countries.

After an agreement has been signed with the government and the investment guarantee program is put into effect, guarantees are issued to the investor in the form of a contract between the investor and AID. The guarantee is backed by the full faith and credit of the United States Government. Standard forms of contract are available in printed form from the Office of Development Finance and Private Enterprise in AID, Washington.

To be eligible for guarantees, the investment must be made by an American citizen or a corporation, partnership, or other association created under the laws of the United States or any state or territory, and substantially and officially owned by citizens of the United States. Ordinarily, a company organized under United States law will be considered an eligible investor if more than one half the total value of its stock is owned by United States citizens.

Whether equity, loans, credits, royalties, or leasing arrangements, eligible investments may be made in the following forms:

Cash: If cash is to be invested, it must be in dollars, credits in dollars, or foreign currency purchased with dollars for the purpose of investment, or otherwise acquired or owned by the investor and transferable into dollars.

Materials or Equipment: Both new and used materials or equipment may be considered investment contributions. Material or equipment will ordinarily be valued at its depreciated original cost to the investor, including transportation.

Patents, Processes or Techniques: To encourage the spread of technology, under some circumstances these so-called intangible assets may also be eligible for guarantees.

Services: As a rule, engineering and management services are considered investments only when performed in conjunction with the transmission of other eligible investments, such as processes and techniques, and provided that such services are not to be currently and separately paid for.

Loan Guarantees: Guarantees of repayment given by investors on loans made by financial institutions may also be eligible investments.

Long-Term Suppliers Credit: The extension of long-term credit by equipment suppliers may also be eligible for guarantees in certain cases.

In general, projects must be approved by AID as furthering the economic development and productive capacities of an economically developing country. This includes most projects which promote trade, increase production, raise standards of living, and improve technical efficiency.

At present there is no restriction as to size of investments which may be guaranteed against specific political risks. Most of the guarantees run into millions of dollars, but some have been written for as little as $1,000. Guarantee contracts usually are written for a maximum term of twenty years from the date of issuance.

Before any investment guarantee contract is issued by AID to the investor, he must secure approval from the foreign government for the inclusion of his project under the investment guarantee agreement between the foreign government and the United States.

It is the investor's responsibility to present to the foreign government the plan and details of his investment, to fulfill the foreign government's requirements regarding the investment, and to request that the foreign government send to U.S. AID Mission or to the American Embassy its written approval of the project for investment guarantee purposes.

When the investor has obtained approval from the foreign government for his project, and when the terms of the proposal are clearly understood and determined by AID to meet the established criteria for investment guarantees, he will be sent a contract for review. After agreement is reached on the terms of the contract, both the contract and the application are submitted to the administrator of AID or his delegate for final approval. If approved, the guarantee contract is then executed on behalf of the United States Government by AID.

A fee is charged of 0.5 per cent of the amount of each of the three coverages in force in any given contract year. There is also an annual fee of 0.25 per cent of the amount of each standby coverage--that is, the difference between the amount in force and the maximum amount which the investor may not yet have put in force on each of the three coverages.

When a prospective investor has decided to make the investment, he may file an application for an investment guarantee. Such an application need not be complete, but should contain the basic facts regarding his proposed investment. Application forms are available upon request from the Office of Development Finance and Private Enterprise, AID, Washington, D.C.

Where it is desirable for an investor to make an investment or to enter into a firm commitment to do so, he may request that AID issue an assurance against prejudice on the application. Such an assurance, sometimes called a "waiver" letter, provides that the investor may proceed with his investment plans or enter into contracts without prejudicing his application for guarantee. This assurance is usually valid for one year but may be extended for successive one-year periods upon request and demonstration of the need for an extension.

This assurance does not commit AID to issue a guarantee contract, nor does it indicate that the foreign government will necessarily approve the project; it does avoid any subsequent objection that the application is untimely.

The Extended Risk Guarantee Program

In certain priority situations, AID may offer United States investors guarantee coverage against any and all risks except fraud or misconduct. AID may cover up to 75 per cent of the investor's risks in investments other than housing and up to 100 per cent in certain housing investments.

AID is interested in investment situations falling under the following categories: loans by professional lending organizations, such as banks, insurance companies, and Edge Act companies to priority projects where a responsible party is prepared to assume a true risk of loss and asks the United States to share in that risk; investments by U.S. companies in industries important to the economic development of the country, in which a substantial equity investment is subordinated to the loan for which the guarantee is requested; investments in priority projects so affected by prevailing political and physical instability in the project country that private investment would not be made without the stimulus of an extended risk guarantee; and prospective investments where use of the extended risk authority might not otherwise be justified, but where the particular investment can yield some substantial benefit to the developing country, such as the planned distribution of ownership of the company on a wider basis in the project country, or construction of housing for workers.

To be eligible, the investor must be a U.S. citizen, a corporation, partnership, or other association created under the laws of the United States or any state or territory, and substantially owned by U.S. citizens.

Formal agreements enabling the U.S. to offer extended risk guarantee coverage have now been reached with over thirty of the developing countries. Specific approval may be obtained on specific priority projects in other countries as well.

The investment must be in a private business enterprise or private institution, although partial government ownership will not in itself disqualify the enterprise. It must be of good repute, have demonstrable management capabilities, and have sufficient capital invested so that, together with the new guarantee financing, it will be able to operate on a sound financial basis. To the extent that the proposed project involves economic, technical, and financial planning, such planning must be completed.

In determining the eligibility of a project, consideration is given to the relationship between the project and the plans and programs of the project country, the priority of the project, and its potential effect (including the balance-of-payments effect, if any) on the local and U.S. economies. Emphasis will also be placed on projects which further social progress and the development of small business enterprises which might not go forward without the guarantee.

AID gives the following guarantees for loans by institutional lenders:

The lender's loss from any cause will not exceed a specified per cent (normally 25 per cent) of the uncollected principal of the loan.

The lender will have the obligation to take reasonable steps to exercise its right of collection.

A guarantee will not be assignable without the consent of AID.

The guarantee will not insure against any loss arising out of fraud or misconduct of the lender.

Periodic reports to AID and prompt notification of defaults will be required.

Disputes under the Guarantee Agreements may be settled by arbitration.

The terms of the guarantee will not exceed twenty years. The guarantee may be terminated at any time at the option of the lender.

The guarantee will be a contractual obligation of the United States. It will not be subject to unilateral termination or modification by the United States except for good cause, such as a breach of guarantee or covenant by the investor.

The borrower will be required to carry the customary commercial insurance such as fire and liability.

AID will charge an annual fee of up to 2 per cent of the guarantee portion of the investment. Where the maximum guarantee coverage under the contract is not required during any year (i.e., before the loan is fully drawn down), a partial standby fee will be charged. Investors may elect to supplement this coverage by using the specific risk program to cover losses over 75 per cent of the investment that may be caused by the specific political risk.

General inquiries on an application for extended risk coverage (except for Latin America) should be directed to Office of Development Finance and Private Enterprise, Agency for International Development, Department of State, Washington, D.C. 20523. Inquiries on applications for coverage for Latin American investments should be made directly to the Office of Capital Development, Bureau of Latin America, Agency for International Development, Department of State, Washington, D.C.

It is strongly recommended that prospective investors make personal visits to AID to discuss their investment in detail with AID representatives before collecting or filling out extensive documentation for their request.

Guarantee for Housing Investments

AID has authority to guarantee coverage up to 100 per cent of investments in demonstration or pilot housing projects.

The program is intended to stimulate private home ownership for middle- and lower-income families by means of guarantees of long-term, mortgage-type financing of housing projects along the lines of the U.S. Federal Housing Administration programs. It is modified to suit conditions in countries where such local long-term financing is not normally available.

Only applications for new housing may be considered, and guarantees may not be granted for investment in rental housing projects.

Guarantees for housing projects are limited to investments made by U.S. citizens, or business entities which are substantially owned by U.S. citizens.

Prospective investors should check with AID to ascertain the eligibility or ineligibility of particular countries in which they are interested.

To be eligible for a housing guarantee, an investment must be in the form of a ten to twenty-year loan to finance mortgages.

No individual guarantee may exceed $5 million.

Guarantees will usually be in the amount of 100 per cent of the principal amount of the loan investment.

Individual mortgage loans made from the proceeds of a guaranteed investment must be held and serviced by an experienced non-U.S. administrator or subsidiary in the country involved.

A fee based upon the amount of the investment guaranteed will be charged by AID for the guarantee. This fee will be between 1 and 2 per cent per annum of the average outstanding balance of the guaranteed investment.

Inquiries regarding housing guarantees should be directed to the appropriate AID Regional Bureau in Washington.

Notes to Chapter 11

1. Much of the information about U.S. Government services for investors is taken from *Memo to American Businessmen: Aids to Overseas Investments*, published by AID. This handbook may be obtained by writing to the Office of Development Finance and Private Enterprise, AID, Washington, D.C. 20523.

PART IV

SOURCES OF FINANCING

CHAPTER 12 THE WORLD BANK FAMILY

Many entrepreneurs never launch their proposed projects because they do not know where to get financial backing. Similarly, many projects, however well launched, fizzle out like spent skyrockets before they attain maturity, for the same reason.

The World Bank family includes the International Bank for Reconstruction and Development (IBRD), commonly known as the "World Bank"; the International Development Association (IDA); and the International Finance Corporation (IFC).

INTERNATIONAL BANK FOR RECONSTRUCTION AND DEVELOPMENT (WORLD BANK)

The International Bank for Reconstruction and Development (IBRD) was conceived at the Bretton Woods Economic Conference in 1944. As a specialized agency of the United Nations, it was originally designed to mobilize capital for the reconstruction of countries devastated by World War II and to assist the economies of the developing countries of the world.

Located at 1818 H Street, Washington, D.C., the World Bank is today one of the principal sources of funds for developing countries and the single largest source of multilateral lending aid.

The Bank loans to member governments for such purposes as construction, electric power, transportation, communications, agriculture, forestry, industry, water supply, and general development.

The Bank averages about three loans a month. Between 1946 and 1965 it made 424 loans for a total dollar value of almost $9 billion to some seventy-seven different member countries.[1]

Of this amount, more than $7 billion was loaned in the areas of electric power, transportation, and industry.

As of June 30, 1965, the emerging countries of Africa had received developmental loans totaling $1,132,450,000; Asia and the Middle East, $3,086,620,000; Australia, $417,730,000; New Zealand, $40,300,000; Europe, $2,005,757,893; and the Latin American countries, approximately $2.25 billion.

By any lending standards, the World Bank loans are large. Of the 424 loans mentioned above, only 92 fell in the $5 million or less range, while 158 loans were for $20 million or more. During the same period, five loans were made of over $100 million each.

The World Bank obtains funds for its operations from capital subscribed by more than one hundred member countries, from the sale of its bonds in the various world markets, and from earnings on its operations. In addition, income is generated from the sale of portions of the Bank's loans to other investors. The World Bank normally finances only the foreign-exchange requirements for specific projects, and does not normally cover local expenditures or provide working capital.

The World Bank, like most banks, expects its loans to be paid back, and accordingly has patterned its banking practices after the best practices of private lending institutions. Before considering a loan, the Bank always satisfies itself that the proposed project is feasible and sound. Normally, the Bank will not loan to a borrower who could obtain the loan from private sources on reasonable terms. A loan from the World Bank carries with it a happy combination of good advice, occasional technical assistance, and, most important, a certain prestige, which gives the borrower a good credit rating.

Most of the Bank loans which have been made to governments have been for infrastructure-type programs of electrical energy and transportation, but "the Bank has always sought to promote the development of private industry. In some cases, it has made loans directly to private industries, contributing to projects such as the production of steel in India, iron mining in Mauretania, and the manufacture of paper in Chile, Finland, and Pakistan. The Bank has also been able to channel funds to private industrial firms in member countries through loans to national development banks which use World Bank funds for their own re-lending operations."[2]

"In the fiscal year 1953-54, the World Bank and the IFC continued their support of industrial finance companies, and committed more than $50 million to create or strengthen companies of this kind."[3]

Over the years, World Bank loan interest rates have varied from 3-6 per cent and have had a maturity geared to the individual loan needs (generally fifteen to twenty-five years). They are "hard loans"--that is, they are repayable in the currency loaned. A significant aspect of the Bank's lending is that, as an independent international organization, its loans are not hampered by reasons of political or commercial convenience. Further, they are not tied to the purchase of goods or services in the lending countries; the borrowers are free to spend the proceeds of their loans in any of the Bank's member countries.

The Bank also runs an economic development institute which offers advanced training in economic management for senior officials of developing countries and territories to enable them to cope more effectively with their responsibilities when they return home. The Bank also helps to mediate international disputes. Its strong international ties and stature have been called upon during the Suez crisis and the India-Pakistan dispute concerning the Indus Waters.

A private company contemplating a loan request to the World Bank should consult with its own government first, for before any loan can be made to an individual company, the borrower's government must guarantee the loan.

INTERNATIONAL DEVELOPMENT ASSOCIATION (IDA)

The IDA, an important member of the World Bank family, came to life as an important lending institution in the fall of 1960. By the end of that year it had total resources of $852 million and thirty-seven member countries supporting its aims.[4]

Under its Articles of Agreement, members of the association are divided into two groups: Part 1 countries, which are those more advanced economically; and Part 2 countries, the less-developed countries. Part 1 countries make an initial payment of 23 per cent and pay the balance in four equal annual installments; all these funds are convertible and usable by the IDA for loans. Part 2 countries make payments on the same installment basis; but of the total only 10 per cent--half paid initially and the rest in four installments--are convertible funds. The remainder is paid in each member's own currency and cannot be used for IDA lending to other countries without the member's consent.[5]

The *raison d'être* for the formation of the IDA is the increasing burden of debt service being carried by many of the developing countries. They need and can absorb more development funds, but find themselves with many loans on the books with unsuitable short-term maturities of three to five years. "This problem of the debt burden has been made still more difficult for most of the developing countries by the general decline in prices of export products upon which they depend to finance the service of their overseas debts."[6] The *U.S. News and World Report* recently reported that debt-service requirements absorbed 12 per cent of their export earnings in 1964 and noted that debt service in the developing countries is rising at the rate of 10 per cent a year.[7]

The 1964-65 Annual Report of the World Bank and the IDA, assessing the seriousness of the debt-servicing problem, notes: "For the developing countries as a whole, total service payments on public and publicly guaranteed debt with a maturity of one year and over are estimated at about $3.5 billion in 1964. A large portion of this outstanding debt consists of medium- and short-term maturities. If allowance is made for the liquidation of commercial arrears and similar short-term obligations, aggregate debt service payments may easily have amounted, in 1964, to well over $4 billion."[8]

In order to ease this problem of debt servicing, the IDA makes long-term loans, or credits of fifty years. "All IDA credits are made to the governments concerned, on identical terms: no principal repayments are to be made for the first ten years; thereafter 1 per cent per annum is repayable for the next ten years and 3 per cent per annum is repayable for the final thirty years. The credits are free of interest, but a service charge of 3/4 of 1 per cent per annum is payable on the amounts withdrawn and outstanding, to meet the administrative costs of IDA."[9]

IDA credits are repayable in convertible currencies. Due to the very favorable terms involved, they are much sought after. With such a low rate of return on its funds, IDA is in no position to finance borrowings from the private capital markets of the world as the World Bank does, nor is it probable that it will accumulate substantial amounts of lendable earnings. Accordingly, in contrast to the Bank, it must look to the Bank and to its member countries for replenishment of its resources.

The majority of IDA members are also members of the Bank and are governed in much the same way, with voting power proportioned to initial subscription. Both organizations have the same officers and directors.

As IDA credits are basically meant to alleviate balance-of-payments problems by easing the debt-servicing requirements, they are made to governments. The IDA insists that if the funds are relent, they must be re-lent on conventional terms to revenue-producing enterprises (whether public or private).

The total of freely usable funds available to IDA from the start of its operations through June 30, 1965, amounted to $1,600 million. By this date the IDA had extended seventy-seven credits, totaling $1,086 million. Significantly, during 1964 the World Bank made a grant to the IDA of $50 million from the Bank's net income for 1963-64. It now appears likely that similar or larger amounts may be granted IDA in future years.

India and Pakistan, the largest recipients, have received credits totaling $95 million and $90 million respectively. The developing countries of Africa during the same period received approximately $63 million; Asia and the Middle East, $189 million; Europe, $39 million; and the western hemisphere nations, $18.5 million. Most of these credits were issued to the poorest of the developing countries. Bolivia, for example, received two credits, totaling $15 million.[10]

Like the World Bank, the IDA does not make small loans, although most of its credits are also for infrastructure purposes. A listing of its loans compiled by the IDA as of March 31, 1965, shows some seventy-four credits issued. Of the seventy-four, twenty-seven were in the category of $5 million or less; fifteen were in the category of $20 million or over, and the balance fell into the $5-20 million category. The largest single credit of $90 million went to India for an Industrial Imports Project.[11]

A developing country considering a credit request should be aware that the IDA is in no sense a "give-away" operation: It applies the same stringent technical and economic standards of assessing a proposed project as does the Bank. While it offers relief from balance-of-payments problems, it will not support uneconomical projects.

INTERNATIONAL FINANCE CORPORATION (IFC)

The International Finance Company completes the World Bank family. Its members, like the IDA, are largely the same as the World Bank's. The executive directors of the World Bank, appointed or elected by member governments, serve as directors of IFC, and the president of the World Bank serves ex officio as chairman of the board of IFC. IFC has its own executive vice-president, a vice-president, and an operational staff.

The IFC was established in 1956 with an authorized capital of $100 million to supplement the work of developmental financing already begun by the World Bank. Its role was conceived as being catalytic in nature, in the sense of marshaling and stimulating the use of private sector funds in the developmental process by making loans and taking equity positions. The World Bank's requirement that all loans, other than those to member governments, carry a guarantee tended to inhibit loans to private enterprise. Also, the World Bank normally finances foreign-exchange requirements only and does not cover local expenditures or provide working capital. This left a gap in the development lending process which the IFC was designed to fill. In addition, traditionally, World Bank loans have been quite large, and it has refrained from taking equity positions.

Although the original concept of the IFC was that it should be able to take equity positions, it was not until 1961 that the Articles of Agreement of the Corporation were changed to enable it to enter into the business of equity financing.

The IFC has made strong efforts to assist in sponsoring and financing joint ventures--enterprises in which local and foreign interests combine to bring local knowledge and capital together with foreign industrial experience and techniques.

TABLE 4

World Bank Loans and IDA Credits, 1964-65, by Area

(Expressed in Millions of U.S. Dollars)

	Bank Loans		IDA Credits		Total	
	Number	Amount	Number	Amount	Number	Amount
AFRICA						
Bechuanaland	–	$ –	1	$ 3.60	1	$ 3.60
Gabon	1	12.00	–	–	1	12.00
Kenya	–	–	3	10.30	3	10.30
Mauritania	–	–	1	6.70	1	6.70
Morocco	1	17.50	–	–	1	17.50
Nigeria	1	82.00	2	35.50	3	117.50
Sierra Leone	1	3.80	–	–	1	3.80
Somalia	–	–	1	6.20	1	6.20
Zambia & Rhodesia	1	7.70	–	–	1	7.70
	5	$ 123.00	8	$ 62.30	13	$ 185.30
ASIA AND MIDDLE EAST						
Afghanistan	–	$ –	1	$ 3.50	1	$ 3.50
China	2	35.00	–	–	2	35.00
India	3	134.00	2	95.00	5	229.00
Iran	2	40.50	–	–	2	40.50
Japan	3	125.00	–	–	3	125.00

Malaysia	1	$ 6.80	–	$ –	1	$ 6.80
Pakistan	–	–	3	90.79	3	90.79
Philippines	2	26.20	–	–	2	26.20
Thailand	2	28.00	–	–	2	28.00
	15	$ 395.50	6	$189.29	21	$ 584.79
EUROPE						
Finland	2	$ 42.50	–	$ –	2	$ 42.50
Italy	1	100.00	–	–	1	100.00
Portugal	1	15.00	–	–	1	15.00
Spain	1	65.00	–	–	1	65.00
Turkey	–	–	3	39.00	3	39.00
Yugoslavia	1	70.00	–	–	1	70.00
	6	$ 292.50	3	$ 39.00	9	$ 331.50
WESTERN HEMISPHERE						
Bolivia	–	$ –	2	$ 15.00	2	$ 15.00
Brazil	2	79.50	–	–	2	79.50
Chile	1	4.40	–	–	1	4.40
Honduras	1	6.00	1	3.50	2	9.50
Jamaica	1	5.50	–	–	1	5.50
Mexico	1	32.00	–	–	1	32.00
Paraguay	1	2.20	–	–	1	2.20
Peru	2	26.00	–	–	2	26.00
Uruguay	1	12.70	–	–	1	12.70
Venezuela	2	44.00	–	–	2	44.00
	12	$ 212.30	3	$ 18.50	15	$ 230.80
TOTAL	38	$1,023.30	20	$309.09	58	$1,332.39

Just as the World Bank seeks to sell portions of its loan portfolio, the IFC sells participation in its investments by private sale to private institutional investors.

Before making a loan or equity investment, the IFC satisfies itself that a proposed project will make a useful contribution to the private sector of the economy; will be a profitable project, properly engineered, managed, and financed; and is unable to secure the funds required on reasonable terms from private sources. IFC does not ordinarily exercise voting rights in respect to the shares it holds, nor does it assume responsibility for management of an investment.

Perhaps the most important role of the IFC is the promotional one of bringing investment opportunities together with domestic and foreign capital. By being able to take equity positions, it provides a base for borrowing by the corporation. In a very real sense, an "equity position" by the IFC carries with it the same prestige as a loan from the World Bank, making the investment more attractive to local development banks and local and foreign investors.

IFC usually invests in private investment opportunities which are predominantly industrial. As a matter of policy, it does not invest in the more developed of its member countries, nor does it compete with private capital where this is available for the proposed investment.

Wherever possible, IFC prefers to invest in private development banks, since they provide a more economical means of assisting small enterprises, rather than make direct private investments. Placing a high value on the work of development banks, IFC aids them with equity investments, loans, and technical assistance.

IFC does not engage in operations which are primarily for purposes of refunding, refinancing, or direct financing of exports or imports. Further, it does not invest in public utilities, real estate development, or land reclamation. It does require periodic progress reports from its loan and equity recipients, and asks for audited reports on a regular basis. The IFC is not permitted to make an investment in a country if the government of the country objects. It thus informs each member government of all proposed investments within its territories. Unlike the World Bank and the IDA, the IFC neither seeks nor accepts governmental guarantees of repayment on its investments. In general, IFC carries on its business in much the same way as a private investor.

Unlike the World Bank and the IDA, the IFC has no uniform pattern of interest rates on its loans. The interest rate in each case is fixed in relation to all the relevant circumstances, particularly the risk involved, the amount of IFC's participation, and the prospective return on its entire investment. The usual terms of IFC loans are from five to fifteen years. IFC's investments are not related to the procurement of specific equipment, and there is no requirement that the proceeds of IFC financing be spent in a particular country.

In its 1964-65 Annual Report, the IFC notes that "the commitments of $137 million made to date by IFC involved 103 transactions." Approximately $35 million has gone to steel companies and metal manufacturing enterprises making a variety of producer and consumer goods. A further $19 million of commitments have been made to pulp and paper producers. Manufacturers of construction materials, chiefly cement, have attracted nearly $17 million of IFC's commitments, while textile companies have accounted for a further $14 million. Other industries in which IFC has made substantial commitments include chemicals, food processing, and electrical goods.[12] Significantly, since its inception, IFC has also made commitments of more than $17 million in private development finance companies and is currently a shareholder in fourteen of these companies in twelve countries. Through its loans and equity positions in development finance companies, it gives much needed impetus to the relending to the small- and medium-

FIGURE 22

IFC'S INVESTMENT COMMITMENTS, 1964-65

	Loan	Equity	Total
INDUSTRIES			
ARGENTINA			
La Papelera Argentina, S.A.	$ 2,500,000	$ --	$ 2,500,000
CHILE			
Cementos Bio-Bio, S.A. (Supplemental Investment)	--	100,000	100,000
CHILE			
Fideos y Alimentos Carozzi, S.A. (Supplemental Investment)	--	153,846	153,846
COLOMBIA			
Industrias Alimenticias, Noel, S.A.	1,000,000	17,254	1,017,254
ETHIOPIA			
Cotton Company of Ethiopia, S.C.	1,500,000	1,003,778	2,503,778
FINLAND			
Huhtamaki-yhtyma Oy	700,000	99,357	799,357
GREECE			
Titan Cement Company, S.A.	1,000,000	501,672	1,501,672

Figure 22 (Continued)

	Loan	Equity	Total
MEXICO			
Compania Fundidora de Fierro y Acero de Monterrey, S.A.	$ --	$ 6,446,250	$ 6,446,250
PAKISTAN			
Crescent Jute Products, Ltd.	1,950,000	--	1,950,000
Ismail Cement Industries Ltd.	1,260,000	416,504	1,676,504
Packages Ltd.	2,310,000	840,001	3,150,001
SPAIN			
Fabrica Espanola Magnetos, S.A.	--	225,444	225,444
UGANDA			
Mulco Textiles Ltd.	2,799,409	713,629	3,513,038
DEVELOPMENT FINANCE COMPANIES			
IVORY COAST			
Banque Ivoirienne de Developpement Industriel, S.A.	--	204,081	204,081
SPAIN			
Banco del Desarrollo Economico Espanol, S.A.	--	291,911	291,911
TOTAL	$15,019,409	$11,013,727	$26,033,136

sized business which might not otherwise qualify for a loan or equity support.

In its 1964-65 Annual Report, the IFC notes that it wrote off as a loss a $300,000 loan to a company in Peru producing lightweight building material. It further states that it is running into serious trouble with an investment of $170,000 to a company in Colombia. These losses might appear to reflect to the detriment of the IFC; however, if kept to a reasonable minimum, they are healthy indications of IFC's willingness to take "calculated risks" in its development financing. Even in the most developed countries, there is no such thing as a "sure thing," and this is particularly true in developing countries. Hopefully, the IFC will continue to broaden its scope of operations and take whatever risks are necessary to further the cause of the small- and medium-sized industrial operation.

Before the IFC will consider an investment proposal, it requires certain preliminary information from the applicant. Because this information is typical of that required by most investment institutions, fourteen items are listed below.

(1) The purpose to which the proposed financing is to be applied--if new construction or purchase of equipment is involved, a brief description, including expenditure to date and an estimate of the time required for completion.

(2) The amount, source, and character of capital which is available or assured and that which is still to be raised in local and foreign currencies. The terms of such financing and plans for application of the proceeds, the amount sought from IFC, and a report of efforts which have been made to raise this capital from other sources.

(3) A description of the company, including name, address, place of business, place of incorporation, history, nature of business, and capital structure. If the company is one of a group of affiliated companies, a brief description of the group and its relationship to the company.

(4) Names, statements of financial condition, and brief biographical notes for principal stockholders, directors, and officers or managers. A description of their relationship, if any, as present or proposed suppliers and customers, including any special arrangements or plans for management, and copies of any relevant agreements.

(5) A description of present and proposed productive facilities of the company, including location, size of plant, nature of equipment, and availability of power and water.

(6) A review of the general operations of the company, including the products being produced and those to be produced, together with relevant information regarding raw materials, markets, labor, and competition. For each of the last five years, to the extent that such information exists, total net sales for each major product, the number of units sold, and sales value thereof.

(7) A report on all presently effective or pending tariffs, import quotas, market restrictions, tax exemptions, and other laws or regulations which may affect the competitive position of the company with respect to each type of product.

(8) Available copies of annual accounts and reports of auditors (including balance sheets, profit and loss statements, and any other financial statements) for the last five years, as well as copies of income tax returns and any circulars to the shareholders of the company during that period.

(9) Copies of special laws or regulations applicable to the company; copies of recent prospectuses, valuations, or other descriptive material; copies of constituent corporate documents (such as character, bylaws, articles of association) and documents on matters which may be material to the judgment of a prospective investor (e.g., loan contracts, options on shares, patent licenses, pending claims).

(10) Estimated balance sheets, as well as estimates of costs, selling prices, sales, manufacturing costs, overhead, taxes, and net profits after taxes for each of the first five years after the proposed financing is completed, showing the major assumptions upon which such estimates are based.

(11) Copies of reports or studies which may have been made by the company, consultants, or others regarding engineering costs, markets, or other relevant matters. If such reports or studies have not been made, a statement of what arrangements, if any, are contemplated for making them; particulars of any arrangements with consultants or for the provision of technical services.

(12) A statement as to whether or not the information is being supplied by the company to be financed; if not, a statement of the capacity in which the person furnishing the information is acting, including the interest, if any, which he has in the proposed financing and the company.

(13) Bank and other pertinent references.

(14) Any related pertinent information and significant facts concerning the enterprise or the proposed financing.

The importance of preparing the above information thoroughly cannot be overemphasized. Such a compilation is not only a tremendous help to the investment reviewer, but it provides the company or individual preparing the application with a valuable document in his search for financial assistance in many quarters.

Notes to Chapter 12

1. Facts About The World Bank and the International Development Association, Pamphlet (Washington, D.C.: World Bank Office of Information, June 30, 1965).

2. World Bank Group in the Americas, Pamphlet (Washington, D.C.: International Bank for Reconstruction and Development, June, 1963), p. 79.

3. World Bank and IDA Annual Report, 1963-64. A Document printed by World Bank in Washington, D.C., p. 7.

4. Eugene R. Black, Financing Economic Development, United Nations Office of Public Information, Washington, D.C. Reprint from United Nations Review, February, 1961, OPI/60.

5. The World Bank Group in the Americas, Pamphlet (Washington, D.C.: International Bank for Reconstruction and Development, June, 1963), p. 80.

6. Geoffrey M. Wilson, Vice-President of the World Bank, "World Bank Operations," A Speech from a World Bank Pamphlet, Paris, France, December 16, 1963, p. 11.

7. U.S. News and World Report, October 4, 1965, p. 95.

8. World Bank and IDA Annual Report, op. cit., p. 21.

9. Ibid., p. 58.

10. Ibid.

11. IDA, Treasurer's Department, Statement of Development Credits (March 31, 1965).

12. International Finance Corporation, Annual Report, 1964-65, Washington, D.C., p. 7.

CHAPTER 13 INTER-AMERICAN DEVELOPMENT BANK (IDB)

The Inter-American Development Bank, a relative newcomer to the field of development lending, was established in 1959 by twenty American nations--nineteen Latin American countries and the United States. Its avowed purpose is to accelerate the economic development of its member states on both an individual and a collective basis.

Since making its first loan in 1961, the Bank's loans and technical assistance have accounted for more than one-fourth of the international public development financing channeled to Latin America.[1]

The Bank's charter is quite flexible and permits a wide scope in the Bank's functions, which include: promoting the investment of public and private capital; using its own capital and funds raised in the financial markets to make loans; encouraging private investment in projects, enterprises, and activities contributing to the economic development of its member countries, and supplementing private investment when private capital is not available on reasonable terms and conditions; cooperating with member countries toward the better utilization of their resources by making their economies more complementary and fostering the orderly growth of their foreign trade; and providing technical assistance in the preparation, financing, and implementation of development plans and projects.[2]

The Bank was originally created with two separate sources of funds: its ordinary capital resources and its fund for special operations. In addition, under the terms of an agreement entered into with the U.S. Government, the Bank is the administrator of the Social Progress Trust Fund, which was established to finance social development projects in Latin America as a part of the Alliance for Progress Program.[3] These three sources of financing are sometimes referred to as the three "windows" of the Bank.

The ordinary capital resources of the Bank are authorized at $2,150 million. Of this sum, $475 million represents paid-in capital and $1,675 million represents "callable" capital.

The callable capital constitutes, in effect, a guarantee of the Bank's securities and thus enables the Bank to borrow funds in the world's capital markets. By the end of 1964, the Bank had sold six bond issues totaling $272.6 million, which was added to its ordinary capital resources.

The Bank uses these resources to make loans, which are repayable in the currency or currencies lent, for economic development projects and programs. Generally, such loans are extended for terms of from eight to twelve years, although they may range up to twenty years for economic infrastructure projects.[4]

These infrastructure-type loans are comparable to those made by the World Bank. The basic lending rate on ordinary capital loans is 6 per cent per annum on amounts disbursed, plus a commitment fee of 1 per cent on undisbursed balances. Somewhat higher rates are charged by the Bank when it lends Italian lire, German marks, and pounds sterling; these higher rates reflect the higher cost of obtaining funds in the European markets.

As of December 31, 1964, the resources of the Fund For Special Operations (the Bank's second window) amounted to $210.474 million, of which $218.921 million had been subscribed by member nations--half in U.S. dollars, and half in their respective currencies.

With this fund, the Bank makes loans on terms

and conditions suitable to the special circumstances which may arise in certain countries or with regard to certain projects. Such loans are repayable on terms and conditions which are more flexible than those applied to ordinary capital loans. Amortization periods are usually longer, interest rates are lower, and repayment may be made in the currency of the borrower's country. Terms for the most part are from ten to twenty years, with interest usually at about 4 per cent per annum. Procurement anywhere in the free world is allowed.

The Bank's third window is the Social Progress Trust Fund. This fund consists of approximately $525 million. It is used principally to provide financial and technical assistance on flexible terms and conditions, including repayment in local currency, to support the efforts of Latin America to achieve improved conditions in: land settlement and land use (including access roads), assistance to agricultural credit institutions, marketing facilities, housing for low-income groups, community water supply and sanitation facilities, and supplementary financing of facilities for higher education and advanced training related to economic and social development.

Interest rates, payable in local currency, charged on loans from the Social Progress Trust Fund vary from 1 1/4 per cent for loans to finance education, housing, and land settlement, to 2 3/4 per cent for projects such as water supply systems and sewerage. In addition to the above interest rates, a 3/4 of 1 per cent service commission, payable in U.S. dollars, is also charged to cover administrative costs.

The proceeds of the Bank's loans have been channeled chiefly into the following fields: industry and mining (26.6 per cent), agriculture (24 per cent), water supply and sewage (17.8 per cent), and housing (17.4 per cent). The remaining 14.2 per cent has been loaned in such areas as electric energy, transportation, higher education, and the financing of exports of capital goods.[5]

There are a number of similarities between the IDB and the IFC and other banks. Like the IFC, loans are generally made for financing specific projects, but loans are also made to development institutions that re-lend to small and medium industry.

The IDB, the IBRD, the IDA, and the IFC normally will not lend to the borrower when loans are available from private sources on "reasonable" terms. Traditionally, the large international banks have taken the position that they want to encourage private capital investment and lending rather than compete with the private sector.

Like the IFC, the IDB only finances projects in which the borrower is to make a substantial investment. As a general rule, it finances no more than 50 per cent of the cost of a project. In the case of loans to governments, this figure may vary in the light of the over-all development effort of the country concerned. As in the case of the IFC, the IDB does not normally seek out or require a guarantee from the government of the country in which the investment is to be made, nor will financing be made unless it meets with the approval of the host government.

The IDB is making a significant contribution in the area of financing of preinvestment studies on both a loan and a grant basis. When circumstances warrant, the IDB may assume all of the costs of the technical assistance involved in a particular project, or it may agree to include the costs of technical assistance in the loan itself. Technical assistance granted by the IDB may be given to governments, official and independent agencies of member countries, and private firms within the countries. It may include formulation of loan applications and feasibility studies as required by the IDB; preparation of national or regional economic development plans; determination of public and private sources of external financing; establishment or reorganization of national or regional financial institutions to promote economic development; and training of personnel in fields related to economic development, including administration of institutions and firms, as well as techniques pertaining to the preparation, evaluation, and implementation of specific projects.

The IDB has no special forms for either loan applications or technical assistance requests. Prospective customers are encouraged to make preliminary inquiries, either in person or by mail. On the basis of the visit or the letter, the IDB and the borrower may determine the desirability and feasibility of conducting detailed negotiations. The Bank deals directly with the borrower or his fully authorized representative. If negotiations are entered into, the IDB will require the same kind of information required by the IFC.

Notes to Chapter 13

1. Inter-American Development Bank, *Activities 1961-64*, p. v.

2. Lincoln G. Sandelin, IDB Director Loan Division, A Speech delivered before the Fifteenth Annual Convention of the Chamber of Commerce of the Americas, Miami, Florida, June 14, 1965.

3. Inter-American Development Bank, *op. cit.*, p. vi.

4. *Ibid.*

5. Sandelin, *op. cit.*

CHAPTER 14 UNITED STATES GOVERNMENT LENDING

THE EXPORT-IMPORT BANK (EXIM)

The EXIM Bank is a wholly owned government corporation which lends, guarantees, and insures where it finds reasonable assurance of repayment in dollars. It has a capital of $1 billion, it may borrow from the U.S. Treasury up to $6 billion, and it is permitted to have outstanding at any one time a maximum of $9 billion in loans, guarantees, and insurance.[1]

The EXIM Bank, whose headquarters are in Washington, D.C., has been in existence for over thirty years. For most of that time, it was the only government agency, domestic or international, that provided long-term financial assistance to other countries. Today it continues to play a major role in such lending, financing the purchase of a wide range of U.S. equipment, goods, and related services to enable private industry and governments to launch new enterprises or expand existing plants. Emergency credits to maintain the flow of U.S. exports are also made to countries faced with temporary balance-of-payments difficulties.[2]

Two recently inaugurated programs of the EXIM Bank designed to aid U.S. exporters are its unique guarantees of medium-term credits extended to exporters by commercial banks and its medium and short-term credit insurance issued in partnership with private insurance companies.

Embracing all parts of the globe, the activities of EXIM Bank are designed basically to aid in the export of U.S. goods and services. Loans issued by EXIM Bank are spent for the purchase of U.S. goods and services. Since it began its operations, the Bank's net authorizations have aggregated over $11 billion, and its disbursements, almost $10 billion.[3]

Like the IBRD, IDA, IFC, and IDB, the EXIM Bank has avoided competing with private capital and has sought its participation wherever possible.

In its major operations, the EXIM Bank makes loans in dollars and expects repayment in dollars. Like all banks, it requires reasonable assurance of repayment. Normally loans are only for specific purposes, and disbursements are made only upon proof that the purposes of the loan have been or are being carried out. The EXIM Bank does not engage in equity financing.

During the fiscal year 1964, EXIM Bank authorizations, including loans, guarantees, and insurance underwritten, totaled approximately $1.7 billion. Of this sum, $570 million were project and equipment loans; $424 million were export and commodity guarantees and credits; $744 million, export credit insurance underwritten; and the balance represented consignment insurance.[3]

The EXIM Bank has no minimum or maximum limits for its loans. Industrial loans have had a tendency to fall in the wide range of $5,000 to $50 million. No particular type of industry is favored, and terms of loans may run from one to twenty years or more, depending on the special circumstances of the individual case. Customarily, the grace period before repayment of principal commences is the time required to complete construction of the project being financed. In determining interest rates, the EXIM Bank takes into consideration the maturity of the loan and the risks taken, as well as prevailing U.S. commercial and government rates. In recent years, rates have run between 4 and 6 per cent, and during the calendar year 1964 they fluctuated between 4 1/2 - 5 1/2 per cent.

Individuals or corporations considering an EXIM Bank loan would be well advised to write or call the Bank for an appointment to discuss their proposal in detail. Often a foreign concern has the prospective American suppliers of goods or services discuss the project with bank officials on their behalf.

Loan Information Required by Export-Import Bank

A. All applications for assistance should supply the following information:

1. A description of the materials, equipment, and services involved; the estimated cost thereof; and the amount of financial assistance sought from the Export-Import Bank.

2. If financing is requested for a United States export, the United States seller and country to which the item will be exported. If financing is requested for an import to the United States, the country of origin and the foreign seller of the import.

3. A description of the use which will be made of the goods and services in the country of import.

4. The repayment schedule and other credit terms desired.

5. Proof that the assistance necessary to finance the transaction is not available from other sources.

6. A statement as to whether the necessary financing could be obtained from private sources under a guarantee by the Export-Import Bank.

7. If the applicant is a private entity, regardless of nationality, and a prospective buyer of United States equipment and associated services for use abroad, the additional information requested under "B" below.

TABLE 5

Export-Import Bank Fiscal Year Highlights, 1963-64

	1964	1963
	(in millions)	
Authorizations	$1,742.5	$1,473.9
Project and equipment loans	570.2	525.0
Commodity credits	177.2	79.8
Exporter credits	30.9	39.9
Emergency foreign-trade credits	--	35.0
Guarantees of exporter and commodity credits	216.8	219.1
Exporter credit insurance		
Foreign-credit insurance association	744.5	569.3
Consignment insurance	2.9	5.8
Loans repaid	$ 617.7	$ 474.1
Sales of bank paper	$ 470.6	$ 362.7
Without recourse:		
For cash	$ 63.3	$ 80.8
Assignment of undisbursed obligations	34.8	31.9
With recourse	372.5	250.0
Disbursed on credits	$ 398.4	$ 498.5
Net earnings (after interest paid)	$ 119.9	$ 113.7
Retained income reserve for contingencies and defaults (see Note 3 of Statement of Condition)	$ 880.2	$ 810.3
Net payments to treasury (interest excluded)	$ 701.8	$ 391.5
Uncommitted lending authority*	$3,459.3	$1,364.0

*During the fiscal year the Bank's authority to lend, guarantee, and insure was increased $2 billion by amendment to its Act.

If the applicant is a government or political subdivision or agency thereof, the additional information requested under "C" below.

B. Additional information from private entities with overseas projects:

1. A description of the project for which United States materials, equipment, and associated services are desired; a statement as to whether it is a new industry or facility or an expansion of an existing one.

2. Present engineering data and market surveys to the extent pertinent for the project.

3. The extent to which prospective United States suppliers might participate in the financing.

4. An estimation of expenditures for the project in dollars and in local and other currencies.

5. A statement as to what portion of the total capital would be provided for the project in the form of equity investment and what form or forms of investment (including the loan requested from the bank) would provide the remainder of the total capital required.

6. If the project is the expansion of an existing industry or facility, balance sheets and profit and loss statements for the last three to five years, and for all projects include estimated balance sheets and profit and loss statements for three years after completion of the project.

7. A statement as to whether a guarantee of repayment of the proposed loan could be offered and, if so, by whom.

8. Where exchange controls are in effect, a statement as to whether the Export-Import Bank could be furnished an assurance by the appropriate authority of the country of import that United States

dollars will be made available, upon payment of local currency, to meet payments of interest and principal to the Bank as they fall due.

C. Additional information from governments or political subdivisions or agencies thereof:

1. A description of the project for which United States materials, equipment, and associated services are desired.

2. Present engineering and economic data and market surveys that are pertinent.

3. A statement as to whether the project would be self-liquidating, or whether repayment would be made from other revenues.

4. The total amount of funds required for the project and the amounts and sources of funds other than those requested from the Bank.

5. An estimation of expenditures for the project in dollars and in local and other currencies.

6. A statement of the external assets of the country in the form of gold and foreign exchange, showing official holdings separately from private holdings, and holdings of dollars and other convertible currencies separately from holdings of inconvertible currencies.

7. A statement of the international investment position of the country for the short term and long term, including major commitments pending or contemplated, and an estimate of the amounts of interest and amortization due in dollars and other convertible currencies on all external fixed-service obligations, as well as on commercial accounts, if any, annually over the life of the loan.

8. Current and prospective balances of payments of the country.

9. If the application is on behalf of a public entity other than the national government, a statement of the financial and legal relationship of the entity to that government and a statement as to whether repayment by the entity would be guaranteed by that government or its central bank.

LOCAL CURRENCY LOANS

Through AID, the United States Government seeks to stimulate economic activity by private enterprise in the developing countries by lending to private firms local currencies generated from the sale of U.S. surplus agricultural commodities. Under this program, up to 25 per cent of the foreign currencies received by the U.S. Government in payment for surplus agricultural commodities may be lent to qualified borrowers to develop business and expand trade. These local currency loans are usually referred to as "Cooley Loans," after Congressman Harold D. Cooley, who originally sponsored the amendment to Public Law 480, the Agricultural Trade Development and Assistance Act of 1954.

Local currencies may be loaned to: U.S. firms and their branches, subsidiaries or affiliates for business development and trade expansion in the foreign country; or either U.S. firms or firms of the local country for expanding markets or consumption of U.S. agricultural products abroad.

Any corporation, partnership, association, or any other legal entity (including an individual United States citizen) is considered a U.S. business firm if it is controlled by United States citizens and is either a profit-making organization or an organization engaged in commercial, manufacturing, or financial activities of the kind customarily engaged in by profit-making organizations. Majority beneficial ownership of an entity by U.S. citizens constitutes control of a firm.

The local currencies are available in countries

where the U.S. has sold surplus agricultural commodities. The currencies may be used by the borrower to develop his business and expand trade, or to finance the expansion of plant and equipment, land acquisitions, and other normal costs of doing business.

Cooley loans may not be made for the manufacture of products which would be exported to the United States in competition with those manufactured there or for the production of commodities which would be marketed in competition with U.S. agricultural products. Cooley loans to foreign firms (non-U.S.-affiliated firms) may be made only if they will be used to expand markets for U.S. agricultural products.

AID Cooley loans usually bear interest at rates comparable to but generally lower than those charged by local development banks. Maturities are related to the purposes of financing, but generally range from three to fifteen years. Loans are repayable in the currency borrowed, without maintenance of value, and usually a guarantee of loan repayment is required. The guarantee requirement may vary from country to country and region to region. Many loans have been made in Asia without a guarantee. In Latin America, the guarantee is almost always required.

Because the loans are repayable in the currency borrowed without maintenance of value, and because they are generally long-term loans at low interest rates, these loans are much sought after when local currencies are available for the lending. Unfortunately, local currencies are generally loaned to medium and large companies, for they promise the greatest security in terms of repayment. Small companies and new companies generally are unable to supply the guarantees or provide the repayment potential of their more mature brothers. Another drawback to the Cooley Loan Program is the rather lengthy, cumbersome process involved in obtaining a loan.

Data on the availability of Cooley funds in countries throughout the world are published periodically in press releases. Individuals and companies wishing to receive these releases on a regular basis may do so by writing to the Office of Development Finance and Private Enterprise, Agency for International Development, Department of State, Washington, D.C. 20523.

General inquiries regarding the Cooley Fund program should be directed to the Office of Development Finance and Private Enterprise. However, inquiries regarding specific Cooley loans to private borrowers for operations in a specific country should be sent to the mission director of the AID mission in that country, as both the mission and Washington work closely together on the Cooley loan programs.

There is no special application form, but the following information is required:

1. Summary of application: The first page of the application should contain the name of the applicant; the name of its United States affiliate, if any; the amount of the requested loan; the requested repayment period; and a brief description of the general purposes for which the loan is sought.

2. Applicant's full legal name, address, form of organization, the country in which the applicant was organized, and the date of organization.

3. A description of the applicant's existing business or proposed business.

4. The names of the principal owners of the applying company and the percentage of ownership held by each individual.

5. A list of the directors.

6. A brief biographical sketch of the principal owners, directors, and officers, as well as key personnel.

7. The amount of the loan requested from AID and a statement showing the specific uses to be made of the funds to be borrowed.

8. The desired repayment schedule.

9. A breakdown of the applicant's existing capitalization and the additional capital required to complete the project for which the Cooley loan is requested.

10. If the enterprise is already in operation, a current balance sheet and balance sheets for the prior three years; a profit and loss statement for the past five years; a statement of sources and uses of funds; and a current cash-flow statement.

11. Pro-forma balance sheets, and profit and loss and cash-flow statements estimated for future years until operations jell. Such statements should indicate clearly the assumptions made in the projections and the basis of these assumptions.

12. The name of the applicant's bank.

13. The total cost of the proposed project, including all equity investment contemplated.

14. The name and address of any proposed guarantor, together with an audit or signed current financial statement of the guarantor.

15. Pertinent economic data, including market studies indicating the benefits which the proposed activity would yield to the enterprise and the country.

16. If the activity will produce items for export, an estimate of the value of such exports and the probable markets.

17. If the applicant is _not_ a U.S. firm or an affiliate of such a firm, an account of how the facilities financed with the proposed loan will aid in the utilization, distribution, consumption of, and market for U.S. agricultural products. An estimate of the increase in the consumption of U.S. agricultural products, both in terms of units and monetary value.

An individual contemplating an application to AID should write to either the AID mission in the country involved or to the Office of Development Finance for a copy of Guide to Preparation of an Application for Cooley Loan Financing. This guide is quite complete. The applicant can also discuss the matter in person with the Office of Development Finance or with the AID mission in the country in which the investment is to be made.

DOLLAR LOANS

Through the Agency for International Development the U.S. Government seeks to increase investments by private enterprise in the economies of developing countries by helping to finance projects which promote economic development. AID encourages investments which contribute to a "marked degree" to development, with emphasis on long-range development assistance.

Dollar loans may be made only with reasonable prospects of repayment. Normally, dollar loans are to be used to cover the U.S. procurement component of the project, but exceptions may be made.

As required by Section 201 of the Foreign Assistance Act of 1961, as amended, the Administrator of AID, before authorizing dollar loans, must take into account the availability of financing from other Free World sources on "reasonable terms." Accordingly, a prospective borrower should investigate a number of private and public lending institutions before making formal application to AID. Also, it is helpful for the potential applicant to discuss his loan with the Office of Development Finance and Private Enterprise, AID, Department of State, Washington, D.C., prior to filling out an application.

The following general terms and conditions may be used as a guideline by the potential applicant:

1. The project must give reasonable promise of contributing to the development of economic resources

or increasing the productive capacities of the country concerned.

2. It must be consistent with the other development activities being undertaken or planned for the country.

3. It must be economically sound and technically feasible, with reasonable prospects that it will pay out satisfactorily.

4. It must not compete with U.S. enterprises.

5. The proceeds of the loan must be used to finance the dollar costs of the project, except where for good cause AID agrees otherwise.

6. Procurement will be limited to goods and services of United States origin, with few exceptions.

7. Loans are generally made directly by AID to the private borrower at an interest rate of 5.50 per cent. While principal and interest are owed in dollars, arrangements may be made for repayment in local currency to the local government, which in turn arranges to pay AID in dollars. The local currency payment schedules usually have maintenance of value provisions at the option of the local government.

8. Borrowers must agree to follow normal, acceptable business practices to assure that the prices paid for goods financed under AID loans are reasonable, and that contracts are awarded on an appropriate competitive basis.

In short, a request for a dollar loan for a project should be supported by all information necessary to determine the equity participation, economic justification, technical feasibility, and cost; by a brief description of how the engineering, purchasing, construction, and management of the project will be carried out; and by appropriate financial projections. It should state whether consultant services will be utilized, and, if not, an explanation should be given.

AID puts out a manual entitled Feasibility Studies, Economic and Technical Soundness Analysis, Capital Projects as a guide for use in the preparation of feasibility studies for loans. It may be obtained by writing to: Distribution Section, AID, Washington, D.C. 20523.

Notes to Chapter 14

1. EXIM Bank, Report to the Congress for the Twelve Months Ended June 30, 1964, p. 3.

2. Ibid.

3. Ibid.

CHAPTER 15 COMMERCIAL FINANCING SOURCES IN DEVELOPING COUNTRIES

COMMERCIAL BANKS

The commercial banks are the most common source of financing in the developing countries. Traditionally, these banks make short-term loans for no more than one year, at interest rates which are excessive by European and U.S. standards. The net effective rate after various charges, stamp taxes, etc., may run from 13-20 per cent or even higher. The security for these short-term loans is quite high, sometimes 200-300 per cent or even higher. High-interest, short-term loans cause a severe hardship, particularly on the undercapitalized, small and medium entrepreneur whose need is for long-term loans at low interest rates. Most entrepreneurs have a tendency to underestimate the many expenses which are incurred in getting their business started. Accordingly, they often find themselves in serious financial trouble with a commercial bank before they have a going business. A typical entrepreneur may start a business with a loan from his family or a few friends. After a year or two he will turn to the commercial bank for help, and not too much later he may find himself insolvent.

However, bankruptcy rates in the developing countries are low compared to business failures in the U.S. This may be due to the fact that it is harder to start a business in the developing countries, principally because of the cost of money. It is also harder to get a job, and accordingly there is more of a tendency "to see it through" than there is in the United States and the other more developed countries.

Traditionally, the commercial banks in the developing countries have been more interested in the safety of the loan than in the loan itself. The high amounts of security required by the banks result in the entrepreneur's discarding many a useful project in search of a proposition which will give him a return of 100 per cent of his investment the first year. With generally limited markets for his products, the entrepreneur will also think in terms of high unit prices for his product in order to recover his original investment as soon as possible. Clearly, this is self-defeating, and the entrepreneur would do well to look elsewhere for his financing. Nonetheless, the commercial banks are here to stay, and will continue to be a source of short-term lending for medium- and large-sized companies.

UNITED STATES COMMERCIAL BANKS AUTHORIZED TO DO BUSINESS OVERSEAS

Corporations organized and operating under Section 25A of the Federal Reserve Act, the so-called Edge Act Corporations, comprise two kinds of financial institutions authorized to do business outside the United States. Banking corporations may engage in commercial banking activities, but may not make equity investments; financing corporations may not receive deposits, but may make equity investments.[1]

In recent years American banks have become increasingly interested in doing business in the developing countries.[2]

Exchange controls, inflation, and economic and political risks generally tend to hold down the part played by U.S. banks in the developing countries, although loans from U.S. banks are eagerly sought after, partly because of the relatively low interest rates obtainable in the Unites States.

However, as the developing countries become more stable, both U.S. and European commercial banks will undoubtedly become more involved in their development process.

ADELA

Perhaps the most significant step forward in private sector development lending was the formation in 1964 of the Atlantic Community Development Group for Latin America (ADELA).

The Adela Investment Company was formed by a group of private enterprises in the United States, Western Europe, Canada, and Japan for the purpose of assisting private enterprise in Latin America with financial, technical, and managerial resources.

To assist private enterprise, Adela invests its own capital (funds raised from shareholders, the financial markets, and other available resources) in Latin American private enterprises which contribute to the economic and social progress of their respective countries.

It provides technical and managerial assistance to enterprises and projects from its own management and professional staff, and seeks cooperation from private enterprises in Europe, the United States, Canada, and Japan, including the shareholders of Adela.

It encourages private investment in Latin American countries with reasonable political, economic, and monetary stability, and assists private investors outside Latin America in their investment activities.

It develops and organizes cooperation among private entrepreneurs in Latin America and private enterprises in Europe, the United States, Canada, and Japan.

It cooperates with investors, entrepreneurs, and organizations in Latin America, Europe, the United States, Canada, and Japan, who are interested and active in development work and development financing in Latin America.[3]

Adela's authorized capital is U.S. $40 million,

of which $16.45 million had been paid in by September 30, 1964. Adela can issue additional shares and thus increase its capital as required. Through its own borrowing power and the borrowing power of the companies in which it invests, Adela will probably exert an impact of several hundred million dollars on the economies of the developing countries of Latin America within the next few years.

Adela has already committed several million dollars of risk capital in plants in Colombia, Peru, Nicaragua, and El Salvador--plants which will turn out such items as steel products, agricultural implements, sugar, and fish meal. Many more projects are being planned, and Adela's success to date augurs well for the future of similar efforts, not only in Latin America but in the developing countries around the world. Through its novel private sector approach, bringing together capital, managerial abilities, and technical know-how, it will vastly extend the scope of investment pioneered by such private investment companies as the International Basic Economy Corporation (IBEC), Deltec Pan American Inversiones Esso de Colombia, S. A., and the Creole Investment Corporation.

Adela has no formal procedures or forms for proposals. It encourages interested enterprises or individuals to make preliminary inquiries in writing. An inquiry should include a brief description of the proposal, which will enable Adela's management to determine the feasibility of conducting further negotiations.

As a matter of policy, Adela deals only directly with interested parties or their authorized representatives. Like most investment companies, it does not wish to pay commissions to intermediaries, nor does it wish to pay finder's fees.

For a preliminary appraisal of the proposal, the interested company or individual should provide the following information in writing:

1. Name, address, and form of organization.

2. General description of the enterprise, stating existing activities, markets, products manufactured or services rendered, financial condition and earnings during past three to five years, banking relationships, information on shareholders, directors, management, and personnel, and other significant data, such as annual reports.

3. Proposed expansion or new activity, market potential, competition, anticipated sales, type and source of raw materials, products to be manufactured or services to be rendered, projected income, direct costs, expenses, earnings and other financial results, and plans for technical know-how and management.

4. Financial requirements and availabilities for proposed expansion or new project, equity capital and financing, with supporting data of cost of project, separated into local currency expenditures and foreign-exchange cost, including working capital requirements and start-up expenses.

5. Studies and surveys of an economic or technical nature prepared by the enterprise or consultants on proposed project, or information on arrangements contemplated for obtaining them if not available.

6. A clear statement of what would be expected from Adela in the form of equity capital, financing, technical and managerial assistance, or other services.

A short preliminary inquiry will save time and effort. Inquiries should be sent to Adela's Operations Office in Edificio El Pacifico, Plaza Washington, Casilla 207, Lima, Peru. The Adela organization maintains a head office in Luxembourg and a branch office in Zurich, Switzerland.

MANAGEMENT ENGINEERING AND CONSULTANT FIRMS

In most of the developing countries a number of management engineering and consultant firms have been created recently. Typically, these firms are small, having from two to ten employees, and most of their work is in the area of management engineering and consulting. Many of these firms have working arrangements with their counterparts in Europe and the United States.

In addition to engineering and consulting work, they also put together joint ventures and serve as a growing source of funds for small and medium business. Working as they do in the private sector, they tend to give emphasis to private sector development. In addition, a number of these firms have worked very closely with AID on developing joint venture opportunities.

Perhaps their most significant contribution to date has been that of bringing in money to the developing countries and re-lending it at rates slightly below the going rates of the countries involved. In Latin America alone during 1966, over $30 million was brought into the economies of Peru, Colombia, Venezuela, and Argentina by this new group of entrepreneurial-minded management consulting firms.

The names and addresses of these firms can usually be obtained from U.S. and foreign embassies located in the capitals of the developing countries around the world, and they should not be overlooked by the small and medium investor in his quest for a joint venture partner, a loan, or equity participation.

Notes to Chapter 15

1. U.S. Government Memorandum to Business from AID, Aids to Business (Overseas Investment), 1963, p. 32.

2. See Appendix A for list of overseas branches and corporations engaged in foreign banking and finance.

3. Adela Investment Company, S. A. Luxembourg (Lima, Peru, November 20, 1964). Pamphlet.

CHAPTER 16 DEVELOPMENT BANKS (FINANCIERAS)

Development Banks around the world are playing an increasingly important role in development lending. Some are private, some are publicly supported, and some receive their financial banking from both the private and the public sector. The financieras act in much the same way as the development banks, except that their support comes primarily from the private sector.

The typical development bank or financiera will take equity positions, make loans, and give technical assistance to the borrowers. Usually, interest rates charged the borrowers are less than the going commercial bank rates and the loans are for longer periods of time (up to ten years) than one may receive from the commercial banks.

It was pointed out earlier that AID, IDA, IFC, and IDB are all interested in making loans to the development banks as a potent re-lending force to small and medium industry. Unlike the commercial banks, the development banks are more interested in the project than they are in the loan security. The complexities created by this rather new approach to lending in the developing countries has created resentment on the part of many small borrowers, since they are accustomed to going to commercial banks and being asked only for substantial security, not questioned as to the purpose of their loan.

The International Banks expect to get paid back when they lend to the development banks. The development banks, in turn, become possibly overcautious. In fact, by the terms of their own loan agreement with the international bank, they often have little option but to require a large degree of security from the borrower; in addition, there is a seemingly disproportionate amount of "red tape."

The result is that the small entrepreneur simply is not being serviced properly by the development banks. A rather typical example is a loan made by AID of approximately $5 million to a development bank in Latin America. Three years after the loan was made, only $250,000 had actually been re-lent, despite the most sincere efforts on the part of AID personnel concerned and the development bank people. The lending procedures simply do not fit the needs of the borrowers.

The situation is gradually changing for the better as the small entrepreneur slowly gets used to loan forms and pro-forma balance sheets and the development banker makes more flexible loans with the international banks, which gives him more flexibility with the end user.

In the final analysis, if the importance of small industry development is acknowledged to be important, the efforts for this type of socio-economic development must be subsidized through the various governments in the developing countries.

Ideally, separate lending institutions should be created employing development-minded individuals capable of making judgment loans rather than bank loans. Unfortunately, in most countries this would be too costly and difficult to administer. Alternatively, "small business loan-windows" should be set up in the established development-lending institutions, and subsidized by the government, with the understanding that these "windows" will probably need continuing assistance. The fruits of such a continued program would yield untold benefits for the developing countries: Planting seeds in the industrial sector today should yield a good crop of successful enterprises tomorrow.

APPENDIXES

APPENDIX A

U.S. BANKING AND FINANCING INSTITUTIONS AUTHORIZED* TO ENGAGE IN INTERNATIONAL BANKING AND FINANCING TRANSACTIONS AS OF SEPTEMBER, 1966 (Edge Act and Agreement Corporations)

Institution	Parent Organization
Bamerical International Financial Corporation, New York	Bank of America National Trust and Savings Association, San Francisco
Bank of America (International) New York	
Bankers International Corporation, New York	Bankers Trust Company, New York
Bankers Company of New York, New York	
Bank of Boston International, New York	First National Bank of Boston, Boston
Boston Overseas Financial Corporation, Boston	
Bank of California International Corporation, San Francisco	The Bank of California, N.A., San Francisco
Chase International Investment Corporation, New York	Chase Manhattan Bank, New York
Chase Manhattan Overseas Banking Corporation, New York	

*Under Sections 25 and 25(a) of the Federal Reserve Act--Edge Act corporations and Agreement corporations.

Institution	Parent Organization
Chemical International Banking Corporation, New York	Chemical Bank New York Trust Company, New York
Chemical International Finance, Ltd., New York	
Citizens and Southern International Corporation, Atlanta	Citizens and Southern National Bank, Savannah
The Company for Investing Abroad, Philadelphia	Fidelity-Philadelphia Trust Company, Philadelphia
Continental Bank International, New York	Continental Illinois National Bank and Trust Company, Chicago
Continental International Finance Corporation, Chicago	
Crocker-Citizens International Corporation, San Francisco	Crocker-Citizens National Bank, San Francisco
First Chicago International Banking Corporation, New York	First National Bank of Chicago, Chicago
First Chicago International Finance Corporation, Chicago	
First National City Overseas Investment Corporation, New York	First National City Bank, New York
First Pennsylvania Overseas Finance Corporation, Philadelphia	First Pennsylvania Banking and Trust Company, Philadelphia
The Gallatin Company, Inc., New York	Manufacturers Hanover Trust Company, New York
International Bank of Commerce, Seattle	National Bank of Commerce of Seattle, Seattle
International Bank of Detroit, Detroit	National Bank of Detroit, Detroit
International Banking Corporation, New York	First National City Bank, New York

Institution	Parent Organization
Irving International Financing Corporation, New York	Irving Trust Company, New York
Manufacturers-Detroit International Corporation, Detroit	Manufacturers National Bank of Detroit, Detroit
Manufacturers Hanover International Banking Corporation, New York	Manufacturers Hanover Trust Company, New York
Manufacturers Hanover International Finance Corporation, New York	
Marine Midland International Corporation, New York	Marine Midland Corporation, Buffalo
Mellon Bank International, Pittsburgh	Mellon National Bank and Trust Co., Pittsburgh
Morgan Guaranty International Banking Corporation, New York	Morgan Guaranty Trust Company of New York, New York
Morgan Guaranty International Finance Corporation, New York	
New England Merchants Bank International, Boston	New England Merchants National Bank, Boston
Northwest International Bank, New York	Northwest Bancorporation, Minneapolis
Philadelphia International Investment Corporation, Philadelphia	Philadelphia National Bank, Philadelphia
Pittsburgh International Finance Corporation, Pittsburgh	Pittsburgh National Bank, Pittsburgh
Provident International Corporation, Philadelphia	Provident National Bank, Philadelphia
Shawmut International Corporation, Boston	The National Shawmut Bank of Boston, Boston

Institution	Parent Organization
State Street Bank Boston International, New York	State Street Bank and Trust Company, Boston
Virgin Islands National Bank, Charlotte Amalie, St. Thomas, Virgin Islands	First Pennsylvania Banking and Trust Co., Philadelphia
Wachovia International Investment Corporation, Winston-Salem	Wachovia Bank and Trust Company, Winston-Salem
Wells Fargo Bank International Corporation, San Francisco	Wells Fargo Bank, San Francisco
Western Bancorporation International Bank, New York	Western Bancorporation, Los Angeles

APPENDIX B

DEVELOPMENT BANKS AND OTHER INTERMEDIATE CREDIT INSTITUTIONS TO WHICH AID HAS AUTHORIZED FINANCIAL ASSISTANCE AS OF SEPTEMBER, 1966

Country of Operation	Name and Principal Address of Institution
	I. Development Banks
Near East-South Asia	
India	The Industrial Credit & Investment Corporation of India, Ltd. (ICICI) (P) 163 Backbay Reclamation Bombay 1
	Industrial Financing Corporation of India (IFCI) Reserve Bank Building Parliament Street New Delhi
	Industrial Development Bank of India Reserve Bank Building Fon and Bombay Bombay
Iran	Industrial & Mining Development Bank of Iran (IMDBI) (P) 204 Boulevard Abe-Karodj P.O. Box 1801 Tehran
Israel	Industrial Development Bank of Israel 22 Rothschild Boulevard Tel Aviv

(P) indicates private institution.

Israel (cont'd.)	Discount Bank Investment Corporation, Ltd. (P) 27 Yehuda Halevi Street Tel Aviv
Jordan	Industrial Development Bank c/o Jordan Development Board Amman
Lebanon	Banque de Credit Agricole Industriel et Foncier (BCAIF) Riod El Solh Street P.O. Box 3696 Beirut
Nepal	Nepal Industrial Development Corporation (NIDC) Judha Road Katmandu
Pakistan	Pakistan Industrial Credit & Investment Corporation, Ltd. (PICIC) (P) Jubilee Insurance House McLeod Road Karachi
	Pakistan Industrial Development Corporation PIDC House Yutcher Road Karachi
Turkey	Industrial Development Bank of Turkey (IDBT) (P) Anadolu Sigorta Han Galata, Istanbul
	American-Turkish Foreign Trade Bank (American-Turk Dis Ticaret Bankasi A.S.) P.O. Box 11 Sisli, Istanbul

United Arab Republic (Egypt)	Industrial Bank of Egypt El Galaa Street Cairo

Latin America

Bolivia	Banco Industrial (P) Avenida 16 de Julio No. 1628 P.O. Box 1290 La Paz
Brazil	Banco Nacional do Desenvolvimento Economic (BNDE) Rua Sete de Setembro, 48 Rio de Janeiro
	Banco do Nordeste do Brasil Rua Senador Pompen, 590 Fortaleza, Cedra
	COPEG Credito e Financiamento Rua da Candelaria 9 Rio de Janeiro
Chile	Corporacion de Fomento de la Produccion (CORFO) Santiago
Colombia	Private Investment Fund (PIF) Banco de la Republica Bogota
Costa Rica	Corporation Costarricense de Financiamiento Industrial, S.A. (COFISA) (P) Apartado 1911 San Jose
Dominican Republic	Private Investment Fund Central Bank of the Dominican Republic Santo Domingo

Ecuador	Corporacion Financiera Nacional Quito
	La Ecuatoriana de Desarrollo (COFIEC) (P) Quito
El Salvador	Instituto Salvadoremo de Fomento Industrial (INSAFI) San Salvador
	Financiera de Desarrollo e Inversiones (P) San Salvador
Guyana	Private Investment Fund (applications accepted through local commercial banks)
Honduras	Financiera Hondurena (P) San Pedro Sula
Nicaragua	Instituto de Fomento Nacional (INFONAC) Managua
	Corporacion Nicaraguense de Inversiones (P) Managua
Panama	Desarrollo Industrial, S.A. (P) Panama City
Paraguay	Banco Central del Paraguay Asuncion
Peru	PERUINVEST (P) (Peruano Suiza De Fomento E Inversiones S.A.) Lima
Uruguay	Banco de la Republica Oriental Montevideo
Regional Central America	Central American Bank for Economic Integration (CABEI) Central Bank of Honduras Building Tegucigalpa, Honduras

Far East

Republic of China	China Development Corporation (P) 181-5 Chung Shan Road, North Sec. Taipei
Korea	Medium Industry Bank Seoul
	Reconstruction Bank of Korea Seoul
Malaysia	Malayan Industrial Development Finance, Ltd. (P) Sentosa Raya 13-15 Arnpang Street Kuala Lumpur
Philippines	Development Bank of the Philippines David Street Manila
	Private Development Corporation (PDCP) (P) CBTC Building Ayala Avenue, Mabati, Rizal Manila
	1st Nationwide Credit Corporation (P) Security Bank Building Santa Mesa, Manila
Thailand	Industrial Finance Corporation (IFCT) (P) Mansion A Rajadamnern Avenue Bangkok
Vietnam	Industrial Development Center Saigon

Africa

Dahomey	Dahomey Development Bank Cotonou
Ethiopa	Development Bank of Ethiopia (DBE) P.O. Box 1900 Addis Ababa
Ivory Coast	Banque Ivoirienne de Developpement Industriel (BIDI) (P) Abidjan
Kenya	Industrial Development Corporation Nairobi
Liberia	Bank of Monrovia Monrovia
Morocco	Banque Nationale pour le Development Economique Rabat
Niger	Niger Development Bank Niamey
Somalia	Credito Somalo Mogadiscio
Sudan	The Industrial Bank of Sudan Khartoum
Tunisia	La Societe Tunisienne de Banque (STB) Palais Consuelaire 1 Ave. Habib Thameur Tunis
Uganda	Uganda Development Corporation Post Office Box 442 Kampala

II. Housing

Latin America

Chile	Central Savings & Loan Bank (Caja Central de Ahorros y Prestamos) Santiago
Colombia	National Housing Institute (Instituto de Credito Territorial) Bogota
Costa Rica	National Institute of Housing & City Planning (INVU) (Instituto Nacional de Vivienda y Urbanismo) San Jose
Dominican Republic	National Housing Bank Santo Domingo
Ecuador	Ecuadorian Housing Bank (Banco Ecuatoriano de la Vivienda) Quito
El Salvador	National Housing Bank (Financiera Nacional de la Vivienda) San Salvador
Mexico	Nacional Financiera Mexico City
Panama	Central Housing Institute (Caja de Ahorros) Panama City
Peru	Mutual Savings & Loan Association (P) (Association Mutual de Creditos para Vivienda "Peru") Jiron Huanacavelica 331 Lima
	Central Home Loan Bank (Barreo de la Vivienda) Lima

Uruguay	Mortgage Bank Sarandi 570, Plaza de la Constitucion Montevideo
Venezuela	Foundation for Community Development and Municipal Improvement (Banco Central de Venezuela) Caracas
	Foundation for Peoples Housing (P) (Fundacion de la Vivienda Popular) Edificio las Fundaciones Avenido Andres Bello Local No. 6 Caracas
	Banco Obrero (National Housing Institute) Caracas
Regional Central America	Central American Bank for Economic Integration (CABEI) Home Loan Bank Department Central Bank of Honduras Building Tegucigalpa, Honduras

III. Agricultural Credit Institutions

Near East-South Asia

Greece	Agriculture Bank of Greece 23 Venezalow Athens
Jordan	Agriculture Credit Corporation Amman
Turkey	Agriculture Bank of the Turkish Republic (Z.I.RA.AT Bankasi) Ankara

Latin America

Bolivia	Agricultural Bank (Banco Agricola de Bolivia) La Paz
Colombia	Agricultural Credit Bank (Caja de Credito Agrario) Bogota
	Institute for Agrarian Reform (INCORA) Bogota
	Livestock Bank (Banco Ganadero) Bogota
Costa Rica	Banco Nacional de Costa Rica San Jose
Dominican Republic	Banco Agricola Santo Domingo
El Salvador	Central Bank (Banco Central de la Reserva) San Salvador
Guatemala	Banco de Guatemala Cuidad de Guatemala Guatemala City
Mexico	Nacional Financiera, S.A., de Mexico Venustiano Carranza No. 25 Mexico 1
Paraguay	National Development Bank (Banco de Fomento) Asuncion
Peru	Institute of Agrarian Reform and Colonization Lima
Venezuela	Agricultural and Livestock Bank Caracas

Africa

Tunisia	Banque Nationale Agricole (BNA) 19 Avenue de Paris Tunis

IV. Cooperatives

Latin America

Chile	Corporacion de Fomento de la Produccion (CORFO) (Rural Electric Coops) Santiago
Ecuador	Cooperative Bank (P) Quito
Uruguay	Banco de Produccion y Consumo Bank of Agricultural Coops (P) Montevideo

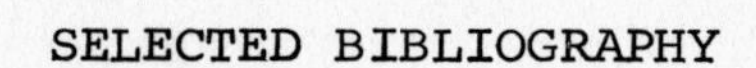

SELECTED BIBLIOGRAPHY

SELECTED BIBLIOGRAPHY

Alpert, Paul. Economic Development. Glencoe, Ill.: Free Press of Glencoe, 1963.

Berliner, Joseph S. Soviet Economic Aid. New York: Frederick A. Praeger, Inc., 1958.

Black, Eugene R. The Diplomacy of Economic Development. Cambridge: Harvard University Press, 1961.

Boskey, Shirley. Problems and Practices of Development Banks. Baltimore: Johns Hopkins Press, 1959.

Bryce, Murray D. Industrial Development: A Guide for Accelerating Economic Growth. New York: McGraw-Hill, 1960.

Buchanan, Norman S., and Ellis, Howard S. Approaches to Economic Development. New York: The Twentieth Century Fund, 1955.

Castle, Eugene W. Billions Blunders and Baloney. New York: The Devin-Adair Co., 1955.

________. The Great Giveaway: The Realities of Foreign Aid. Chicago: Henry Regenery, 1957.

Clark, Collin. The Conditions of Economic Progress. London: Collier-Macmillan, Ltd., 1957.

Coffin, Frank Morey. Witness for AID. Boston: Houghton Mifflin, 1964.

Currie, Lauchlin. Accelerating Development: The Necessity and the Means. New York: McGraw-Hill, 1965.

Diamond, William. Development Banks. Baltimore: Johns Hopkins Press, 1957.

Doane, Robert Rutherford. World Balance Sheet. New York: Harper & Row, 1957.

Forde, J. S. An International Trade in Managerial Skills. Oxford: Basil Blackwell & Mott, Ltd., 1957.

Galbraith, John Kenneth. Economic Development. Cambridge: Harvard University Press, 1964.

Hagen, Everett E. Handbook for Industry Studies. Glencoe, Ill.: Free Press of Glencoe, 1958.

Harris, Seymour E. International and Interregional Economics. New York: McGraw-Hill, 1957.

Higgins, Benjamin. Economic Development: Principles, Problems & Policies. New York: W. W. Norton & Co., 1955.

Hirschman, Albert O. The Strategy of Economic Development. New Haven: Yale University Press, 1958.

Hoffman, Paul G. World Without Want. New York: Harper & Row, 1962.

Hyde, Louis K. The United States and The United Nations. New York: Manhattan Publishing Co., 1960.

Kaldor, Nicholas. Essays on Economic Policy. New York: W. W. Norton & Co., 1964.

Kindleberger, Charles P. Economic Development. New York: McGraw-Hill, 1958.

Kurihara, Kenneth K. The Keynesian Theory of Economic Development. New York: Columbia University Press, 1959.

Leibenstein, Harry. Economic Backwardness and Economic Growth. New York: John Wiley & Sons, Inc., 1957.

Lewis, W. Arthur. The Theory of Economic Growth. Homewood, Ill.: Richard D. Irwin, Inc., 1955.

Liska, George. The New Statecraft: Foreign Aid in American Foreign Policy. Chicago: University of Chicago Press, 1960.

Loeber, Thomas S. Foreign Aid: Our Tragic Experiment. New York: W. W. Norton & Co., 1961.

Meier, Gerald M., and Baldwin, Robert E. Economic Development. New York: John Wiley & Sons, Inc., 1957.

Mikesell, Raymond French. U.S. Economic Policy & International Relations. New York: McGraw-Hill, 1962.

Millikan, Max F., and Rostow, Walt W. Aid, Trade and the Tariff. New York: Crowell Publishing Co., 1953.

Morgan, Theodore, Betz, George W., and Choudhry, N. K. (eds.). Readings in Economic Development. Belmont, Cal.: Wadsworth Publishing Co., 1963.

Myrdal, Gunnar. An International Economy. New York: Harper & Bros., 1956.

Patterson, Minos Ernest. The World's Economic Dilemma. New York: McGraw-Hill, 1930.

Polanyi, Karl. Trade and Market in Early Empires. Glencoe, Ill.: Free Press of Glencoe, 1957.

Robock, Stefan Hyman. Brazil's Developing Northeast. Washington: Brookings Institution, 1963.

Stead, William H. Fomento--the Economic Development of Puerto Rico. Washington, D.C.: National Planning Association, 1958.

Tinbergen, Jan. The Design of Development. Baltimore: Johns Hopkins Press, 1958.

Walinsky, Louis J. The Planning and Execution of Economic Development. New York: McGraw-Hill, 1963.

Ward, Barbara. The Rich Nations and The Poor Nations. New York: W. W. Norton & Co., 1962.

Wolf, Charles, Jr., and Sufrin, Sidney C. Capital Formation and Foreign Investment in Underdeveloped Areas. Syracuse: Syracuse University Press, 1958.

ABOUT THE AUTHORS

Richard S. Kaynor is an independent industrial development consultant, specializing in business problems related to small and medium industries in developing countries. Most recently, as Director of Special Projects of the Center for Advanced International Studies of the University of Miami (Florida), he supervised a project involving the transfer of advanced technology to developing nations. Prior to that he was Industry Officer with the Agency for International Development in Peru, and from 1961-63 he was Deputy Director of Placement for the Cuban Refugee Program in Miami. He holds several patents and has owned and operated his own company. Mr. Kaynor received his master's degree from Massachusetts Institute of Technology and has done postgraduate work at the University of Havana and the University of San Marcos, Peru.

Konrad F. Schultz is serving as the industrial development advisor to the Arequipa Development Corporation in Arequipa, Peru, under the auspices of the Economic Development Division of the Stanford Research Institute (in Menlo Park, California). The project is concentrating on improving the Peruvian economy by the expansion of existing industries and the development of new ones. Like Mr. Kaynor, Dr. Schultz specializes in medium- and small-industry development. Prior to joining the Stanford Research Institute, he was assistant to the president of the Ingersoll Milling Machine Company in Rockford, Illinois and also served as a liaison between that company and its European partner. Dr. Schultz received his master's degree from the University of the Saarland in Germany and his doctorate in economics from the University of Madrid.